Dear Reader:

The book you are about to read is the latest bestseller from the St. Martin's True Crime Library, the imprint *The New York Times* calls "the leader in true crime!" Each month, we offer you a fascinating account of the latest, most sensational crime that has captured the national attention. St. Martin's is the publisher of Tina Dirmann's VANISHED AT SEA, the story of a former child actor who posed as a yacht buyer in order to lure an older couple out to sea, then robbed them and threw them overboard to their deaths. John Glatt's riveting and horrifying SECRETS IN THE CELLAR shines a light on the man who shocked the world when it was revealed that he had kept his daughter locked in his hidden basement for 24 years. In the Edgar-nominated WRITTEN IN BLOOD, Diane Fanning looks at Michael Petersen, a Marine-turned-novelist found guilty of beating his wife to death and pushing her down the stairs of their home—only to reveal another similar death from his past. In the book you now hold, DEAD BUT NOT FORGOTTEN, Amber Hunt explores a tangled web of cold-case murder . . .

St. Martin's True Crime Library gives you the stories behind the headlines. Our authors take you right to the scene of the crime and into the minds of the most notorious murderers to show you what really makes them tick. St. Martin's True Crime Library paperbacks are better than the most terrifying thriller, because it's all true! The next time you want a crackling good read, make sure it's got the St. Martin's True Crime Library logo on the spine—you'll be up all night!

Charles E. Spicer, Jr.
Executive Editor, St. Martin's True Crime Library

Dead But Not Forgotten

AMBER HUNT

St. Martin's Paperbacks

Acknowledgments

To say there are two sides to a crime story is an understatement. In reality, there are dozens. I aimed to keep this in mind while writing this book, and I owe a great debt to the people who helped me tell as many sides to the story as possible. I would specifically like to thank Macomb County Prosecutor Eric Smith, Assistant Prosecutor Steve Kaplan, Joe Kowynia, Clinton Township Police Lieutenant Craig Keith, defense lawyers Carl Marlinga and Joe Kosmala, and Renee George. Their perspectives vary greatly, and it was no easy task to sift through their sides to tell as balanced a story as possible. Their cooperation and patience helped immensely.

On a personal front, I owe an enormous thanks to Elijah Van Benschoten, whose love, encouragement and dinner-fetching was instrumental in this book's completion. To my friends, I say thank you for understanding why I disappeared for more than a year.

Among others I'd like to thank, for a variety of reasons: Missy, Luke and Roland Piotrowski; Sarah MacKusick; Bruce and Amy Hunt; Bill Cataldo; Jamie Cook; *The Comics Journal* (specifically Kristi Valenti, Michael Dean and intern August Williams); Jane Dystel, my agent; the Detroit *Free Press*; Tom

Henderson; Allison Caplin, my editor; Barbara Ontal; Shawn Starkey; Emily Batcher; Fred Rothenberg and Dennis Murphy of *Dateline*; the Powell House in Lexington, Michigan; the Parador Inn in Pittsburgh, Pennsylvania; and Geraldine Peterson.

Finally, I'd like to dedicate this book to my mother, Marcia, who died of cancer in 1991. It perhaps seems a macabre dedication, but Mom was my writing's biggest fan, and her death imparted in me an empathy that will forever drive my work.

Book One

Book One

Chapter 1

Barbara George's Murder

As Tom and Lenora Ward pulled into the parking lot of the Venice Square Shopping Center in Clinton Township, Michigan, they spotted a dark car speeding behind the strip mall and exchanged puzzled glances. It was a Friday night, a thirteenth even, and they had stopped by Comics World to browse through the new selections and see if anything caught their attention. It was a ritual of sorts: get off work, grab some dinner, hit the comic book store. This night, in July 1990, they got there about 6 p.m. Something seemed off. That speeding sedan was out of place in a parking lot that was otherwise quieter than usual.

Tom squinted. He wanted to get a glimpse of the driver, but the car was too far away and moving too quickly. Maybe it wasn't breaking the speed limit, he figured, but it was still going too fast for the parking lot of a strip mall marked with stores that drew children—the comic book store, a pizza-and-sub shop. He could tell one person was in the car—a man, it seemed—but that's all he could make out. As he and his wife got out of the car, Tom noticed a second person, this one thin and odd-looking—was that a fake beard? he wondered—wearing a short-billed Greek fisherman's cap and walking away from the store. The bizarre fellow shot a

look back toward Comics World. Ward shrugged and followed his wife into the store.

No one was behind the counter, but that wasn't unusual.
The store was owned by Michael and Barbara George, a sub-
urban Detroit couple who treated customers like family.
Inside stood racks of comics, from the usual X-Men and
Spider-Man fare to the less mainstream Neil Gaiman cre-
ations. Lenora and Tom made their way past a few customers and thumbed through the bins of new arrivals, but after
a few minutes, they began to feel uncomfortable that no one
was staffing the store. The other patrons grew antsy, too. A
teenage boy waited in line, tapping his cellophane-wrapped
selection on the counter. Peter Corrado and his brother, there
to kill time while waiting for a nearby dry cleaner to finish
their shirts, picked through the bins as well. After a few
minutes, the customers looked around, puzzled. One of the
kids leaned over the front counter and tried to peek into the
store's back room, the employees-only zone. The door was
partway open.

"Hey, mister, somebody's back there!" he shouted, apparently to Peter.

Peter walked toward the room and saw a hand through the
doorway. At first, he thought the hand belonged to a downed
mannequin. But when he pushed the door open, he saw a
woman's body on the floor. Lenora and Tom sensed his panic
and rushed into the room. Immediately, they recognized
Barb. Lenora shook off the shock of seeing her friend on
the floor and let her training as a nurse kick in, getting on
her knees beside Barbara's body to feel for a pulse. Barb
was lying on her right-hand side, her arm stretched out
beneath her.

"Barb, are you OK?" Lenora asked. No answer.

She moved Barb onto her back and saw that her lips were
blue, her pupils dilated and fixed.

"Call nine-one-one," she said to Tom, who rushed to the
phone behind the store's cash register to call for help.

Lenora couldn't find a pulse. There was a small amount of blood and no obvious injury, so Lenora figured that Barbara must have suffered a heart attack or a seizure, then fallen backward and hit her head. "Please, God, let this be OK," Lenora thought. "She's a mother." The nurse had performed CPR hundreds of times, but never on someone she considered a friend. She thought of Michael, Barbara's husband, and the couple's two young daughters. She caught her breath and thought again, "Just let this be OK."

After Tom made the 911 call, he knelt beside his wife. Lenora pulled Barb's head back and began breathing for her. Her hands moved to the center of Barb's still-warm chest and started compressions. She worked for ten minutes, her arms growing tired, until she heard the sirens. Medics rushed into the store and took over. Lenora stepped back and stumbled out of the storage room. Medics pulled Barbara's body from the store on a stretcher and loaded her into an ambulance. Police officers began to fill the store. Lenora jotted down her and Tom's names and phone number on a piece of paper and set it next to the cash register on the counter.

As she and Tom left the hectic scene, their innocuous date night suddenly tragic, Lenora continued to pray, but she couldn't ignore what years of nursing training told her. She knew that Barbara was in dire straits. The color had never come back to the thirty-two-year-old woman's face despite the chest compressions and puffs of breath. Unless God Himself intervened, Barbara George was dead.

At the hospital, doctors and nurses worked feverishly to get a pulse. They pumped more air into Barbara's lungs and tried to zap her heart back into rhythm. Nothing worked. After fifteen minutes, they declared her dead. Kris Kehoe, an emergency room nurse, came to clean up Barbara's body so the family would be less disturbed when they saw her. She wiped down Barbara's face and began to straighten her shoulder-length hair. That's when she saw the blood.

Kris leaned in for a closer look and saw a hole. She called

the Clinton Township police, and word quickly spread that Lenora had jumped to the wrong conclusion: Barbara George hadn't simply hit her head. She had been shot. Soon, even more police officers and evidence technicians descended on the store. The scene was chaotic. Clinton Township doesn't get much violent crime, and when cops learned there had been a shooting, they dropped everything. Even off-duty officers arrived, as much to gawk as to assist.

Outside the hospital room, Barbara's family and friends began to gather. Several had stopped by the comic book store around 8 p.m. to attend a surprise birthday party Barbara had been planning for her husband. She'd had friends sneak in throughout the day with decorations, and the shindig was supposed to start about an hour before the store closed. Michael, too, showed up as Barb had instructed, but instead of being greeted by his wife and a store full of partygoers, he saw flashing sirens and police tape. He walked toward the store and was stopped by an officer. Michael said he was the store owner and asked what had happened.

"Your wife has been hurt," replied the officer, offering few other details. He summoned another cop to take Michael to his wife.

Barbara was dead by the time Michael arrived. A doctor approached the family, glumly shook his head and shared the news. Michael did not cry. He hung his head and refused to look at his wife, so her brother, Peter Kowynia, went into the hospital room to identify the body. Barbara's sister, Christine, asked Michael what all the other family members were thinking:

"Do you think Renee's husband had anything to do with it?"

Renee Kotula was one of the Georges' employees. She was also Michael's lover. Christine had already suspected the affair. So did Barbara. Even customers could tell.

Michael shook his head. "No, he wouldn't be the one," he said quietly. "He didn't do it."

Christine thought he answered too quickly.

The story of Barb's death soon hit the newspapers and rocked the quiet Macomb County township. There were a few murders a year in the burg of 89,000 people, but most were quickly solved and usually linked to crimes spilled over from the big city twenty miles to the south, Detroit. This case was different. Barb George had no enemies. She was a bubbly, curly-haired woman who knew her customers by name and devoted her life to daughters Michelle and Tracie, ages two and four, respectively.

There was something off about Michael George, though. Customers could tell one off-color story or another, like the time he allegedly emerged from the back room—the same room his wife would later die in—and announced that Renee had just performed oral sex on him. After Barb's death, he seemed both overly emotional and unaffected at once. He cried when he spoke of her, but didn't seem too invested in finding the killer, even discouraging friends from offering reward money to find the person responsible. He also couldn't seem to shake the flirt in him and passed a note to a female customer who offered him condolences to tell her she looked pretty that day.

None of this was lost on the police. Most murders are committed by people familiar with the victims, and when a woman is found dead, her husband is the first to be questioned. But this case was tricky. Police hadn't found the murder weapon; there were no witnesses. Michael said two boxes of high-priced comic books had disappeared during the shooting, so robbery might have been a motive, but more than $700 was left in the store's two cash registers, another $400 was in Barb's pants pocket, and her jewelry, including her diamond engagement ring, remained on her body. Investigators were at a loss. A gut feeling told them Michael George was the killer, but they had no proof. The case would languish for eighteen long years.

In March 2008, during Michael George's trial on murder

charges, Lenora Ward was asked to relive those moments she spent on the floor with his dead wife. She described her desperate attempt to save Barb's life, and said she had braced herself for a frantic phone call from Michael the night of the shooting. Surely he would want to talk to the couple who had found his wife's body. He would want to know every detail of what had happened. But the night of July 13, 1990, came and went without a phone call. So did the next day. And the next. Lenora and Tom spoke several times to police officers, but never once to Michael. Lenora at first dismissed the lack of contact as Michael grieving in a way she couldn't possibly comprehend.

Eighteen years later, however, when the cold case was resurrected and police and prosecutors finally levied charges against Michael George, claiming he'd gotten away with murder for nearly two decades, Lenora admitted she'd found the lack of contact to be disconcerting. They weren't close friends, but Lenora's life had been forever affected by those ten minutes she spent on her knees, trying to breathe life back into Barbara George's body.

"I was special in Michael George's life," Lenora Ward said at his trial, "because I put my mouth on his wife's bloodied mouth."

When she didn't hear from Michael, Lenora, like police, grew suspicious of the supposedly grieving widower.

Chapter 2

Barbara George, Mother & Wife

Barb George had always been known as headstrong and confident. Her coming-of-age was in the '70s, a fact reflected in the way she feathered her curly hair, but she was far from a girlie-girl. She played volleyball and softball, competing valiantly in the latter as she and her younger sister, Christine, brought home tournament championships throughout high school. The girls shared a bedroom in their 1,200-square-foot ranch home on 10 Mile Road in Warren, Michigan, a suburb just north of Detroit. Barb was the oldest of four children, two years separating each birth. The younger two, Peter and Joe, shared a room, too, and the four grew up athletic and competitive with an Archie Bunker–type millwright father and a homemaker mom.

Because Barb was the oldest, she got her share of talking-tos from dad Peter for typical teenage stuff—missing curfew or forgetting to fill the car up with gas—but the elder Peter Kowynia was a bit of a hothead who liked to argue, so the kids shrugged much of it off. In hindsight, Barb's family would say it likely helped shape her personality more than they had realized. In high school, Barb was unusually focused. She wasn't interested in college, but she wanted to own and run her own business. She landed a job at a Tubby's

Sub Shop and worked her way up to management, then saved up her money to buy her dream car: a red Chevrolet Camaro, which she cared for like the pride and joy it was, regularly washing and buffing it and urging her dad to change the oil when due. She and her father even talked of joining forces and getting a Tubby's franchise—Dad as the owner, and daughter as the manager. That plan changed when a man with a handgun walked into the shop while Barb and her sister were working. Other employees were at the store, too, and by all accounts, Barb stayed cool and kept her panicked employees calm. Afterward, she admitted the incident shook her up. She quit soon after the robbery.

After graduating Mott High School in Warren, Barb skipped the college route and went to beauty school instead, graduating a few years later. It seemed an odd career path for a woman who was far more sneakers than pumps growing up, but Barb was proud of her schooling. Her graduation was commemorated with a gold pendant of hair-cutting shears that she wore around her neck. After school, she didn't seem particularly driven to land a job at a beauty salon. It was more of a side interest, a hobby to earn extra money, so she chopped hair for friends and family at her home while working at Farmer Jack, a grocery store in Hazel Park. It was there where she met Michael George, who worked stocking shelves. Their flirtation began simply at the store, but soon they were properly dating. Before Michael, guys just hadn't been much of a priority for Barb. She maybe had a handful of dates in and after high school, said youngest brother Joe Kowynia. She went to the prom, but it wasn't a big to-do; there was no puppy love romance that defines (and torments) so many teenage years. Within a few months of dating Michael, Barb took him to meet her family. Joe was sixteen when he first met Michael, who he decided was, well, a nerd. For a too-cool teenager, it was the big tinted glasses that did Michael in for Joe.

"I always thought he was kind of different," Joe said. "I

always thought of him as a dorky kind of guy, but he was all right. He seemed nice."

Michael didn't seem to have many friends of his own. Around the Kowynias, he was generally quiet, and he and Barb seemed to click. They weren't the type of couple to turn heads and make others envious with their good looks and overtly loving relationship, but they seemed happy. After less than a two-year courtship, they got married on September 12, 1981. They didn't bring in much money at Farmer Jack, but Michael soon got a job at John Hancock Life Insurance Co. The two moved into a mobile home together near M-59 and Garfield in Macomb Township—a standard, single trailer in a well-kept park with friendly neighbors—and had two daughters: Tracie, in 1985, followed by Michelle two years later. The girls quickly became the center of Barb's life. She was a doting mother, but firm as well. Her headstrong attitude translated to how she raised first Tracie, a bright-eyed baby destined to follow Mom's footsteps as an athlete, and then Michelle, who would inherit Barb's reddish hair and round cheeks. Barb often sat outside and chatted with neighbors as the girls played. "We stayed outside and talked and she would be with her children," neighbor Anita Dukich would later testify.

Joe doesn't recall much arguing during the marriage's early days.

"He was always nice to her, especially at the beginning," Joe said.

But sometime later, rumors began to swirl. "You'd hear about some arguments and stuff like that," Joe recalled, "but all couples argue, so I didn't really think about it. I never saw anything that I thought would be a threat to her life or well-being."

Within a few years, however, the rumors got more pointed. Joe heard that Michael was fooling around. Barb was either oblivious or in denial, her brother recalled, because even when someone would tell her straight up they thought Michael was having an affair, she would shrug it off. "He's just messing around," she would say.

Joe wouldn't learn until years later that "messing around" was an understatement. Michael, then twenty-five, had begun having an affair with a twenty-three-year-old blonde coworker, Patrice Sartori. The two worked in a building on Stephenson Highway in Troy with about thirty other employees. Patrice got the job in 1988, and met Michael, a full-time insurance agent. She knew he was married with a child—at that point, just Tracie—and Barb was pregnant with Michelle. The two had flirted in the small office space, where employees sat at one long table to do their paperwork. After a few months, the relationship changed. Michael told Patrice he was separated from his wife and took her to an apartment on Mound Road near 14 Mile in Sterling Heights, a sparsely decorated bachelor pad where she thought he was living during the separation. Michael told Patrice he was frustrated with how fat Barb was getting with the pregnancy. He and Patrice began an affair that would last six months. The whole time, she thought he was readying for a divorce; Barb, meanwhile, told no one of any discord during her pregnancy— nothing about a separation, talk of divorce, or Michael's private apartment.

The trysts, steamy at first, ended about the time Michael asked Patrice to babysit Tracie while he went to the hospital to pick up his wife and their newborn, Michelle. Patrice complied, but called off the affair. Michael was not happy. He and Patrice had made a videotape of themselves having sex and Michael threatened to make it public if Patrice didn't rekindle the relationship, she would later tell police. She balked and Michael backed down. In truth, Barb, a Catholic, wouldn't be likely to grant him a divorce anyway. He returned to Barb, to their plans of opening a comic book store, to their ever-more cramped mobile home in Clinton Township, and seemed to move on. How much Barb knew of this affair is still a mystery to her family.

Though they had started making a bit more money, Michael had a long-term goal to open a comic book store, feeding off a passion he'd had since childhood. It fit with Barb's dreams, too; she had always wanted to become a business owner, dating back to the days she and her dad had talked about getting a Tubby's franchise. She just never seemed to settle on what to pursue, never getting the idea—or the start-up money—off the ground. Now, her mate had the business plan, and they as a couple could set out together to fulfill the dream.

The couple asked Barb's dad for a $7,000 loan to open the comic book shop in a township strip mall on Garfield. Peter Kowynia complied, and helped the two do something he himself had hoped to accomplish someday: open a business. Barb's family pitched in with a lot of manual labor. Joe and Peter even helped build the interior walls for the shop.

"We all chipped in," he recalled. "We were all supportive. We didn't know much about the business because no one knew a lot about comic books and baseball cards and all that, but Michael had a lot of that stuff already. After talking with Barb, and with people I knew who collected, it sounded like a pretty good up-and-coming business."

Barb took a buyout from Farmer Jack and began working at the store full-time. She handled much of the daily operation, working the cash register, handling orders, helping to stock. Michael, meanwhile, researched like crazy, made contacts with other metro Detroit comic book shops, and focused on the then just-blossoming Internet fad. Barb made a good impression as the customer-friendly face of the business. She was friendly, pleasant, and clearly proud of the new store. She took customer service to a new level, not only treating patrons politely, but often taking a personal interest in their lives. She treated some regulars as friends, stepping out from behind the store's counter to greet them with hugs and chitchat rather than a simple, "How may I help you?"

"She was bubbly, she was sweet, she was extraordinarily kind," Lenora Ward said. "She was always joking. She joked around with the kids a lot. She kept us coming to that store, actually."

Outwardly, she and Michael initially seemed a good pairing. But that began to change. After the second pregnancy, Barb gained even more weight, which, on her athletic frame, made her look frumpy and a bit older than her thirty years. Michael disapproved and became vocal, telling customers that she was overweight and becoming increasingly less attractive. To Michael Benson, who first was a customer, then later an employee at Comics World, he snottily complained that she didn't even try to be attractive anymore, wearing nightgowns that went to her ankles. Benson recalled Barb as being the backbone of the store who fulfilled Michael's requests. Michael gave the orders, and Barbara carried them out, Benson said. He spoke to his wife curtly, far more like a business partner than a loving spouse.

"They didn't appear happily married," Benson said.

Whatever the problems, Barb seemed determined to keep them quiet. Unlike Michael, she didn't unload her marital problems onto customers and employees. She kept them largely secret from friends and family until just months before her death, and even then, she was absolute in her resolve to hold the marriage together.

Employees at neighboring businesses began to hear the two arguing. The back-and-forth was never overly heated, but it became a regular thing. His flirtatious side became more apparent, too. Benson noticed he seemed to pay special attention to attractive female customers, some of whom would later tell police that something about the shop owner just seemed off. One woman quit going into the store with her comic-loving son because Michael gave her the creeps. And Joe's girlfriend, Mary Shamo, always got the impression that Michael was hitting on her.

Joyce Selke, who was married to Barb's cousin and would go to Barb's house for haircuts, began sensing that the marriage was in trouble. Joyce was nine years older than Barb, who was just a teen when the two met. Despite the age difference, they became friends.

"She had the most bubbly personality," Joyce said. "She lit up a room when she walked in it, always with a smile on her face, no matter what. She talked to everyone who was around."

And she was ambitious. Beauty school was just one example. "Barb had her hands into a little bit of everything," Joyce said.

Joyce helped with babysitting duties when Tracie was a toddler, watching the girl two or three times a week for nearly a year as the Georges began hatching their plan to open the comic store. As the plans progressed, the store became a reality, and their business grew, but it seemed Michael and Barb were fighting more and more. One day, about a year before Barb died, Joyce stopped by the couple's mobile home for a haircut and found Barb in tears. Michael didn't say a word and stormed out of the house. Joyce already had decided Michael was a strange bird; he had once tried to sell life insurance to her and her husband and suggested about $100,000. When the couple balked, saying it was overkill, he said he had the same amount out on Barb. Something about the way he said it didn't sit well with Joyce.

Despite the obvious bickering, the store was doing well—so well, in fact, that Michael and Barb could finally move out of the dinky trailer and into a real home. The one they had in mind was a significant step up northwest in the county in Sterling Heights. It was about 2,500 square feet, a split-level. Tracie and Michelle would get their own rooms—something Barb didn't even have growing up. They had picked out the model of the floor plan that, to Barb's delight, was named Barbara.

"She was tickled pink at the time," Joe said. "She took the whole family on a tour."

Meanwhile, Michael set his sights on expanding Comics

World into a multi-store franchise peppering metro Detroit. Business was healthy, and even the Garfield store was becoming too hefty for them to handle alone. Barb set out to hire help on top of the handful of teenage boys who lent a hand on occasion. She met Renee Kotula at Tracie's preschool, which Renee's son Josh attended. Renee, recently separated from her husband and a single mother of five, needed work, so Barb brought her into the business, both as a franchise investor and to help shelve the order arrivals in the Garfield store one night a week.

At five-foot-three and some one hundred pounds, Renee was petite and cute, and she quickly caught Michael's eye. The fighting between him and Barb escalated. Customers and the teenage help could tell something was up: It was clear the two were having an affair, and that Barb was a stooge. While Michael barked work demands at his wife, he was smiley and flirty with Renee. He chastised Barb about her weight and appearance, while openly complimenting Renee on hers. Then there was that time he supposedly announced that Renee had just pleasured him in the back room of his store, some customers would later report to police.

Even Joyce, who hadn't been in contact with Barb as often after the store opened, sensed fireworks during an unannounced visit to the shop. Barb wasn't there, but Michael and Renee were.

"They were the only two in the store," Joyce said. "The way they laughed and smiled at each other—it made me uncomfortable. At that time, nobody knew anything, then later on, we found out he was having the affair with her."

Barb suspected he was cheating on her, but she didn't seem to know with whom. Maybe she could tell he thought Renee was pretty, Joe said later, but Renee was among Barb's best friends, and when Barb set out to plan that surprise birthday party, she brought Renee in on the ruse. It was the mistress's job to bring soda to the store for the party. Whatever Barb knew, she fought hard to avoid burdening her friends and family with it. But after a while Barb began to speak more openly about the trouble her marriage was in. She told a friend not a month before she died that Michael had asked for a divorce. Barb refused. She wanted to save the marriage. She told her little brother the same thing.

"She wanted to work on it," Joe said. "She didn't believe in divorce. She wanted to work on her marriage."

She went so far as to plan the party, followed by a romantic weekend getaway in northern Michigan. The girls would stay with Michael's mother; Barb packed something frilly to wear. But come 8 p.m., when Michael was supposed to be walking into the shop and greeted by a dozen of his closest friends, he instead was being whisked to the hospital, where Barb's lifeless body was being wiped down and readied for family identification.

Chapter 3

A Murder's Impact

Barb George's plans—the surprise party, the weekend get-away, the move into her dream home—all ended with a bullet to her head. Her family had gathered at the hospital—Mary, Joe's girlfriend, went to pick up father Pete, while Joe called sister Christine. The only person missing was Barb's mother, who had suffered a stroke about three months prior. She was bedridden, in bad shape. She couldn't walk or talk. Barb had been visiting daily since it happened, and now that she was gone, her family had to break the news to a woman whose mental faculties were waning.

"It wasn't good when we had to tell her," Joe said. "You could tell she was sad, but she couldn't do anything. She couldn't speak. She had a feeding tube."

Dad Pete took it hard, too. He never thought he'd have to bury one of his children, and he was still in shock from his wife's stroke. It was all too much.

At the hospital, Michael seemed to just shut off. He didn't react.

"He didn't come up and hug anybody," Joe recalled. "He just sat there and really didn't do much of anything."

Despite that, it initially didn't cross Joe's mind that Michael might have been involved. His girlfriend Mary, however, felt something was off. She and Joe had gone to the store early to help with the birthday party. They were the first to arrive, and later that night, they stopped by the Georges' mobile home to offer comfort. Michael seemed theatrically inconsolable. He spotted a vacuum cleaner and ran to hug it. "This is Barb's vacuum," he cried, Mary would later testify. "He was hugging it and crying—pretending to cry," she said. "No tears were coming down his face."

More disturbingly, she said that Joe briefly left the room, and Michael took off his glasses, tossed them on the table, and nonchalantly asked, "What do you think about all this?" It gave Mary the creeps.

The next day, Patrice Schemansky, who worked at a Big Boy restaurant with Michael's mother Janet, brought food to the Hazel Park home where the Georges had gathered. She figured Janet wouldn't be up for entertaining, so the restaurant donated some meals to be dropped off to help feed the slew of people who inevitably would end up at the house. While there, a priest arrived to offer Michael condolences. Michael, like Barb, was religious, so the offer seemed appropriate, but Michael did not react as Schemansky expected. Instead of greeting the priest, he ran out the back door and didn't return.

The midweek funeral was well attended, not only because Barb was well liked in the community, but also because her brutal slaying had reached many in metro Detroit. She was a young mother of two taken too soon, with no suspects in sight. Michael arrived in dark sunglasses, which struck many as a bizarre fashion choice. He occasionally let out a moan as he sat on a couch positioned in front of the open casket, but no one saw him cry. Tracie and Michelle ran around the funeral home, playing under the casket. Michelle at one point ran up to her mother and shook her, demanding that she wake up. Michael, witnesses said, just sat there, unresponsive.

Bob Reams, a comic book shop regular, was struck by

how flat Michael seemed at the funeral. He was "emotion-
less and robotic," Reams later testified. A longtime friend of
Barb's, Kathy Treece had known Michael, too, for years. She
was a bridesmaid in their wedding and chatted with Michael
as he watched the women bowl in a league. But when she arrived at the funeral, he seemed to avoid her. More bizarre,
she overheard him talking to his mother, and it didn't seem
like typical grieving widower talk.

"He said, 'Mom, did you call the insurance company today?'" Treece later recalled. "She didn't hear him and he
asked the question a second time, 'Mom, did you call the
insurance company?'"

Theresa Danieluk, who regularly took her then-twelve-
year-old son to Comics World every Saturday, heard about
the slaying and was disheartened. She had been at the store
less than a week prior—the Saturday before—and remembered that Michael, yet again, volunteered how dissatisfied
he was in his marriage. She had walked inside and Michael,
who had been behind the counter, came out to greet her. The
conversation turned to Barb, and it was not flattering. Michael
said his wife was heavy and unattractive, and that he
wouldn't be with her if it weren't for the two daughters, she
later told police. He said he wanted to take the girls to Florida and leave Barb behind. "It was every conversation when
I went into the comic book store," she later testified. "It was
the same thing."

After the death, Danieluk attended the funeral to pay her
respects. She saw Barb lying in an open casket. She spotted
Michael sitting on the couch in front of it, wearing a dark suit
and sunglasses. When he spotted her, he got up and approached her and gave her a hug that made her uncomfortable.

"It was a hug that I would give my husband, not that I
would give to someone else," she later said. Barb's body lay
not four feet away. She could see the corpse over Michael's
shoulder as he embraced her. Not wanting to make a scene,
Danieluk hugged back, said she was sorry for his loss, and

left. A few weeks later, she stopped by the store again and told Michael how sorry she was. He described that the customers who found her body at first thought she had suffered a heart attack. He said Barb was on her knees when she was shot in the skull. He didn't know why it happened, he told her. There were expensive comic books in the store, but nothing was taken, he said. After Danieluk left the store, Michael followed. He handed her a slip of paper that she accepted, then read later. It was a childish note, the type a twelve-year-old boy shyly hands to the girl he's crushing on. It read: "You look very, very, very pretty today. Thanks for coming in. Sincerely, Michael." Under his name was his phone number.

Danieluk never called Michael, but he called her, she later said. In August, she began getting late-night phone calls at her house when her fiancé was out of town. She recognized Michael's voice. "I saw you today," he said. "You looked pretty." The phone calls were disturbing, prompting Danieluk to call the police, but she never mentioned her conversation with Michael shortly after the slaying—the one in which he denied to her the motive that he'd given police: robbery.

No money was taken, Michael told police after they pestered him for nearly a week for information about his wife's death—but two boxes of moderately priced books had disappeared from the backroom. He filed an insurance claim for the supposedly stolen goods and received $30,000.

When Mary heard within a few months after Barb died that Michael and Renee had moved in together, her uneasiness about Michael's role in Barb's death turned into certainty. She was sure Michael had killed his wife.

Chapter 4

Word Spreads

Headlines about the slaying seized on the happy-occasion-turned-tragic angle: "Shop owner gunned down before party," read the write-up in Saturday's *Macomb Daily*, a county-wide newspaper that had the luxury of dedicating more ink to water rate hikes than murders, unlike the Detroit papers to the south.

The printed details were scarce: Barbara Marie George, thirty-two, dead of a single gunshot to the head. Police said there didn't seem to be a struggle; her death was more like an execution. She'd been organizing a surprise thirtieth birthday party for husband Michael, the story read, but was found ninety minutes prior by customers who thought she'd had a heart attack. The short story foreshadowed trouble to come, however. While Clinton Township Police Lieutenant Donald Brook said police were considering robbery a possible motive, a family friend told the newspaper that the timing was suspect.

"If it weren't for this party, there would probably have been a bunch of people in the store at the time of the shooting, and this whole thing would have probably been deterred," the friend said. And the story noted that employees of the nearby pizzeria—the only other store in the strip mall open at the time of the shooting—heard nothing, no gunshots, no struggle, even though the stores were just fifty feet apart.

As news spread to Dave Stuart, the Hungry Howie's manager, he realized he'd been among the last to see Barb alive. Not an hour before her death, she'd come in to order food for the party. "She was going to pick them up around nine-thirty p.m.," Stuart told the *Daily* the day after the murder. "She was fine that day, her usual friendly self, without a care in the world. We were all shocked. . . . Nothing like this is supposed to happen in this part of town."

The other storeowners began locking up early. Several in the area had been targeted in a rash of recent robberies, though none had turned violent. Now customers were chit-chatting about a killer on the loose—not exactly a boon for business.

"Every customer that comes in here has been talking about it," Michael Stilber, owner of Pro Printing Center, told the *Daily* at the time.

Michael George, meanwhile, posted a note on the door of his store saying it was "closed due to unforeseen circumstances." It would reopen July 20—a week after the slaying.

The murder barely got mentioned in the bigger papers of Detroit; the *Free Press*, the bigger of the two dailies, wrote two stories after the slaying. But the death caught the attention of the comic book world. An August 10, 1990, story in *Comic Buyer's Guide* listed the identifiable highlights of the three-hundred-some comics—specifically the Mylar-bound Silver Age books—that Michael said were stolen. Among them were *Action Comics* No. 6; *Amazing Spider-Man* Nos. 9, 42, and 50; *X-Men* Nos. 4, 5, 6, 9, and 10; *Incredible Hulk* No. 102 (three copies); *Iron Man* No. 1 (three copies, as well as Nos. 3–10); *Iron Man & Sub-Mariner* (two copies); *Daredevil* No. 6; and *Fantastic Four* Nos. 9, 20, 48, 49, and 50.

A few *Turok* books, as well as *Green Lantern, Adventure,* and *Thor*, were also missing. Detective Sergeant Donald

Steckman, one of the lead investigators in the case, told the CBG that those books were the ones cops had the most hope of identifying. He asked that shop owners and sellers keep an eye out, but he warned against drastic action. Try to get the name of whoever's showing the item, he suggested, but do it without raising suspicion.

The comic world was shocked. Their stores were rarely targeted by anything more than kids slipping books down their pants because that week's allowance didn't quite cover their comic-reading habits.

"We hear about robberies from time to time, but very seldom armed robberies," said Brian Hibbs, a founding member of the Board of Directors of the Comics Professional Retailer Organization, owner of Comix Experience in San Francisco and author of the Tilting at Windmills column published at www.comicbookresources.com. "Nine out of ten times, if there's a robbery, it will be break-ins when the store is closed."

Usually, money would be stolen from the cash register along with obvious high-ticket targets on display on the store's walls (not a single box in a back room while the registers and walls were untouched). And it certainly was rare for someone to be killed over comics—especially when the books stolen weren't considered key by avid collectors. There was no *Amazing Fantasy* No. 15, marking the first appearance of Spider-Man, or *Detective Comics* No. 27, which introduced Batman. The most valuable was *Action Comics* No. 6 featuring Superman, which at the time was worth about $2,700, providing its pages, spine, and cover were virtually blemish-free. That magazine, first printed in November 1938, centered around "Superman's Phony Manager," in which Clark Kent's superhero alter ego has to save damsel reporter Lois Lane after she discovers the existence of a phony Superman. Jimmy Olsen also appears as an office boy.

The other *Action Comics* that were on the missing list—numbers 22, 24, 25, and 33 being the oldest—were worth at most $700. No. 22's cover is noteworthy in that it features an *S* on Superman's cape and is the first issue to boast being the "World's Largest Selling Comic Magazine"; it was printed in March 1940. The remainders on the list ranged in value from less than $100 to up to $500, assuming they were in mint condition, according to 1991's *Overstreet Guide*.

"They were Silver Age comics, but it wasn't like they were highly visible," Hibbs said. Someone trying to sell the items might find it easier in that most of the books weren't so highly sought-after that they would stand out. Were an *Action Comics* No. 1 to appear on the for-sale scene, for example, heads might turn, Hibbs said. But not the books Michael George reported as missing.

"These wouldn't necessarily be hard to sell," Hibbs said. "If all the books showed up at one time from one buyer, that would be extremely suspicious, but flipping an *Action* 6, if someone were to do it individually and in an intelligent way, wouldn't be hard whatsoever."

Michael didn't include descriptions of the books' conditions, which would cause the values to vary widely. The only missing *All-American Comics* issue, No. 29, featured "The Patent Medicine Racket" and starred the Green Lantern. In simply good condition, it could bring in some $80. In fine, $210. In mint, a flat $500. And in between, there's an array of mid-grades—fair/good, fine/very fine, near mint, etc. Grading the books is subjective, but dealers are told to check the book thoroughly, from the inside pages to the spine to the cover, for tape, tears, marks, and soiling. Even page brittleness deteriorates a book's worth. Based on *Overstreet* information, it would be unlikely that Michael George's dated collection would be in anything better than near mint condition.

Police sent a list of the stolen books to comic dealers in

Michigan, who then shared it nationwide. It was a tight-knit community, and George had been making a name for himself with the three metro Detroit stores and a fourth on the way. The story published in *Comics Buyer's Guide* quoted Tim Allison, co-owner of the Comics World franchise in Madison Heights: "A lot of the regular customers had been planning a surprise birthday party for Michael, and my partner and I were here running the Madison Heights store. . . . At 5:45, my partner's fiancée was on the line with Barbara, who had locked the cash register and taken the keys out of it."

Barb put the Madison Heights store on hold, sounding as though she were agitated, and never picked the phone up again. Allison said no one heard anything on the phone when it happened. When police arrived, the handset was still off the phone cradle, apparently where Barb had rested it when she stepped away.

The story also quoted Renee Kotula, the future second Mrs. George, with whom Michael George later admitted he'd been having an affair when his wife was killed. Renee said she was readying to open the fourth store at summer's end: "Everyone was so excited for Barbara and Mike," she said. "She was planning on taking them to a golf outing for the weekend, and things were looking great for them. Her brother and I were going to run the store for the weekend, during the outing."

The plan, she said, was for Renee to help decorate the store while Barb and Michael were at dinner.

"She had been planning it for a month," Renee said of the party. "That made it even more traumatic."

Allison told the publication that Comics World staffers met the week after the death to start figuring out how to fill in the gaps left by Barb's absence. She'd handled a lot of the "nuts and bolts on the store, so things are complicated," he said. Everyone seemed to agree that the store should stay open—a plan that Barb's family supported, Renee said.

"It's really nice to see that everyone's pulling together,"

she said. "Everyone's asking if there's anything they can do to help; it's been really impressive."

That may have been Renee's take on things, but behind the scenes, Barb's family said they were growing increasingly suspicious of Michael and his mistress.

Chapter 5

The Scene

On that humid July night in 1990, Barbara George was carried from the store on a stretcher and loaded into an awaiting ambulance. As it sped away, police began scouring the scene for clues. Immediately, they were perplexed. They spotted two cash registers, but neither was open. A safe in the back room seemed undisturbed. The rear door leading into the store's back room was closed and didn't appear to have been futzed with, and first responders had already noticed Barb George didn't seem to be missing any jewelry; her pockets, unrifled. What exactly had happened here?

Sergeant Donald Steckman was put in charge of the investigation, making it his job to figure out exactly what happened and to try to bring to justice the person who did it. By then, he had worked with the Clinton Township Police Department for twenty-two years—after having worked his way up in just six years to detective sergeant. He got the phone call to head to Comics World within minutes of Barb's murder. By 7 p.m., he was en route.

The scene was secured when he got there. Officers were roping off the area, and one evidence technician already was inside taking photographs and gathering clues. Steckman was still absorbing everything that had happened when he saw a man walking toward the store on foot. Steckman stopped him and asked who he was. It was Michael George. Steckman noted it was 8:10 p.m.

The sergeant told George there had been a problem, that his wife was in the hospital. Another detective would drive him to her, Steckman said. George asked if his wife was OK.

"No, she's not," Steckman replied. He intentionally was vague about Barb's injuries, and Michael didn't probe further. The sergeant asked where Michael had been and where he was headed. His mother's house, he replied, and he was returning to meet his wife for dinner. Steckman would need more details on his whereabouts, he explained—a specific timetable of what happened and where he had gone—but first, he suggested Michael go to the hospital. He summoned Lieutenant Brook to drive him there.

Michael stammered. "Something must have fallen and hit her on the head in the back room," he said.

Steckman and Brook both took note. What a strange, unsolicited comment. How did he know where Barb had been found inside the store? Steckman intentionally had not told him.

In the car, Brook began carefully approaching the "where were you when" questions. Michael said he worked the morning at the store until Barb came with their two girls. She then took over and he left with the children to go to his mother's around 4 p.m. and got there by five. He hadn't been back since he'd left Barb at the store.

How is the marriage? Brook asked. Your finances OK? Yes and yes, George replied. He'd just left the store briefly and headed back to go to dinner with his wife to celebrate his birthday. The two were to meet by 8 p.m.

Brook asked if Michael kept money at the store. Sure, George said; they sporadically deposited money throughout the day, then Barb would sometimes take the cash home in her purse or he would put it in his pants pocket. The safe in the back room was kept unlocked and open, he said. George was cooperative, almost chatty. The men began their talk in the squad car on the way to the hospital and continued it until nearly 9 p.m. in the waiting room, where Michael learned his wife indeed was dead. From George's descriptions of his home life and finances, he seemed to have no reason to want to hurt his wife.

At that stage, Brook knew he was dealing with a suspicious death, though he didn't know the cause. But soon, he would learn that an emergency room nurse, while cleaning Barb's face and hair of blood, discovered the bullet hole in the top of her head. That made Michael George's comment about a head injury even more suspicious.

Back at the scene, Sergeant Douglas Mills, then a sixteen-year veteran with the Clinton Township department, arrived about 8 p.m., armed with an RCA Pro Wonder video camera. It wasn't department-issued; he brought it from home, at Steckman's request, to film the room so that detectives could look back at the scene to refresh their memories as the investigation unfolded. He videotaped for nineteen minutes, dryly narrating as the video scanned the unkempt store.

The camera work was shaky. Back then, video cameras were bulky, not the cell phone–sized devices they are today. Mills's camera was about two feet long, about a foot tall and weighed a good two pounds. He stopped and started the tape to keep view of his footing, making sure he didn't trip and fall or disturb evidence.

Evidence technicians also worked the store, carefully taking pictures to document the scene. They shot a wide picture of the back room, showing how plastic crates lined the room from floor nearly to the ceiling so that there was just a pathway leading to the back wall. There, a safe sat on the floor. Some Mylar bags, used to wrap the comics, jutted out from a nearby box and obstructed access to the safe. Above the safe was a push-pin board covered in extraneous papers, a photograph of Barb and Michael and a calendar featuring popular swimsuit model Kathy Ireland in a barely-there bikini.

There was a bullet hole in Kathy's left eye.

Click-click-click. The photographers excitedly snapped away. A bullet hole in the wall could translate to important evidence. It could mean the gunman fired a warning shot to startle a perhaps uncooperative Barb. Or maybe he missed the first time. Or maybe it was a test shot fired before Barb was even there—to check out his aim, to see if neighbors noticed the noise, to build up some courage. The only possibility investigators didn't want to pan out was that the bullet hole was somehow unrelated to the shooting—because then it would mean nothing to them.

Mills set down the video camera and began helping process the scene. First, he concentrated on the floor, hoping to lift footprints from the carpet using an electrostatic dust print lifter. The device, still used nearly twenty years later, uses electrodes to shoot a low-grade electrical current through a film sheet. The current ignites static electricity to lift dirt and debris onto the sheet. The dirt keeps its form, allowing technicians to lift footprints, tire marks, or other impression evidence, which then is analyzed forensically. At the time, the Clinton Township Police Department was ahead of its time in using the lifter. Mills used the lifter around the cash registers. He decided that using it in the back of the store would be useless, though, because of the slew of medical personnel and law-enforcement agents who had been there.

Then Mills turned his attention to the safe. It sat in the back room in the northwest section near a furnace. The room was unkempt, with piles of comic books inside the stacked plastic bins. It was like a maze, Mills marveled. Those bins made it tough to see the safe straight away. They were situated so that there were aisles to walk through, but Mills noted that someone who didn't know the store and its layout probably wouldn't even see the small, beige safe sitting on the floor.

The safe door was closed, but it was unlocked. Inside was empty.

Mills set out to find fingerprints. The surface of the safe was fairly slick, a decent home for the prints left behind by skin's natural oils collecting at the raised ridges of the fingers and palms. He didn't find a full print, however, just a ridge structure, or partial print. He used a laser and camera another evidence tech had borrowed from the nearby Macomb Community College and photographed the mark on black-and-white film. He wasn't sure how useful the print would be, though. It wasn't ideal quality and it didn't appear as though there had been any ransacking of the store at all. There was a good chance this print would just belong to one of the owners, he figured. He snapped some pictures and moved on.

Some of the boxes in the back room indeed had been tipped, possibly by the killer, or perhaps by Lenora and Tom Ward and subsequent medics who tried to breathe life back into Barb as she lay blue-lipped on the floor. Mills snapped more pictures.

Officers discussed whether they should run tests for gunshot residue, but they had had bad luck with the tests in the past. The tests search for certain heavy metals—barium and lead, for example—that are expelled from a gun when it's fired, but in the 1990s, the threshold was pretty low for a law-enforcement agency to conclude the test was positive. So long as the test site had two of the elements present, it could be deemed gunshot residue. Because of that, police hit a lot of false positives. As years passed, the courtroom standards for declaring positive identification of gunshot residue would become more specific. They want the presence of barium, lead, *and* antimony in at least one spot, as well as more supporting particles elsewhere. Mills shrugged off the test as useless and set out to look for the shell casings—the cartridges that encase the lead bullet and are expelled when the gun is fired—to send to the Michigan State Police for GSR testing. A shell casing would clear up any confusion over potential false positives, so the state police had begun asking for them to beef up the evidence. Mills got on his hands and knees and combed the floor but found no casings.

Mills stayed at the store for more than eight hours—from 8 p.m. to 4:30 a.m. Aside from walking out the back door briefly for some air, he never left. He had videotaped, searched for shell casings, dusted for fingerprints, lifted shoeprints. Outsiders saw the men inside working and felt sorry for them. They dropped off coffee and soda. By the time he left as the sun rose Saturday, Mills was exhausted and left the scene.

But on Monday, when he was back on regular road patrol, he swung by the store again. Something about the case bothered him. He found some officers still perusing the scene. He went inside and decided to take another look at Kathy Ireland. The afterthought paid off. The bullet had pierced Kathy's eye, passed through the corkboard, cleared the dry-wall, and had gotten lodged in the brick and mortar of the north wall of an adjacent vacant building. The bullet was mangled. Mills couldn't even tell what caliber it was. But it was something.

Lieutenant John Neal knew Clinton Township as well as anybody at the department. He became a cop April 1, 1968, as one of the original twenty-one members of the department. When it became clear that Barbara George's death was no heart attack or accident, he was called in to handle the inevitable interview of her husband. Michael arrived at the station about 11 p.m. and Neal joined Steckman in the routine interview. Michael said he'd left the store between 4 and 4:30 p.m. and gone to his mother's house, and when he returned for the planned dinner with his wife—which he didn't know was actually a ruse for a surprise party—police had already pulled her body from the store.

Steckman repeated many of the questions his colleague Brook had asked in the car: How was your marriage?

"He said everything was fine," Steckman later testified.

Any extramarital affairs police should know about? No.

George said that when he left the store in his wife's care, two men were with her—Joe Gray and Matt Baczewski. Detectives at the scene had noticed a Pinkerton Security hat in the store that seemed out of place, so Neal asked George about it. No, no, George replied. The hat was his; it had been a gift from a few years prior. Were you and Barb having any problems? No, he insisted. Were you concerned about the safety around the store? No.

The conversation lasted no more than a half-hour. Michael wasn't treated as a suspect. His hands weren't swabbed for gunshot residue. Neal didn't take his clothing for blood spatter or GSR testing. These were all decisions that would come back to haunt investigators nearly two decades later.

After the interview, Steckman took George to the comic book store and asked him to look around and see if he spotted anything missing. The detectives hadn't been able to open the cash register—neither could Renee Kotula, who had shown up to drop off soda for the party—so Michael popped the registers open and said the money was still there. But, he said, there was about $2,000 missing from the safe in the back room, and two cardboard boxes missing from on top of the safe that had held expensive collectors' comics books.

Steckman asked what kind of books. If stolen books began circulating the comic book world, maybe they could be traced back to the seller—who, with any luck, might also be the killer. George didn't know the titles offhand, however. He'd have to get back to detectives.

"We kept pushing Mr. George to give us a list of the comic books," Steckman testified. It took nearly a week before George turned the list over. Police sent the list to sellers across the area; no one had seen any pop up recently for sale.

George was just as slow writing up a specific timetable for officers. In the days after the slaying, Steckman repeatedly

tried to get back in touch to have George spell out specifically what he had done that day.

"It took six days to get that," Steckman later said. "Every
time I talked to him he kept putting me off."

He finally got it midweek, after Barb's funeral. Michael's
day began about seven, he told police, when he woke up for
work. He went to the store about 9 a.m. to open up for customers around ten. Barb showed up at 4 p.m. with the children. She was there to tag-team with the kids so that he
could take them to his mother's and she could watch the
store while he was away. He left the store between 4:15 and
4:30 p.m., fell asleep on his mother's couch, then left to return to the store about 7:30 p.m.—a slight variation from his
earlier estimate of an intended 8 p.m. arrival. When he arrived, he was greeted by yellow police tape and milling
officers.

In the days that followed, Neal handled several interrogations. He talked to longtime customer Michael Renaud (whose
information about a phone call he made close to the time Barb
died would be lost in the case file), a Michigan State Police
crime lab technician, Barb's sister and one of her brothers,
Christine Ball and Joe Kowynia. And he interviewed Jea-
nette Renee Kotula, known by friends simply as Renee; rumors had begun circling that Michael was sleeping with her.
She denied any affair. So did Michael.

Neal sent a letter to John Hancock Life Insurance Co.
asking about the policies Michael had on his wife. He had
two, one for about $100,000, and another for $30,000, the
combination of which in 1990 was a hefty amount. Michael
was the sole beneficiary. That alone didn't seen too suspicious, as Michael had worked for the same insurance company in his mid-twenties, before quitting and fulfilling his
dream of opening up a comic book store. Insurance salesmen
are known to buy the kinds of policies they want to sell—
the heftier, the better, when it comes to honestly reassuring a

customer that they're purchasing the same type of insurance the seller has on his own loved ones. Curiously, though, Neal noticed that while Barb's life insurance was up to date and substantial, Michael had let his own lapse. As the primary breadwinner in the family, he had no life insurance at all.

Neal's suspicion was piqued, but he simply did not have enough on Michael to get any warrants, he thought. And Michael, who had initially been so cooperative the day of the slaying—chatting in the squad car and hospital with Brook, then back at the detective bureau with Neal—clammed up after the funeral. That was particularly odd when coupled with people's descriptions of the supposedly grieving widower at the funeral itself. As Neal, Brook, and other detectives moved forward in their investigation, they heard again and again that Michael had worn sunglasses to Barb's funeral, that he seemed aloof and unaffected. One woman said he'd grabbed her near his wife's coffin and held her tightly in such a sexually charged embrace that she'd left, mortified. He'd also slipped her a strange note when she offered condolences at the store, telling her that she looked pretty that day and including his phone number on the note. It was all odd behavior.

As George steadily became less cooperative, the bits of information police gleaned from him seemed to become more and more contradictory. Like that $2,000 he initially reported missing to Steckman: later, he told other officers that he and Barb never kept money in the store. He phoned Steckman a few days after the slaying to say that no, he was mistaken, there hadn't been money in the safe after all.

"This is where we had the problem with the statements that he was giving me," Steckman later testified. "He told other officers . . . that particular day he had I believe two or three bank drops that he had made, that there was never money kept in the safe."

Barb's family noted at the hospital that he seemed off, too, though they dismissed it as a grieving husband not knowing how to react to the horrific news. When a nurse came out to finally confirm that yes, Barbara George had died, the family was invited to view the body if they so wished. Brothers Peter and Joe agreed; Michael stayed behind. Joe walked in and saw his sister's lifeless body lying on a gurney. Her face and body had been washed clean of the blood that had spewed from her head and mouth, but her hair was in a bonnet and her hands had been bagged to preserve evidence. Aside from an abrasion on her head, apparently from falling to the ground after she was shot, Barb was injury-free.

Her family was lost. Barb had no enemies. She didn't use drugs. She didn't gamble. Perhaps the store had been robbed, but whoever shot her left behind the diamond on her left hand and a few hundred dollars in her pocket. Nothing made sense.

Michael didn't seem interested in trying to make sense of it all, either. Two weeks after the investigation began, he quit cooperating with police. He refused a polygraph test and stopped answering the cops' questions. The investigation was already stalling.

Chapter 6

The Investigation Hits a Dead End

The angle of the bullet in Barb George's head, matched with the bullet hole through Kathy Ireland's eye on the wall calendar behind her, led Steckman to believe one of two things: Either Barb dove to the floor after the gunman fired an errant first round, or she was ordered to her hands and knees and shot from above. The gunman had to be in the back room, too, the sergeant reasoned, based on the angle of the bullet and how narrow and cluttered that room was.

Elements of Michael's timeline didn't sit well with Steckman. While the skeleton of it was plausible overall, little things didn't mesh with what others had told police. Barb, for example, didn't show up anywhere near the store, per Michael's description, until between 4 and 4:30 p.m., but a woman who worked at a nail salon in the strip mall recalled seeing Barb there about two hours earlier. Kimberly Koliba was outside smoking a cigarette and had come to recognize the sight of Barb and Michael fighting over the past few months. They had been arguing more and more often, and the nail techs in Venice Square had started to gossip. Usually it was about money or gambling. Michael was known to bet on football and liked to play poker, which Barb found upsetting. The two just didn't make the kind of money to throw away on gambling, she complained. She wanted him to stop.

As loud as some of the other fights had been, the one Friday before Barb's death was the worst. Koliba noticed Michelle, the youngest, outside the front door, pounding to get inside. Michael opened the door, allowing the sound of yelling to waft down the alleyway, grabbed Michelle, and slammed the door.

But there was a problem with Koliba's statement. While she said she saw the fight the day Barb died, she told police it was July 12—the day before the shooting—and specifically said that on July 13, she saw nothing. She would later say she'd simply mixed up the dates, but it was enough to undermine her credibility. Plus, witnessing an argument is hardly the same as witnessing a crime. Couples argue, and the Georges were no exception. Steckman would need to piece together the day's events if he wanted to solve the crime. He, Lieutenant Neal, and Lieutenant Brook divvied up the interviews. Based on the information they got, here is how the day reportedly unfolded.

Michael opened the store about 10 a.m. with Matt Baczewski, a nineteen-year-old who worked part-time helping the Georges out. Matt began the day with a secret: He knew about Barb's plan to close the store early and surprise Michael with a party to celebrate his thirtieth birthday. Matt remembered Barb arriving between 4 and 4:15 p.m. with the girls, and Michael leaving soon after, apparently to take them to his mom's house. Matt left by five to grab a bite and set about gathering party supplies for the night's event. He never saw Barb alive again.

Janet George, Michael's mother, told investigators that Barb called her around 5 to 5:30 p.m., saying Michael was on his way. Janet's job, aside from taking the girls overnight, was to keep Michael occupied at the house for as long as possible so Barb could get the store ready for the surprise party. Janet's recollection matched Michael's: Once her son got there, he fell asleep on the couch, she said, while she took the girls to the park at the Henry Ford School down the street. At some point he called the store but didn't get an answer. After that, he headed out to return to the store. She wasn't positive what time he had left, but she remembered warning him that traffic would be a pain at that hour. Her son, she said, had been at her house the entire late afternoon, leaving no time for him to drive a half-hour each way back to the store to kill his wife.

Barbee Hancock was just a teenager while dating a comic book guy who regularly dragged her into Comics World, where she met Barb, a friendly woman who seemed interested in the teen's everyday problems. Even though she and the guy had broken up, Barbee still swung by the store on occasion to chat with Barb. She did just that on July 13, arriving sometime between 5 and 5:30 p.m. The door was locked and she had to wait a few minutes for Barb to arrive. The harried storeowner said she had been down the street ordering food for the night's party. She let Barbee inside and the two chatted a few minutes about Barbee's pregnancy. Then the phone rang.

Barb answered and seemed uneasy. Someone was asking about expensive comic books, and Barb told the person on the line that she wouldn't discuss the matter over the phone, that they'd have to talk in person at the store. Barbee left the store after just a few minutes' chat.

Around 6 p.m., Barb was on the phone again. This time, she placed a call to Renee Balsick, who helped run a Comics World franchise in Madison Heights. Barb began chatting about the evening's surprise party. Renee and her then-fiancé were supposed to attend. Barb wanted to know when they planned to show up. After a few minutes, Barb said to hold on a second, she'd be right back, and placed the phone down. Balsick could hear background noise, but nothing out of the ordinary—no yelling, no scuffling. Balsick waited a minute, then began helping customers while occasionally checking back on the line to see if Barb had returned. She never did.

Eventually, Balsick decided Barb had forgotten about her, so she hung up the phone and called back. The line blared busy.

Soon after, when Tom Ward would call 911, he would find the phone handset placed carefully on top of the wall-mounted base, apparently where Barb had left Balsick on hold.

Ward hung up the phone so he could get a dial tone and called 911 shortly after 6 p.m.; Patrol Officer Ross Amicucci got the call at 6:22 and was the first unit to arrive. It had been reported simply as a medical run. When he arrived, people in the store directed him to a woman down in the back. Lenora Ward was performing CPR. Amicucci took over on chest compressions while Lenora continued to do mouth-to-mouth. Within fifteen minutes, the ambulance arrived and rushed Barb to the hospital. Soon after that, Amicucci and other first responders used Barb's own keys to lock up the store and leave.

"It didn't appear to be any crime or anything unusual," Amicucci later testified. "Basically, it was a heart attack. The lady fell, maybe possibly hit her head, and that was about it."

Police would rush back within minutes once they learned that the death was a homicide, not a heart attack, and the search for clues would begin.

A couple of people reported seeing bizarre characters the day of the slaying. Police didn't know what to make of the descriptions. One teenager, Douglas Kenyon, described a man wearing a baseball cap and sunglasses inside the store who made him uneasy. Kenyon was there picking up a comic he had put on reserve in one of the baskets for regular customers that Michael and Barb kept in the back room. Kenyon didn't see the man's face, couldn't estimate his age or even pinpoint what about him seemed off. Detectives took and filed his statement, but wondered if the teenager's imagination had gotten a little carried away after he learned he was in the store less than an hour before Barb was killed.

Then there was the man the Wards saw driving away from the shopping center. They weren't able to describe him in detail, either, nor did they see him physically at the store. They simply saw him driving away at a speed they felt was too fast for the strip mall parking lot. And, finally, there was the strange character Tom Ward described—slightly built, in a Greek fisherman's cap, perhaps wearing a fake beard and mustache. Police never got a line as to who those people might have been and what role, if any, they played in Barbara George's death.

For the officer-in-charge, it seemed like Michael George was the only person with motive and means to kill his wife, and as Michael grew increasingly reluctant to help investigators, Steckman became more and more certain the husband was to blame. But Steckman found nothing—no physical evidence, no witness statement, nothing—that placed George at the scene of the crime. The case grew cold. Police were certain that Michael was a killer, but the system relies on evidence, not gut feelings, so they never even sent the case file to the prosecutor's office to see if the county's top law-enforcement agent deemed there to be enough evidence to file charges against George. It simply faded in people's memories.

A story that ran Aug. 17, 1990, in the *Detroit Free Press* was more prophetic than its author could possibly have known. "It may be long after Tracie George turns 5 next month before information surfaces to help the little girl understand what happened to her mother," the story, written by staff reporter Marty Hair, began. "Police say they have loose strands of information but, as yet, no fabric of facts to make sense of the violent final minutes of Barbara George's life."

Lieutenant Neal told the paper that leads were coming in but simply weren't going anywhere.

Hair interviewed Michael George as well. He said he'd moved with his two girls out of the trailer and in with his mother. Michelle, at just two, was too young to understand, he said, but Tracie was less fortunate.

"I just told her, 'Momma went to Heaven,'" George told the paper.

The previous Sunday, he said, he and Tracie were alone in the store and cried for an hour together. He was considering taking her to see a psychiatrist.

George said the two containers of stolen comics were worth $30,000, that he had had no inkling about the surprise party Barb had been planning, and that the fourth store in Rochester Hills still was on track to open Sept. 1 despite the business taking such a hit with Barb's loss.

"She did all the book work, all the running around," he told the paper. "She did a lot."

Michael George closed the Garfield store soon after the slaying and opened a new one on Hayes Road instead. The building was bigger, and Renee Kotula was now his partner. By then, they were no longer hiding their affection. Renee had stepped in to help care for Tracie and Michelle, and the families were quickly merging together.

Joe Kowynia, Barb's brother, finally listened to his girlfriend's suspicions once he learned that Michael and Renee indeed were a couple. He and Mary had gone by themselves to search for the murder weapon outside of the strip mall, hoping they would uncover something police had missed. They turned up nothing. Joe made a point to swing by the new store on occasion, curious to see how the couple would react to him catching them off guard. Within two years, Michael and Renee closed that shop, too, and moved to Pennsylvania with the girls. Joe never confronted Michael about his suspicions; nearly twenty years later, he would say that perhaps he should have, but he was trying to keep the peace for the sake of Michelle and Tracie. Still, that wasn't easy. In his eyes, they were living with the man who had killed their mother—and gotten away with it.

Chapter 7

Michael George's New Life

Police knew Michael George was a player. They'd heard stories about Michael the flirt, Michael the philanderer, even Michael the borderline stalker. Some female customers said he gave them the willies by complimenting them a little too enthusiastically and even passing along his phone number to a few of them. But detectives were most intrigued by rumors about a relationship that Michael denied—with employee Renee Kotula. She was pretty and petite, though as a newly divorced mother of five, she was hardly the quick-hit score that most bosses would high-five their friends about.

In the days after Barb's death, Renee comforted her apparently grief-stricken lover. Neighbors saw her with the two girls, taking them into her brood. Tracie was Joshua's age; Michelle, at just two, was a redheaded handful. Renee knew how to handle a full house.

It was a strained start to what eventually would be a lasting marriage, Renee would say nearly two decades later. Her relationship with Michael budded in chaos and blossomed through sorrow. She had been Barb's friend first. They'd met through the children's preschool. Renee, a newly separated mother, needed a job; Barb, a working mother of two, needed help at the store. She hired Renee to keep shop.

Renee worked one evening a week at the store when the comic order came in. She'd staff the register and get the orders ready for the other stores. She also ran a franchise in Rochester Hills for the couple. She was no comic book buff naturally, but her oldest son, Joey, was a collector, and the new job earned her some "cool mom" points as well as extra money.

Michael was flirtatious, but it was more than that. He was kind and funny, and while Renee would never publicly say anything bad about her ex-husband—"He's the father of my children," she says as an almost apologetic explanation for her lack of candor—she acknowledges simply that the two men were "different."

"Have you ever seen *The Office*? The joke in our family is that Michael *is* Michael Scott," said Renee, describing the good-natured but painfully oblivious boss on the NBC sitcom. He's the type to jokingly talk smack about whooping his athletic daughters at basketball—he could if he wanted to, anyway, he'd claim—while also being so proud of the girls that he covered his office with every newspaper clipping that mentioned their names and accomplishments.

"You know at graduations, you see some men quietly wiping away a few tears?" Renee described with a laugh. "Not my husband. He's sobbing, wiping away handfuls."

After Barb's death, Michael denied the rumors about him and Renee. He and Barb were fine, he told investigators; he wasn't cheating. Seventeen years later, when investigators told Michael they were reopening the case, he would finally admit the truth: He and Renee had been having an affair, and it was more emotional than physical. Barb knew he was cheating and had demanded he stop. She found out, he said, by "just being smart and me being stupid."

"She confronted me with it, and I said I would stop," he told detectives later. "I'm sure it wasn't one confrontation. It was over a period of time."

Even Barb's family knew about the affair. As Christine,

Barb's sister, sat next to Michael at the hospital July 13, 1990, she verbalized the question everyone else was too shocked to ponder: Could it have been Renee's ex-husband?

Michael's response was telling: simply "no." Not "Why would he have?" because everyone knew the answer to that.

Everyone except the police.

Before Barb's death, she and Michael had been planning to move from their cramped trailer into a nice-sized home that was still under construction. Barb had taken family members there shortly before her death. She was excited about the move and what it meant, both practically and symbolically, for her family. After she died, Michael moved in with the two girls. Renee might have joined him, were it not for Joe Kotula.

"I don't think she would have been allowed to," Michael told police, "because Joe Kotula would have said something."

Instead, Renee lived in a townhouse with her five children as her relationship with Michael continued growing. The next two years became a blur, she said: "Ours was a relationship bonded in sorrow," she said. "I would do anything for him now, but we were on and off. It wasn't a normal start to a relationship." The two forged ahead, closing the Venice Square Comics World and opening another, but only briefly. Slowly, she said, they'd fallen in love and wanted to leave Michigan to raise their merging families somewhere else—somewhere safer than crime-ridden metro Detroit.

Renee's family had roots in a small Pennsylvania burg called Windber. About ninety minutes east of Pittsburgh, the town was known for its coal-mining past. A set of railroad tracks cuts through the quaint downtown; its lack of railroad crossing barricades serves as a reminder that the tracks went cold decades ago. Today, the occasional train again crosses through town, and residents get so excited to see it alive again that they gather trackside, watch and cheer.

In Somerset County, less than ten miles south of larger

Johnstown, Windber is one of those small towns that seemed destined to always be a tiny dot on the map, partly because Johnstown never took off itself. It seemed poised for greatness in the mid-1800s when the Pennsylvania Main Line Canal made it a port city, but soon the railroads made the canal superfluous and Johnstown lost its status as a key cargo transfer point. Next came the iron, coal, and steel. Johnstown boomed with the latter toward the late 1800s thanks to the Cambria Iron Co., which dwarfed the ironworks of bigger cities such as Pittsburgh and Cleveland. This brought prosperity to the region, and Windber was founded in 1897 as an offshoot. In 2000 Johnstown to the north had a population of about 76,000 and offered decent public transportation for a town its size.

The city had shouldered its share of tragedy even before it was officially christened. Disaster struck with the Great Flood of 1889 when the South Fork Dam collapsed during heavy rains, killing 2,209 people from the area and temporarily leaving Johnstown reeling. Still, the area forged ahead, and Windber officially was born eight years later. Another devastating flood hit in 1936. This time, in the midst of the Great Depression, times weren't so prosperous. President Franklin D. Roosevelt toured the city and greenlighted a federally funded project that allowed the U.S. Army Corps of Engineers to channelize the rivers through town—and allowed Johnstown to declare itself "flood free" for nearly four decades. That came to an end in 1977, when a line of thunderstorms carved new channels and leveled apartment buildings and homes. Streets were flooded; expressways, damaged beyond repair. Though officials at the time said it could have been worse—the FDR-ordered channels likely kept the water levels significantly lower, and thus saved lives and real estate—that came as little consolation to the area. Eighty-five people died; property damage tolls reached some $300 million. Somerset County in general, and Johnstown in particular, already was struggling as steel competition had grown stiffer overseas. The '77 flood nailed Johnstown's coffin closed.

Windber was far from insulated. In 1940, about 9,000 people lived in its 2.1 square miles—a decent population for a burgeoning town. In 2000, the population was about half that, the U.S. Census counted. Median household income: about $23,000. Though founded by a couple of coal barons, its success was linked to Johnstown's, and when the steel industry faltered, so, too, did coal. Today, its downtown is a smattering of cute, colloquial, and historic businesses, most notably the Arcadia Theater, which still shows movies advertised on an old-style marquee. Up a winding road on the town's outskirts is an overlook that highlights the remnants of a coal-mining town, including the bathhouse where miners tried (usually in vain) to clean themselves of the soot so as not to track it back home.

Lest their hometown be written off as a dead mining town, Windber residents are quick to point out that in recent years, it's diversified, opening a sought-after cancer center and medical facility. And while that image of cheering residents at the train tracks might seem simplistic, it's symbolic, too, they say: The tracks aren't cold anymore. Windber is alive and well. It's the type of town that unites to face tragedy. When infamous Flight 93 crashed in a field in Shanksville on September 11, 2001, in a thwarted terrorist attack, parents and teachers in Windber, about a forty-minute drive from the crash site, banded together to keep tabs on children, who were under lockdown at schools while authorities sorted out what had happened and whether it was safe to send kids home. Everyone in Windber knows everyone else, and they tend to look after their own.

Renee's roots were deep in the city. Her father lived in a brick house across the street from the high school. Her grandfather's name adorned a memorial dedicated to the many men who'd died mining-related deaths. His ailment: black lung. Renee wanted to be somewhere familiar, a place more steeped in history than defined by sprawl. And she wanted to raise her children farther away from homicide-heavy Detroit.

Two years after Barb's death, Renee and Michael married and moved to Windber, where he and the girls had tagged along on a few family trips already. Renee's parents gave them two plots of land. The plan was to open a store, and being in a sleepy borough was no problem. "We sold so much product online that it didn't really matter where our location was," Renee recalled. Even in 1992, at the time of the move, a Web group called Sports Net facilitated the sale of caseloads of sports cards, so the couple was doing fine from a business standpoint. One of the chunks of land was in a business district along Graham Avenue, where they decided to build a store from scratch. Unlike the Clinton Township store, this one would have a full basement for storage and two showrooms upstairs. For Renee, it felt comfortable: Her grandparents' furniture store was next door, and her grandmother's beauty shop was to the other side.

About a half-mile away on 9th Street, they focused on renovating a triplex built at the turn of the century into a home big enough for the *Brady Bunch*–like brood. The two extra kitchens were converted into bedrooms. By the time the project was finished, it had eight bedrooms and four bathrooms, so all the kids had their own space—a priority for Renee, who said her biggest concern in merging the families was ensuring there was enough room for everyone. Financially, Windber was a significantly cheaper place to live and do business than Michigan. Their property tax was cut by about one-third, and building a new store cost less than renting one in metro Detroit.

The most promising aspect, Renee said, was the crime rate. Pittsburgh and Philadelphia had hefty crime rates, some years on par with Detroit's post-Murder City days of the 1970s, but both big cities were far away—Pittsburgh about ninety-five miles east, and Philly some 230 miles west. Even in 2007, the year Michael's case was reopened, Windber logged just ten violent crimes, according to FBI statistics. There were no murders and no rapes and just a handful of robberies and aggravated assaults.

As the couple settled in, Michael decided to pursue another comic-oriented dream: to launch an annual convention. The Detroit area already had its Motor City Comic Con, but Pittsburgh had none. In 1994, after building some word-of-mouth momentum, Michael and Renee drummed up support for an event that in part was designed to raise money for the Make-A-Wish Foundation. Renee had been introduced to the organization through some family members in Pennsylvania when she learned of a little boy needing an organ transplant at the Pittsburgh Children's Hospital. The boy wanted to be a comic book artist and loved baseball, so Michael and Renee organized a trip for the boy to a Pirates game with some artists. The couple also used the Pittsburgh Comicon to set up a fund-raising silent auction that would become an annual event staple. Michael served as auctioneer, and the first year, the event raised about $2,800 for the charity.

"We thought we were kicking butt," Renee later joked, noting that the money wasn't enough to grant even one wish. The subsequent years gained momentum, and the silent auction was padded with a fund-raising casino night that allowed Michael, a gambling man, to play Vegas for a cause. In 2001, the event raised more than $30,000, and by 2008, the Comicon in total had donated $280,000 to Make-A-Wish, Renee said.

In Windber, Michael George carved a reputation for himself as a "tremendous family man, a respected businessperson in the community," the Rev. Brad Westover would later say on *Dateline*. People knew that Michael's first wife had been murdered, but they didn't know the circumstances—nor did they have any clue that nearly four hundred miles away in Clinton Township, Michigan, a handful of cops would consider him not a philanthropist and shopkeep, but a cheating husband who had gotten away with murder.

* * *

Though Renee and Michael say they never talked about his wife's death, Renee said she saw the aftereffects firsthand.

"When we were building the store, Michael was still concerned about security. A better word may be in a state of panic," she recalled. "He had a security system installed with a panic alarm by the register. After the first year, it had gone off so many times accidentally that the police department asked us to turn it off."

Michael also asked the contractor to put bars on the store's windows, Renee said, but the city's building department would not allow it.

"Thank goodness, because it would have looked so out of place in this small town," Renee said.

At first, Michael worried about Renee's family accepting him and his girls, she said, but there was no strife. They opened their arms and quickly became part of the family.

"He just wanted a safe environment for them to grow up in," she said. "Windber provided that for us. This is a place where the whole town comes to see your kid play in a football game or basketball game and there is a parade for every occasion."

Michael helped coach the girls' basketball teams and refereed basketball at the community recreation center. Both Michelle and Tracie went on to play college basketball; two of the mixed brood were All-Staters in sports—Tracie in basketball, Joshua in football.

"We were blessed to be able to raise them all here," Renee said.

Fifteen years after the couple moved to Windber, however, the small-town familiarity would become as much curse as blessing. That's when a determined detective decided to reopen the dusty case, uncovering a long-misplaced clue that had slipped by investigators the first time around. Michael and Renee's quiet life was about to change forever.

Book Two

Chapter 8

Enter Eric Smith

Barbara George's murder was one of those cases that people couldn't seem to let go. Around the Clinton Township Police Department, it had become known as the Comic Book Murder—a cop-speak title that among long-timers needed no further explanation. A quick reference conjured the gnawing details: woman killed, husband suspected, case frozen in time.

Police Chief Robert Smith was officer-in-charge, Steckman's boss, and, thus, the true overseer of the Michael George case. He was a gruff man's man who always seemed to be chewing a cigar. Immediately after Barb's death, he was on the phone constantly, keeping in touch with the detective sergeants and lieutenants to whom he had delegated the case. He didn't say much to his family, despite their keen interest in the unusually high-profile case, recalled his middle son, Eric Smith.

"He might've grumbled, 'Ehhh, a murder,' " Smith said, his voice dropping low and husky. "My dad didn't talk about work a whole lot. He was a big guy with a big personality and a big presence, but he didn't discuss things from work with us at all."

In 1990, Eric Smith was a second-year law student and

an intern working for the prosecutor's office in neighboring St. Clair County. Though his focus mostly was on school and work, the George case caught his attention. He was still living in his parents' three-bedroom ranch while in school, and random crime just didn't happen in Clinton Township. It's all anyone could seem to talk about.

"Back then, you didn't have random crime, period, much less random murders," Smith recalled. "People just didn't get shot in Clinton Township."

Immediately, suspicion was cast on the husband, as is usually the case. And while the elder Smith was tight-lipped about the details in 1990, as the years passed, he became more candid with his son, who graduated law school and was hired at age twenty-six to work as a Macomb County assistant prosecutor by then-bigwig Carl Marlinga. Marlinga has said it was Eric's ear-to-ear grin that helped get him the job: After the job interview, the prosecutor asked Eric if there was anything else Marlinga should know. "He flashed that smile," Marlinga would recount later, as his protégé's star began to rise, "and said, 'Generally, people like me.' " Eric got the job.

As Eric climbed the ladder in the office, working his way up to the head of the sex crimes unit, his father's career was winding down. About six years after the George slaying, Robert Smith retired as police chief, spending more time at home with his wife and at their condo in Florida. He and his children were close, though, with daughter Lisa moving across the street from her parents and oldest son Bobby becoming fire marshal in Clinton Township. The Smiths tended to stay close to the family's ranch-style home, and because Venice Square plaza was on Garfield—a main drag in the area—they regularly passed the storefront that had long ago been vacated by Michael and Renee George, the site of Barb's unsolved shooting. The case was never far from Eric's thoughts.

"I noticed it more after I became a prosecutor," Eric Smith

recalled. "George's name would pop up, or we would drive by the comic book store and he'd say 'that guy' or 'that husband.' It'd be something like, 'Ehhh, we're gonna get that guy one day.' He knew there was an unsolved case there, and everyone in the department thought Mike George was the one who committed this crime."

Robert Smith died in 2000, the case file still dusty. Eric, meanwhile, began setting his sights on higher office when his boss ran into some legal trouble that threatened to force him out of office: Marlinga was accused of accepting campaign contributions in his failed bid for U.S. Congress in exchange for intervening in two rape cases. The turmoil divided the office, with half standing by their longtime, nice-guy boss and the other half at least questioning his leadership. Some flat-out believed he was a criminal. One of Marlinga's own underlings, Eric Kaiser, reportedly assisted federal agents with their investigation.

"Every day, you'd hear a new rumor," Eric Smith recalled. "It'd be, 'This week, Carl's gonna be charged.' Or 'Eric [Kaiser] was wearing a wire.'"

Smith backed Carl, though he thought his boss had used bad judgment and opened himself up to criminal charges. Marlinga was up for reelection in November 2004, and in April, the federal government indeed indicted him on charges he'd swapped prosecutorial favors for money donated to the failed congressional bid he'd lost two years prior. Marlinga at first was steadfast in refusing to withdraw from the campaign, but Smith saw an opportunity to move ahead and announced he would run. Backed by area builders upset with Marlinga for employing an environmental prosecuting attorney, Smith threw a $500-a-head fundraiser dinner, his first ever. It raised $55,000, and suddenly a virtual no-name became a formidable opponent.

As Eric had predicted, Marlinga ended up withdrawing from the race anyway, saying he needed to focus on the mounting legal challenge he faced. Eric stepped up his campaigning, hitting every gathering in the county he could fit into his schedule.

"If there were ten people gathered somewhere in the county and I heard about it, I was there with them," Eric later said. People he met seemed to mostly fall into two categories: seniors who had been scammed—a problem he pledged to address with a senior crimes unit—and people who had lost loved ones in cold cases that were never solved.

"I heard from mothers and fathers and brothers and daughters saying someone was murdered and no one was prosecuted in the case," he said. "You could see the anguish in their faces. They clearly haven't been able to let go of the pain."

That was 2004, and cold cases seemed to be gaining popularity thanks to forensic-focused shows on TV and the proliferation of cases reversed after DNA evidence had cleared the prime suspect by pointing to a different culprit. If Eric wanted to be prosecutor, he felt he needed to address those people who thought law enforcement had passed them by, he said.

"It wasn't just that someone was murdered and no one had been arrested," Eric said. "It was that their loved one didn't mean anything to law enforcement, to the government."

Eric promised he'd set up a cold case unit to shine new light on those forgotten cases. He figured that area police departments would appreciate the backup, too, as chats with distraught family members resurrected memories of his old man, puffing on a cigar, lamenting the case that got away. He knew that plenty of cops take their work home, and when a case goes unsolved, they can take it hard.

In August, after facing off with some hefty names in Macomb County politics, Eric Smith won the primary election and was pitted against another big name, David Viviano, whose father was then the chief judge in the county's circuit court. Viviano's name carried extra recognition points because his family had long owned a well-established flower shop business. But Viviano ran as a Republican in a largely blue-collar county rife with auto-plant workers who made the daily commute from downtown Detroit and Dearborn to the more sedate suburbs to raise their families. Eric, meanwhile, drummed up support from the local unions and police organizations. Having Smith as a last name perhaps wasn't useful, but being the son of a well-liked police chief was. And when it came to the prosecutor's office, Viviano was an outsider, while Eric had worked there for ten years.

After a showdown like no other in twenty years in the county's history, Eric triumphed. He would be the county's first new prosecutor since Marlinga's election in 1984. Now it was time to make good on some of his campaign promises.

Chapter 9

Cold Case Unit

Eric Smith took office in January 2005 and, after settling in a few months, decided it was time to launch the cold case unit he had touted during the campaign. He called on Assistant Prosecutor Steve Kaplan, then an eighteen-year fixture in the office, to head up the unit. Kaplan had a solid reputation as a go-getter in the courtroom, and Smith thought that if he put that kind of manpower behind the unit, area police would know he was serious about wanting to tackle the long-dormant cases.

"Steve is not only one of our best prosecutors, but he's one of the best prosecutors in the state," Smith said. "He's tireless. He has more energy than the rest of the office combined. He'll have one homicide jury out, getting ready to pick another homicide jury and running his own district court, and he'll come in my office and say, 'Things are kind of slow. You got any other cases?'"

In the courtroom, Kaplan was a character, with a quirky waddle reminiscent of Laurel and Hardy's Ollie character. A self-described history buff, he read some thirty nonfiction books a year and was as known for his seemingly photographic memory as he was for his bah-dah-dum one-liners. ("You know what you should write about me in the paper?

That I have a face for radio.") He could memorize dates and names, spellings and locations, without hesitation, and his memory was rarely flawed. In the courtroom, he used his indexical memory to his advantage, citing case law in his objections that left most defense lawyers flipping through law books.

"He quotes cases and gives you the page number to look for. The guy's crazy," Smith said.

And persuasive: In 2001, he won over a jury in the high-profile murder case against Robert Pann, whose estranged girlfriend had disappeared nine years earlier from St. Clair Shores. Bernice Gray had last been seen dropping off the couple's twenty-two-month-old daughter at a day care center the day after Christmas. No one ever heard from her again, and while police believed Pann killed her, they didn't feel like they could make a case without a body. Kaplan took on the challenge, however, piecing together circumstantial tidbits from witnesses who thought Pann was tracking Gray's daily routine near the time she disappeared. Pann was sentenced to life in prison without parole.

"God and Kaplan, that's my motto," Bernice Gray's mother, Jean Gray Ulmer, said after the verdict. "We had God and Kaplan."

Smith and Kaplan crafted a one-page memorandum in July 2005 announcing their intent to back departments' efforts to reopen and solve cold cases. A handful of departments responded, but most were initially silent. Even if they had cases to tackle, they weren't ready to prosecute. Plus, Smith was a newbie in town, and they weren't sure whether the memo was sincere or simply post-election rhetoric.

When Kaplan got bored, he would grab the phone and call a department or two to check in: "Hey, ya got anything for me?" Steadily, departments did. The first case the office tackled was out of Shelby Township, another small Macomb burg that didn't see many homicides. In 1998, Karen Deleon was found dead in her home of a gunshot wound that at first looked like a suicide, though that finding never sat well with a lot of cops on the force. Township Detective Terry Hogan was already re-examining the case when Smith sent his memo announcing the new cold case unit. After poring over the old case files, Hogan and Kaplan felt confident that Deleon's husband, Anthony Deleon, had killed her, then staged the scene. The case hit trial in 2005 and secured the unit's first conviction.

"There was a lot of significance to that," Smith said. "It was our first one, and we were certainly hopeful it'd be successful. Everyone believed Deleon had murdered his wife. His family, the detectives—every one of them said he did it."

By 1990, when Barbara George was killed, Kaplan had worked in the Macomb office for four years. After graduating Michigan State University's College of Law in 1981, he'd worked three major jobs: as a staff attorney for a circuit judge in Oakland County, the more affluent county next door to Macomb; as a staff attorney for a judge with the Michigan Court of Appeals; and as a staff attorney for a federal judge. Ever since law school, however, when he had his first job working under George La Plata, the first Hispanic judge on the bench in Oakland County, he'd set his sights on becoming a prosecutor. During his time there, he'd run into a then up-and-coming lawyer named Carl Marlinga, who was elected Macomb prosecutor in 1984. After Marlinga settled in, Kaplan called him up and asked for a job.

"He said, 'Sure, sure,'" Kaplan recalled. "It was easier than it'd be now. Now, there's a lot more competition."

Kaplan, wearing his trademark three-piece suit and neatly kept mustache, worked under Marlinga until the prosecutor left amid the federal scandal of 2004. He'd handled everything from basic misdemeanors to high-profile murder cases. His first murder trial was a cold case in 1989 against Ronald

Feazel, a man accused of answering a help wanted ad to become a manager at a small Clinton Township factory. Feazel was convicted of killing his boss, Robert Dave. The case was particularly diabolical, Kaplan said, because Feazel answered the ad with the end goal of murder in mind. Feazel got life in prison. In another Sterling Heights case, Kaplan successfully prosecuted a man for murder even though authorities were never able to find the victim's body, similar to his 2005 success with the Deleon case.

"You know why I like cold cases? Because they're history," Kaplan said. "I'm interested in history, and cold cases are historical. You have to return in time a ways and capture what happened then."

Kaplan, too, was long fascinated with the "almost perfect crime." That's what a cold case is more than anything: a crime that would have gone unpunished had it not been resurrected by someone determined to catch the bad guy. In the cold case unit, Kaplan was already having undeniable success by early 2007. More than a dozen cases had been reopened, and each had resulted in either a plea deal or jury conviction—meaning someone was found guilty one way or another. Some were lesser crimes such as arson or robbery, but several were murder cases. The Michael George case would prove to be among the most difficult.

It was November 2006 when Kaplan first heard that Clinton Township police were interested in breathing new life into the case. He regularly stopped by Blimpie Subs & Salads, a sandwich shop at 15 Mile and Gratiot in the township, for lunch. This day, he ran into township Police Captain Gary Franey and started chatting. He told him about the cold case unit and asked if the department had anything it might want to reopen. As a matter of fact, they did, Franey said.

"We're working on one now," he said. "Remember that case where the woman was shot in the comic book store?"

Kaplan did remember the case, though his office was never

asked to authorize warrants in it. Back then, in the early 1990s, the police and prosecutors didn't do much investigating together, so the prosecutor's office waited until cases were turned over before they got involved. In the George case, police never felt like they had enough evidence to charge anyone, so Kaplan knew of the case only through hearsay and from reading newspaper reports in the days after the slaying.

"There had been very little publicity about the case," Kaplan recalled. "It wasn't a hot topic. There was very little discussion in the office in 1990. I learned about the case when I read about it in the local paper either Saturday or Sunday. I remember my initial instinct was the husband did it."

Most murders aren't committed at random, after all, he said, and comic book stores just aren't targeted often for robberies, much less violent ones.

"A small store of that nature rarely is the subject of an armed robbery," Kaplan said. "A store that carries cash is far more likely."

Franey told Kaplan that Lieutenant Craig Keith, who was in charge of special investigations, was re-examining the George case. After lunch, Kaplan got on the phone.

Chapter 10

Lt. Craig Keith Reopens the Case

A few months earlier, Lieutenant Craig Keith had just wrapped up a couple of narcotics cases and found himself with an unusual luxury: time. With all the recent talk of cold cases, he stuck his head in his supervisor's office and asked if he could take a look at the Comic Book Murder, which, for old-timers on the force, needed no further explanation (on par with the township's Moravian Drive Granny Basher or Sherwood Forest Hit). Captain Richard Maierle said sure, so Keith grabbed the case file—a single, manila-colored accordion-style folder—from a back storage room and took it home.

He didn't know what to expect. He had been on the force for less than four years in 1990 and wasn't part of the investigating team. His job back then was street patrol, and the big-time murder case was being handled by the veterans. Still, he thought it might be worth a look. The Barbara George murder case had haunted more than her family and the police who couldn't solve it. It had affected the entire community.

The case file was a mess. There were no headings or methods of sequencing the information within. The reports basically had been shoved into the folder. It was not how Keith tended to file his own case reports. His were organized, with notes that cross-referenced tips he had checked out with tips

that were still outstanding. He used headings and broke tidbits down by name, date and importance. As Keith pored
through the documents, he came upon a handwritten report
outlining a phone call police had received the day after the
murder. It was from a Comics World customer who said he
had called the store at nearly 6 p.m. and Michael George
had answered the phone. The customer, Michael Renaud,
had called back soon after and said he had checked with a
coworker, pieced things together better and realized he had
made the call slightly earlier than he initially thought. It
was somewhere between 5:15 and 5:45 p.m., not quite as
late as six. Renaud called one more time on Monday, July
16, to say he was certain of the last time he'd given police;
he'd even seen a time card his coworker punched that served
as the benchmark for his chat with George the day of the
murder.

Nothing else in the file referred to the report. There was
no documented follow-up with Renaud. Keith found this
curious, but moved onto other reports. Tips had come in that
George was having an affair with Renee. A few months after
the slaying, the tips shifted: George had actually moved in
with Renee. Keith touched base with Steckman, the now-
retired lead detective from 1990, and Steckman said, yes,
police knew the two were having an affair, but George had
denied it and no one had found enough evidence against him
for it to become a bigger issue than a lie about adultery.

Keith set the file aside and digested what he'd read. It was
how the officer—a steely-eyed husband and father of two—
handled his work load: His eureka moments came in the
calm and quiet when he was jogging or mowing the lawn,
not while he was hunched over his desk straining for an
epiphany. It was during one of the quiet times that the significance of Renaud's phone call grabbed hold of him: If
Michael had said he was at his mother's house from 4:15
p.m. to nearly 8 p.m., he couldn't have been at the store to

answer Renaud's phone call at sometime around 5:30 p.m. And if he was there, he was likely the killer.

It was enough to warrant further scrutiny, he figured, though the case itself still seemed thin.

"Nothing in the file stood out like, 'Why the hell haven't we charged?'" Keith said.

Keith went back to Captain Maierle with the update: He wanted to explore the case further, but he'd need help. Maierle agreed to free up detectives James Hall and Lenny Hrecho. The three men met for the first time in early 2007. Keith laid out his intentions: He didn't know if there would be enough to file charges in the case, but he wanted to take a look at the Comic Book Murder with fresh eyes.

"I asked them to read it and give me their impressions, and I left it at that," he said. "I wanted their clean view. I knew back then that there was a rumor about who did it, but I didn't want to get tunnel vision in going down that road."

Hall and Hrecho took turns taking the case file home, and the three men would squeeze in meetings to talk about the possibilities of moving forward. They all still had to carry out their regular caseloads. Solving the George case would just be gravy. Over the next few months, they'd fit in an hour meeting here, three hours there. Someone would pipe up that he had time, and the other two would see if they could carve out some breathing room as well.

"Once we met to look at the pictures, another time to look at the video," Keith said. "We all have families and other cases and everything else, so we just did what we could."

They whittled away at the case bit by bit. Michael George was a suspect, but to move forward, they needed to weigh out the other possibilities equally. After reorganizing the existing police reports into a better system, they set about reconnecting with earlier witnesses to piece things together. The video they reviewed showed the condition of the store—its cash registers untouched—in the hours after Barb's body was rushed away. In 1990, Keith was a relative rookie, but more than fifteen years later, he felt he knew what an armed robbery typically looked like.

"When someone goes in to rob a business, they're looking for quick, easy cash and no violence," Keith said. "They want to just get in, do it, and be done. They don't spend a lot of time taking people into back rooms and supposedly grabbing comic books or fumbling with safes."

For someone to have committed this crime, he said, someone would had to have known where Michael kept his high-dollar comics—beyond the easily spotted ones showcased in the glass display out front—and have access to the back of the store.

The three men had barely scratched the surface when Kaplan's phone call came in. Keith knew Kaplan from earlier cases—"He's got a genuine interest and an unbelievable mind," Keith said—but he felt it was premature to get the assistant prosecutor excited about the case.

"We're looking at it, Steve, but it's just not there yet," he said. "It's going to be real slow."

Kaplan sounded enthused and asked Keith to keep him posted. Keith promised he would.

"We didn't talk every day; we didn't talk every week," Kaplan said. "Slowly, it progressed, and then in March [2007], the talks started to become more regular."

At that point, Keith and Kaplan began chatting weekly, and every other week, the lawyer met up with the other investigators on the case as well to keep apprised. They huddled in a conference room at the township's police department and floated scenarios past each other. Soon, they were scrawling out theories on a dry-erase board. Their biggest concerns were the timeline and the person disguised in a beard and Greek fisherman's cap. Kaplan, who tended to organize his thoughts in list form, decided there were four possible explanations for the disguised loiterer: 1) The witnesses were wrong and thought they saw someone suspicious but they didn't; 2) that was the killer and Michael George was innocent; 3) the person was an unknown accomplice to Michael George; or 4) it was Renee serving as Michael's lookout. By the end of the discussions, Kaplan believed it was the latter. The witnesses described the person as slightly built, either male or female, in a fake beard and mustache. Renee and Michael were having an affair. Kaplan decided that it made most sense that Renee would help Michael get rid of Barbara, who was reticent to get divorced and, in fact, wanted so badly to fix the marriage that she was planning a romantic getaway without the kids.

The other major element was the timeline, which would prove to be the prosecution's main obstacle. Michael told police he'd left the store by 4:30 p.m. and had fallen asleep at his mother's a half-hour away in Hazel Park. When he got back to the store at nearly 8 p.m., the area was cordoned off and swarming with officers. Michael's mother said she'd taken the girls for a walk to a nearby park and hadn't been gone an hour before she returned to find Michael still asleep on a couch in the living room. If that were true, it would have given Michael barely enough time to drive to and from the comic book store, and certainly wouldn't have given him enough time to ambush Barb, shoot her execution-style, and sneak away without being spotted. But Janet George could be mistaken, Kaplan reasoned. Maybe she'd taken longer at the park than she remembered. Or maybe she was lying and Michael wasn't still home at all when she got back.

There were enough maybes in the case to make everyone uneasy. Too much relied on someone fibbing or inaccurately remembering. They needed something concrete, Kaplan said, or they wouldn't be able to file charges.

That's where Renaud's phone message came in. If its contents were true, it proved that Michael was inside the store

between 5:15 and 5:45 p.m.—long after he'd told police he'd
left, and right before his wife was fatally shot.

The entire case hinged on a former Comics World customer
who'd made a seemingly benign phone call on an early Friday
evening. Keith decided it was time to track Renaud down and
see if his story was still the same nearly twenty years later.

Chapter 11

The New Investigation Unfolds

The only phone number Lieutenant Keith had for Renaud—
the witness who potentially could make or break a case against
Michael George—was nearly twenty years old and scrawled
on the police report that described his death-day chat with
the shopkeeper. Keith figured he'd have to hunt down a new
number for the witness when he had the time, but he found
himself with a few extra minutes one afternoon while sitting
at his secretary's desk waiting as a colleague borrowed his
own office for a minute.

The lieutenant punched in the digits. Mike Renaud answered.

Keith found himself fumbling. It's a rarity for someone
to keep the same phone number for nearly two decades, especially now that cell phones had replaced so many land-
lines. The lieutenant began chatting with Renaud about the
case. He kept his tone level, so as not to betray just how
crucial the former customer's phone call might be to the
case. Renaud rattled off details as if he were talking about
an event that occurred the other day, not the other decade:
His coworker, another man named Mike, had punched in to
work at the Crowley's department store at 4:53 p.m. and
shuffled to Renaud's office to chat comics. The coworker

mentioned that a book Renaud owned—*Captain America* No. 241, the issue in which a Spider-Man villain called The Punisher crosses over—had gone up in price, so after the two wrapped up their chitchat, Renaud picked up the phone and dialed Comics World. He knew the number by heart. He was, after all, a fanatic.

Renaud told Keith he was certain it was Michael George who answered the phone. He had spoken to him before on the phone and the two exchanged basic pleasantries. This time, though, George seemed rushed, so the chat was short—far less than five minutes, Renaud recalled.

Keith jotted down Renaud's statement and asked few follow-ups.

"His memory was so vivid that he basically gave me a free-flowing statement," the lieutenant later said.

Renaud's memory matched what he had told officers in his corrected statement back in 1990. His first statement had placed George at the crime scene right at the time of Barb's death, and when he realized that he might have been off by as much as forty-five minutes, he called back to clarify. Surely they would want to know that the dead woman's husband wasn't at the scene of the crime when it was committed, he reasoned.

"I give the guy all the credit in the world," Keith said. "He didn't want to lead anyone astray."

Not only that, but he had been persistent, calling a third time to make sure his corrected time reached the right hands. Somehow, however, every version of Renaud's statement to police slipped past Detective Steckman, the officer in charge. As Keith sat on the phone with Renaud, he could only guess as to why the man's seemingly damning report had gotten lost in the shuffle. Maybe the detectives were too harried or the case files too disorganized. Perhaps it was a timing issue: George hadn't provided police with a definitive timeline of his whereabouts until six days after the slaying, and Renaud's calls came in the Saturday and Monday after Barb's death. Maybe the officers who took the report simply missed the significance of the phone call because they didn't yet know that George had claimed to be at his mother's house, making it impossible for him to also be at the store chatting with Renaud.

"Mistakes are made. We're people," Keith would later reason. "As much as we try our best, we mess up."

Those mistakes would ultimately prove to be more plentiful than Keith initially realized—and they came complete with ripple effect. Because Renaud's phone call was lost, so, too, was the opportunity to crosscheck his claim of a 5:30 p.m. phone call with his coworker's time card. By 2007, Crowley's no longer existed, and any hope of recovering that potentially crucial time stamp had disappeared.

Keith hung up the phone finally feeling as though the case might be doable.

Renaud hung up the phone caught equally off-guard. He had never forgotten that fleeting phone call he had made, but it had been years since he talked about it. He had known Michael George fairly well, stopping by the comic shop several times a week. Renaud only made about $100 a week at Crowley's, of which he turned around and spent about $25 at Comics World. Spider-Man was his passion.

That *Captain America* had shot up in value from about $10 to $40 seemingly overnight. It didn't make sense to Renaud. The book, released in 1980, has Captain America cross paths with The Punisher as the two fight organized crime in Brooklyn. While Renaud liked the Spider-Man crossover, he couldn't fathom why the value would skyrocket. He didn't get an explanation from George, who said he didn't know what warranted the hike.

"He said he didn't know why it went up in value, he wasn't really sure, and he had to go, he was in a hurry," Renaud said.

The next day, Renaud read about Barb's death in the

newspaper. He knew her, too, from his stops in the store, and remembered George telling him that her dad was the one who ponied up the money for him to open the store. At first, Renaud thought their phone chat on the day Barb died happened right after 6 p.m., which, based on the newspaper story, would have been right after Barb was killed. Renaud called the police right away. He knew even before then that Michael was fooling around with the pretty employee, Renee. He had caught them mid-snuggle more than once when he would stop by the store midday after his college classes wrapped up and before his shift at Crowley's.

"I even asked him one time, and he just kind of smiled at me," Renaud later said. "I didn't think he'd kill his wife over it, though. I just thought he was having sex with somebody aside from his wife."

With a rush, Renaud picked up the phone. The call was anticlimactic; Renaud left a message with a detective saying he had talked to Michael George right after six o'clock. After he hung up the phone and thought harder about the day he'd had at work, he realized he was off by almost an hour. The phone call was before six, not after, possibly by as much as forty-five minutes. He called police again to clarify. On Monday, when he got back to Crowley's, he and his coworker, another man named Mike, looked up the time card to see for sure what time Mike had clocked in. There it was: 4:53 p.m. Renaud called police again. He had his suspicions about George, especially in light of his obvious affair with Renee, but he didn't want to place the man at the crime scene if he wasn't there.

A detective called Renaud a few times to pick his brain, he would tell a reporter nearly two decades later, and Renaud was asked to go to the Clinton Township Police Department for an in-person interview.

"Can I bring my baby down?" asked Renaud, then a newlywed. His firstborn, Cassandra, was still in a car seat, so Renaud bundled her up, put her in the car and headed to the department, where he spoke to a detective for between ten and fifteen minutes. The cop asked questions, jotted down Renaud's answers and sent him on his way.

There were elements of the case that just didn't sit well with the then-young man, particularly when it came down to the types of comics he learned George had reported stolen. The *Action Comics* No. 6 was one to covet, and George supposedly was missing an *Amazing Spider-Man* No. 50—a book that Renaud didn't think he would keep in a box in the back room rather than show off in the glass display case out front.

"He would have shown those to me," Renaud said. "If he'd had those, he would have showed them to me to see if I wanted to buy them. He was in the business of selling; he wasn't in the business of storing them in his back room."

Renaud expected to hear back from police following his interview with a detective, but he never did. He assumed that his rushed phone conversation with George was deemed irrelevant. Renaud remained a Comics World customer after the shooting and watched as George's relationship with Renee went from flirtatious lovebirds to man and wife. The two moved in together soon after Barb's death, and while it all seemed shady to Renaud, he figured the cops had ruled George out as a suspect.

In the years that passed, Renaud and his wife, Kirsten, had another daughter, Monique. Renaud left Crowley's and became an accountant and girls' softball coach. He continued building his comic collection, never losing his affinity for Spider-Man in particular. It was a pastime his wife regularly razzed him about, but Renaud always distanced himself from most collectors, whom he describes as "nerds." By mid-2009, Renaud estimated he had about 1,000 books, including the *Captain America* he had called about so many years prior. He was a collector, he explained, not a seller.

"When I die, my wife and daughters can finally sell this stuff off," he joked.

But four years before Lieutenant Keith reached Renaud

by phone, he had almost died. In 2003, at a pool party cele-
bration with his young softball players (ages twelve and
younger), Renaud playfully announced he was going to rob
the girls of an annual tradition—throwing the coach in the
swimming pool. He tossed a couple of girls into the water,
then dove into the pool over their heads to avoid hitting them.
His dive was too steep, and Renaud slammed into the pool's
bottom headfirst. Renaud was pulled from the water by his
frantic players. His daughter Monique, then eleven, flipped
her father onto his back. Renaud was rushed to the hospital,
where his heart stopped thirteen times. He pulled through,
but was left a quadriplegic.

Keith didn't know it during that phone interview, but the
case he was trying to build against Michael George wouldn't
have been possible had that unfortunate dive turned fatal.
Without Renaud to expound on his statement on the stand,
the timeline he had given police would have been deemed
inadmissible as hearsay.

After finding Renaud, the investigators pored over the
reports to find possible explanations for George being at the
store to answer the phone so close to the time Barb died.
They still couldn't find one. They brainstormed whether that
mystery man in the Greek fisherman's cap could be the killer,
but there was no evidence pointing to anything suspicious
about the man except that he was in the area and his cap was
distinctive. Nothing suggested he was the gunman.

The investigators sat down again with Kaplan, grabbed
the dry-erase marker and set out to thoroughly exhaust the
SOD defense—Some Other Dude did it. After sketching
out every scenario they could think of, they decided there
could be only two possible killers: Michael George or Renee
George—or both in concert. As lovers, they both had motive. Renee had left her husband just weeks before Barb's
death, and based on witness statements, the two were having
a pretty heavy affair by then.

"You've gotta look at Renee if they're having an affair," Keith said.

Based on early police reports, Renee had acknowledged being in the area at the time of the slaying buying soda for the party. Thus, she knew about the surprise party that her friend and boss was throwing for her lover.

"You can only imagine the kinds of conversations Renee and Michael must have been having," Keith said. "He's feeling frustrated and backed into a corner because he wants to be with Renee, but Barb is not letting him get a divorce. She's even planning a weekend getaway to try to rekindle their marriage."

Keith didn't think he could rule Renee out, but he also had nothing to justify charging her. The early investigators didn't bother tracking down a receipt tape from the store where Renee said she had bought the soda. All Keith knew was that Renee and Michael were intimate, and had even married after the slaying, which seemed a little too convenient.

That left Michael. The detectives decided it was time for a last-ditch barrage of interviews to see if they could shake anything loose before levying the charges.

And that meant it was time for a road trip.

Chapter 12

Michael George Is Interviewed Again

On Aug. 7, 2007, the detectives divided up the tasks: Hrecho and Hall would surprise George in his Windber shop, while Lieutenant Keith and Detective William Furno hit Renee up at the couple's home not far away. Back in Michigan, two more investigators—Sergeant Kevin Kline and Detective John Friedmann—would interview Janet George, Michael's sole alibi witness, all at the same time.

The ambush was to keep them from round-robin calling each other and coordinating stories. No one gave them any heads-up. They synchronized their watches and planned to begin their chats exactly at the same time.

That plan was flubbed by a couple of minutes when Hrecho and Hall got to the comic book store and decided to wait while some customers headed out. They walked into the store about two minutes later than planned. Michael was on the phone, his back to the door. They overheard him saying, "What? No one's here," his tone confused. Then he turned around, spotted the men and hung up the phone.

Michael and his oldest daughter, Tracie, were running the Graham Avenue store. Hrecho and Hall felt uncomfortable questioning Michael in front of his daughter, but their job was straightforward: to see if he gave up any new infor-

mation that would help either nail or exonerate him, though
they weren't hopeful he'd do either. The men introduced
themselves, and then Hall fumbled in his pocket to turn on a
tape recorder in case George said anything useful. In Pennsylvania, as in Michigan, tape recording conversations is
legal so long as one of the parties knows they're being taped,
though Hall's subterfuge use would be later questioned in
court. The detectives introduced themselves and said his
wife's murder case had been reopened. Michael seemed to
go pale.

"So we have reopened the case. We have a few questions
for you," Hrecho began.

Michael barely made eye contact. "OK," he said.

"What did the police tell you back then, our department?"

"They had leads," Michael said. "They never, um, told me
what the leads were. I saw a police psychiatrist for a while, or
psychiatrist that they—"

"—that you had seen at their request?" Hrecho finished.

Michael agreed: "At their request."

He took them back to 1990. He'd thrown up when he saw
Barbara's body at the morgue, he said. He hadn't seen her at
the hospital or in the store. He hadn't even been allowed inside the store; rather, he was driven to the hospital straight
away when he'd arrived to police tape and sirens and detectives milling around the strip mall. He didn't remember much,
he said.

"I don't even know if they told me she had passed away
then, I don't know," he said. "All I know is I remember showing up anywhere, it was sometime in the evening, anywhere
from like five to eight I showed up."

Hrecho perked up. The timeline would be key. Barbara
died at 6:30; Michael had told police he left at four and didn't
come back until about eight.

Michael returned to the subject without prompting, sounding like he was correcting himself.

"Four to eight, about four to eight I showed up. Because I

was at my mom's, and I think I was with my girls, and we all fell asleep, and later to find out that she was planning a surprise birthday party for me."

Hrecho somberly said, "That must have broke your heart."

Michael nodded. His birthday had turned into a bad anniversary date, he said. He described going back to the gravesite every six months, maybe more, laying flowers and cleaning off the site. Barb's buried near a big cross, he said.

"I will be buried with her. I bought a plot," he said. "I haven't bought a stone because I don't know what the girls would want me to get on the stone or anything."

He introduced the men to Tracie, one of those bright-smiled young women who strikes the balance between athlete and girlie-girl with success. She'd been an All-State basketball player and a stellar student. Newspaper clippings about her achievements lined her father's office, and her picture hung in her high school's hallway in honor of her athletic prowess.

Hall noticed her physique right away. "You look like an athlete," he said. She smiled and said she was.

"Sorry to meet under these circumstances," Hrecho said.

"I know," she replied.

Michael began talking about the gravesite again, but Hrecho wanted to steer the discussion back to the shooting. He asked when Michael learned that his wife had been shot, rather than suffered a medical condition, like the heart attack that initially was phoned in to emergency dispatch.

"I don't know if I learned at the store, or either at the morgue or hospital," he said. "I don't know when they told me."

Hrecho subtly hit on the time frame again: "That would have been dependent on what time you showed up because for a while they thought there was a medical emergency," he said.

"OK," Michael said.

"And they didn't find the bullet until later," the detective continued.

Michael shook his head. He couldn't remember, he said.

The conversation came around to the life insurance policy—what detectives considered half of Michael's motive. Barb had two policies worth $130,000 total. Without prompting, Michael said that his now-adult daughter had one worth that much, and that he was currently insured for about $350,000. Renee, he said, had about $175,000 on her through several companies because of some health problems that made her harder to insure.

Barb had worked at Farmer Jack's a bit before she died, but she'd quit. The girls and the store were enough. She cut hair on the side but couldn't get a job in a salon that fit with her schedule, Michael said, so she worked with the scissors a bit from home.

"Nothing like on a big-time basis," Michael said.

Hrecho stopped him: "We're not here on your tax records. I don't care if people work for cash under the table."

Michael stammered. "No, no, I'm just saying, though, but that wasn't a major income."

Barb's completion of cosmetology school had been a big accomplishment for her. She'd been wearing the pendant of golden shears—a gift after her graduation—when she was killed. Officers had found it in the puddle of blood on the floor of the comic book's back room. Michael said he couldn't remember it.

Hrecho thought this was odd. If his own wife were murdered, he thought he'd remember the pendant she'd worn daily around her neck.

The detective switched gears back to the SOD defense: Did Barb owe anyone money, do drugs, have enemies? Was anyone disgruntled with her—past Farmer Jack employees, ticked-off comic store customers, anyone?

"Not that I know of, no," Michael said.

"Neighbor troubles?"

"Not that I know of, no."

"Jealousy things, anybody stalking her, or anything like that?"

"Not that I know of."

"So in your mind, who do you speculate would have had something to do with her death?" Hrecho asked.

"I would think somebody that hated me a lot more than her, I would think, because I was supposed to be at the store," Michael said.

Hrecho wanted to smile. In seventeen years, Michael had never offered a possible motive. Now, in the detective's mind, he was shifting stories, even if slightly, to present a new theory. In his years of interrogations, Hrecho had seen suspects take this tack before, and it usually meant they were trying to make sure the focus stayed off themselves.

Michael continued: "That's why I still blame myself for her death, because I was the one who was supposed to be there, and she didn't want to be there at that time."

"So quite possibly, in your mind, you think somebody might have had it in for you?" Hrecho asked.

"I'm not the most . . . uh, how do you say it?" Michael stumbled. "I got rid of a lot of employees. You can check the police records. I've called the police if I ever had problems with kids stealing. There was a lot of stealing going on. . . . I had a lot of employees I fired."

"Yeah, and any business owner does," Hrecho said. "But anything stand out in your mind as really a nasty situation where somebody would be so pissed off as to take another human being's life?"

"No," Michael said.

"You know what," Hrecho said, "I must have talked to something like probably forty people that knew your wife. And every one of them has said—without any rehearsal, or without even hesitating—she was just the kindest, easiest person to get along with."

"She was," Michael agreed. "We still fought and argued because, you know, we were married. But there was no reason for that, uh-uh. We still talk about it an awful lot." He motioned to Tracie. "This is good therapy for her. We still have a lot of problems, we do, and people don't understand that."

Hrecho asked about Michael and Barb's relationship when she died. It was rocky, Michael acknowledged, because he'd quit his job to open the store and they were both feeling the pressure. Then there was his extramarital activities.

"On your side or her side?" Hrecho asked.

"That would be my side. That was my fault and I take responsibility for that," Michael said.

It was the first time Michael admitted to police that he'd been unfaithful. Hrecho and Hall's interest was collectively piqued. They now had on the record that Michael stood to gain not only money, but a new wife, if Barb were out of the way. They tried to sound nonchalant, asking how Barb found out.

"Just being smart and me being stupid," Michael responded.

Hrecho tried to joke. "Women will know, no doubt about it," he said. "They have like X-ray, like radar—that's a good thing, keeps us straight. So when she found out, what did she confront you with?"

Michael said she asked him to stop and he said he would. It had been more an emotional affair than a physical one, he said, and that hurt Barb more than anything. What was worse was that it was with Renee, the store employee and one of Barb's best friends. The couple fought for months over it.

The detectives and Kaplan felt the SOD defense was nearly useless save for two key players: Renee and her ex-husband Joe. First, Renee: She could have been a jealous lover who wanted Barb out of the picture so she could have Michael to herself. Or, in a scenario they considered more likely, she could have worked with Michael to help him kill Barb. There was always that slightly built man in an obviously fake beard that freaked out witnesses the night Barb was killed; Kaplan theorized that it could have been Renee in disguise. So Hrecho turned his questions to Renee.

"How did Renee react when she found out about Barb?" he asked.

Michael said he couldn't remember. The time around the shooting was a blur.

"I don't remember the day after, I don't remember the week after," he said. "All I remember is me raising these two girls."

Then there was Joe, Renee's ex-husband: "Somebody described in a statement at the hospital . . . that Joe Kotula may have shot her," Hrecho said.

"Joe Kotula hates my guts," Michael said quickly.

"I talked to Joe previously."

"He hates my guts," Michael repeated. "I mean, he is one person who's always hated me, he always will hate me, we've never gotten along."

Hrecho pressed. "So emotions were running really high at that point, I would imagine, because I know if my wife caught me doing something, or if I caught my wife doing something, it would just devastate both of us, really," he said.

"Right," Michael responded.

Hrecho asked if there ever was a showdown between Barb and Renee, any threats made or heated arguments. If there were, Michael said, he didn't know about them.

"Well, you talk to Renee," Hrecho said. "I mean, you see her."

"I've never, ever specifically asked her her opinion of my wife's death," Michael said.

Hrecho was shocked. "I'm sure you talked to her about who may have caused it?"

"No," Michael replied.

"Never?"

"Never."

This seemed odd to the detectives. Even in smaller crimes—robberies, larcenies, carjackings—the victims always ponder who would have done it and why. How could Michael and his new wife—a woman who had once been among Barb's best friends—have never discussed who they thought might have killed her?

"To me, my life with Barb . . . She gave me two beautiful girls, and she never did anything wrong to me," Michael said. "I don't care what Renee thinks, I don't care what anybody thinks. She never did anything wrong to anybody.

"I would never want to start arguing over something, you know. I know you don't understand, but—"

Hrecho interjected. "I understand a lot more than you believe I do, trust me. Seems like there's something you want to tell me a little bit more about, about that between Barb and Renee."

"They did a lot together," Michael said. "I mean, we were over to their house for barbecues all the time. They went places with people."

A customer came to the door. Michael told Tracie to handle it. Hrecho and Hall felt the dynamic switch—Michael might say he had to leave to take care of the store. They could lose this chance to try to nail the final questions.

"Now here's the thing," Hrecho began. "We've reopened the investigation. We've looked at a lot of things that happened back then. And our main crux is to find out why it happened. Now, originally it was made to look like an armed robbery, or suggested an armed robbery, but on us investigating all that, and talking to people, we don't believe it was an armed robbery. We think—"

"I know I had it wrong," Michael interrupted. "I knew something was wrong."

Hall and Hrecho stumbled over each other a second.

"OK," Hrecho finally said. "What was taken, maybe the cops are missing something?"

"Very old books," Michael said.

"OK. What kind of books were they?"

"They were golden-age books, and that's all I can tell you," Michael replied. He seemed to be getting weary of the conversation.

The detectives prodded. Which books specifically? In what kind of box were they kept? Were they from his private collection or were they for sale? Michael rattled off the answers: He didn't know which books; they were kept in a white magazine box; they were the store's, not his. But he couldn't remember the details. Hrecho recalled the missing comics report saying one of the comics was an original *Superman* with Jimmy Olsen. He recalled the value at around $3,000.

"I, honest to God, don't know," Michael replied. "I have no idea."

Hrecho asked if Michael had made a claim to the insurance company. If he could back him into admitting the claim was made—and it was false—the detectives would have the basis of their murder case. After all, if Barb wasn't killed as part of a robbery, then Michael was the only person with reason to want her dead. Michael said he assumed he'd filed a claim and that he likely was paid for the missing comics. But he acknowledged that he remembered nothing else being stolen from the store. Cash was in the register and in Barb's pocket. It appeared Barb was killed simply for a case of comic books.

"The whole thing didn't make sense to me," Michael said. "It still doesn't make sense to me. I'll be very honest with you."

"So, in having said that, what do you think happened?" Hrecho asked.

Michael shook his head. "I think Barb was at the wrong place at the wrong time," he said. "I think somebody wanted to get back at me. I don't know who it was, but I should have been there so they could—so they could get back at me. And so she could raise these two girls instead of me."

But Barb was there, Hrecho said. She was there, planning a birthday party and a trip to northern Michigan for a retreat in hopes of getting the marriage back on track. Renee, as a

store employee, knew about the plans. Michael said he had
no idea until after the shooting.

"Barb was trying to make it work, wasn't she?" Hrecho
asked. "No matter what, that's what people have told us."

"Yeah, they're telling you the truth," Michael said.

Hrecho asked why Michael was being more forthcoming
now than in 1990. He said he'd tried to talk to the psychiatrist police recommended, but that the guy didn't seem like
much of a doctor. More like a cop.

"He didn't even care what I said," Michael complained.
He went maybe ten times, he recalled. He'd never gone to
another psychiatrist. But he thought of Barb "every day of
my life."

"If I didn't think of her, you wouldn't see me going to the
gravesite. You wouldn't see me buying flowers for her. . . .
You wouldn't see me taking tools to clean it up and stuff,
you wouldn't see me getting a grave next to her."

Renee didn't know any of that, he said. He didn't share
that part of his life with her. He talked about Barb to the
girls, but Michelle was too young to remember her mother.
Tracie had a few memories and took pictures of Barb with
her when she went to college to put in her dorm room.

The men were talking about Michael's role in raising the
mixed family—Joe Kotula had finally kicked the kids out of
the house and given up battling for custody about ten years
prior—when Hall got a phone call. He left the room to talk
to another detective out of Michael's earshot.

"I just flipped my tape," Hall said. "He's not giving up
nothing yet."

Hall came back in the room. The conversation mean-
dered back to the psychiatrist, then to Barb's health, then to
the night she died. One statement Michael had made had
been gnawing at the detectives. When officers told him his
wife had been injured, he made a seemingly off-the-cuff comment about how perhaps something had fallen on her head

in the back room. It struck the officers as curious because
Barb indeed was found dead in the back room. How could
Michael know that?

"I can see why it would jump out at you," Michael told
Hrecho, but he said he didn't remember making the comment. There was a lot he couldn't remember, like whether
Renee had moved into the house he and Barb were building. Or whether he'd ever passed a suggestive note to a
female customer telling her how pretty she looked. Briefly,
he couldn't even remember Patrice, the woman with whom
he had an affair while he worked at the insurance company.
After some prodding, however, Patrice came back to him.
Their breakup was messy, he recalled, and he'd had a videotape of them having sex. Neither Barb nor Renee ever knew
about that escapade, he told the detectives.

"Did you ever own any firearms?" Hrecho asked.

"You know what, never," Michael said definitively. Neither had Renee. Her father owned some rifles, but the couple
didn't like guns and never kept them in their house.

The detectives knew this was at least partly wrong.
Michael's father had left him a handgun in his will, and
Michael had sold it to a neighbor soon after he moved to
Pennsylvania.

Hrecho and Hall decided to begin zeroing in. They came
back around to the supposed motive: robbery. They wanted
to know if Michael had ever looked for the missing comics.
It's not hard to track down rare books, they reasoned, especially nowadays with the Internet. And comic book stores
nationwide were given a list of the missing items in hopes of
finding anyone trying to sell them—a move that investigators
reasoned could lead them to the killer. But none of the books
were ever recovered. Not one. Detectives found that odd.

Michael said he couldn't remember which ones were
stolen, so he never searched for them.

"You gave the police a list," Hall said, "because I have a
copy of that."

"I'm sure I gave the police a list, and I'm sure I gave the insurance company a list," Michael said.

"One of the actual comics was a number six of seven," Hrecho said, somewhat incredulous. How could he forget such a rare book?

"OK," Michael said dismissively.

The detectives weren't getting anywhere. His explanation for not remembering the books didn't wash with them. He either genuinely had blocked out all memory related to his wife's murder or those books had never been stolen to begin with. Hrecho and Hall were getting impatient. They'd seen the pictures of the store from the time of Barb's death. Nothing was stolen from the front. If someone had taken the comics from the back room, they had to have known they were there. But when the detectives asked Michael if he'd taken anyone to the back to show them the goodies he had stored in the white magazine bin, he said he hadn't.

Hall didn't know if Michael was being dense or elusive. He decided to spell it out for him.

"You had expensive books in the back that nobody knew about, that you don't know anybody knew about, because you never took no one back there," he began. "But if there was a robbery, and the books were taken, why didn't they hit the cash register, take the money and take the expensive books that people *knew* were up there?"

He continued: "I mean, to go in there and take a box of comic books, as opposed to hitting the cash registers . . ."

A customer walked out. Michael called out to him: "Thanks, Alan. I'll see you tomorrow."

Hall tried to refocus him: "But they couldn't find nobody that knew about the ones in the back, yet everything wasn't touched except for those ones there, right by where Barb was found."

Michael sensed he was being accused of something. "So what are you—"

"I'm trying to . . . I'm asking," Hall stumbled.

"So what are you?"

"Help me understand it," Hall said, almost pleading. "That's what I'm trying to say. Is there anybody that you could have taken back to show them the books?"

Michael said he couldn't remember. If someone had wanted to see books that he'd kept in the back, he likely wouldn't have brought them to the back room, but rather brought the books out to the front.

"As an investigator, you in my shoes—" Hall said.

"I would think—" Michael interrupted.

They were reaching a head. There would be no more small talk, no more discussion about the gravesite or how the kids are faring. It was time to tell him what they thought of his robbery claim.

"They weren't taken," Hrecho said.

"They weren't taken," Hall echoed. "It was insurance fraud."

Michael bristled. "So you're saying I'm lying now."

The detectives tried to hedge. We have to look at all the options, they explained. But Michael knew what they meant, and he was having none of it.

"So now you're saying that I lied about the books being gone. So now what you're saying is I better get a lawyer."

"We didn't say that, though," Hrecho said.

"Yeah, you did," Michael shot back. "If you're going to show up tomorrow, let me know, and I'll get a lawyer because this is bullshit now."

Michael got up, left the room and began fumbling around the store looking for a phone number to a lawyer. The detectives tried to chitchat with Tracie, who asked if her uncle Peter, Barb's brother, was the one calling for the investigation to be reopened. Hall tried explaining what they'd said to make Michael so upset.

"I don't want to make you feel bad," he said. "There was no comic books. He wanted the insurance money. That's why the question was brought up."

"You mean there were no comic books stolen?" Tracie asked. "Oh."

"And that's why I think he got mad, it's because it was an insurance fraud," Hall said.

"Oh," Tracie said.

"And . . . from reading the report, there was a lot more going on then with just your stepmom and your dad then you probably know about."

Tracie agreed. "Yeah, there's a lot going on."

The detectives got nervous. Michael was still rushing about. Finally, he emerged and spoke only to his daughter. "Tracie, watch the store. I'm going to get a lawyer." With that, he left.

Hall got on the phone to alert the investigators at Michael's house. "He left to get a lawyer, but he might be coming up the hill, just to let you guys know," he said. He wanted to let the investigators with Renee know that Michael could be headed home. He explained that the conversation turned sour when the detectives began asking about insurance fraud.

"He goes, 'You're fucking accusing me now, I'm out of here,' and he stormed out of here," Hall said.

Hall hung up. He asked Tracie if her dad had any guns at home. She said he didn't.

"OK, good," he said. "I didn't want him to come back down and something happen, you know. I'm not saying he would. . . . You never know, because he is pretty mad."

"Oh, my God," Tracie said.

Chapter 13

Renee and Janet Interviews

Up the street, Renee had been stopped by two other investigators—Lieutenant Craig Keith and Detective William Furno. Though she invited them in, she was clearly uncomfortable and suggested they follow her to the store down the hill. She thought it odd that they wanted to talk to her alone. The officers said they already had detectives talking to her husband.

"I'll still give him a call," Renee said, and picked up the phone over Keith's protests.

"He said nobody's down there," she said after she hung up. "We can all go down to the store."

Keith danced a second. He wanted to check with his people first, he said, to make sure they got into town OK. Renee persisted. Finally, he admitted they simply wanted to talk to the two separately.

Back in Michigan, two more detectives were knocking on Janet George's door. Sergeant Kevin Kline and Detective John Friedmann were greeted by the now-elderly Janet, who seemed happy to cooperate.

"I just wish they'd get whoever done it before I die," she

said as she led the investigators into her Hazel Park home. "You know her children were just babies then."

She pointed to a photograph of Tracie.

"She's going into her fifth year of college," Janet said proudly. "She's going to be a pediatrician. . . . And that's Michelle," she said, pointing at another photograph. "She's going to be a surgeon. She's in her first year."

The detectives steered the conversation back to Barb. Janet said she didn't like to talk about it. She'd been watching the girls that day, she said, because Barb wanted to throw the surprise party and she'd been out of town on Michael's actual birthday—July 2—and couldn't accommodate the kids then. So she and Barb worked out an arrangement for her to watch the girls a few weeks later, and Barb would surprise Michael with a trip up north.

"He dropped the girls here," Janet recalled, "and when he got back to the store, he was just thrown into a police car, and they called me to come to the hospital. So I don't know what happened."

Michael had fallen asleep on the couch after he brought the girls over, Janet said. She'd taken the girls to the playground—she walked them, she emphasized proudly, because even at seventy-three, she still works forty hours a week. Kline laughed. "Me, I would have drove."

Janet said she'd tried to keep Michael at home. It'd been her charge so that Barb and her friends could get the store ready for the big surprise. She'd taken the girls to the park, but hadn't stayed long, she recalled. Michael was still on the couch when she returned.

"I more or less tried to keep him," she said, "because Barbara says keep him there so she could get ready and everything. And then he left. He left at a busy time, I know, though, he left about five-thirty, I think, because traffic is heavy at that time." She remembered telling him that the expressway would be busy, she said.

Kline recalled that Janet had told police some things in 1990 that didn't seem to add up. Like that Michael had called his house to talk to Barbara during his brief layover to drop off the girls but he hadn't been able to reach her, that he thought his wife was in the shower. And the reports said that Janet suggested Renee might have had something to do with Barb's murder.

"I don't think she was involved," Janet told Kline.

"Do you know why you said that at that time?" he asked.

"You suspect everybody," she reasoned.

Janet George seemed old and frail, and she could rattle on. But she was sharper than the detectives gave her credit for. While it appeared to take her son a good hour to piece together the possibility he might be a suspect in his wife's death, it took her just minutes.

"Mike didn't have anything to do with it," she said.

The detectives were taken aback. "No, no, no," Kline stammered, as if to say, "Of course he didn't."

"I know that," Janet continued, "because he was— When I went to the hospital, I went in to see Barbara and he was almost collapsing. His legs were just . . . And the priest kept following me around and I said, 'Why are you following me around? Take care of my son.'"

When detectives circled back to Michael asleep on the couch, she cut them off.

"I know what you're getting at—that he ran home and came back," she said. "That's a long way from here."

She and her son were close, she said. She saw him and the girls more often than she saw relatives who lived in Michigan even. The Mother's Day prior, she was told at Big Boy's, where she worked, that someone had sent her bubble bath at the front desk. When she went to pick it up, there were Michael and Michelle with flowers. He was a sensitive, caring son, she said. He was no murderer.

* * *

Back in Windber, Keith and Furno were taking Renee back to 1990. Her most vivid memory, she said, was pulling up to the store because they were planning a big party. Her van was full of wine coolers and beer. But instead of a jovial crowd, she was greeted by police officers in front of the store.

She'd met Barb first, she recalled, and felt she knew the couple fairly well. Because Tracie and her son John were both about three, she'd babysit when Barb and Michael needed help. Barb would bring the girls by to go swimming at Renee's place, too. She had a pool and moms would swing by with their kids around 4 p.m. to socialize and let the kids play. That summed up their afternoons: pool, mom chat, and wine coolers.

"Nothing wrong with that." Keith smiled.

Renee had never been into comics herself. She went into Comics World the first time to get a present for her oldest son, Joe, whom she affectionately called a "pure comic book little freak." Soon, Barb was pushing her to buy the Rochester Hills franchise. Renee eventually agreed, using the money she'd gotten from her divorce from Joe Kotula to make the buy.

She'd liked Barb. Michelle, the youngest girl, had grown up to be Barb's spitting image, she said. Barb was always laughing and bubbly. She always seemed to be in a good mood, and she was a hard worker. Just like Michelle.

"When I see her, that's who she reminds me of," Renee said of her stepdaughter.

In Michigan, Janet George described the days after the slaying. Police had come to the house, but family and friends wouldn't let the officers question Michael. Two days after Barb died, he took the girls to the park to explain that Mommy was in heaven and wasn't coming home.

"And if looks could kill, I swear," Janet recalled. "You should have seen the look on Tracie when she walked in after she was told."

She held onto newspaper articles about the slaying, she told detectives. Michael wouldn't read them until several years later.

Renee told her two detectives that merging the families was difficult. She and Michael started out as friends; she didn't let on that they'd become more than that while Barb was alive, and when Keith asked specifically, she denied the relationship was more than platonic.

"When I look back on that, I think that was two people grieving," she said. "I was grieving in a divorce, a marriage, and he was grieving a loss. I think it started out just good friends that merged families.

"I can remember him calling and crying and saying he didn't know how to put this hair-doodle thing in his daughter's hair, you know. And, you know, I called his mother saying I think he needs to be with you because he's falling apart. . . . It's a whole different story having a dad raise two girls."

The conversation didn't get much further before Renee heard a familiar sound.

"That's Tracie—maybe Michael, too, is it?"

Keith shrugged. "I didn't see anybody; I heard a truck."

"Somebody pulled into my driveway," Renee said.

It was Michael. The detectives' chat with Renee was officially over.

Chapter 14

Charges Are Filed

After Michael stormed out of his comic store, leaving Tracie behind with the cops, he drove straight to Tim Leventry, the man who had represented him when he had incorporated Comics World. Michael was frazzled, confused, nearing tears, when he walked into the office asking for help. By chance, Leventry was still in the office. Oftentimes, lawyers in the Richland Township office pack up early on Friday afternoons, and it was past the official quitting time of 5 p.m. But Leventry was there, and he was about to learn details of Michael's past he never would have imagined.

"He was very panicked," Leventry recalled. "He came to our office to ascertain what was happening, how did these police from Michigan end up in Pennsylvania, how could they legally be here. He had all the questions a person who had just been threatened with being arrested would have."

His voice unsteady, Michael laid out the back story for Leventry: His wife had been murdered, no one had been arrested and now it looked as though police were going to charge him with the crime. Leventry was shocked. Though he had worked with Michael for years, he'd had no idea about the execution-style slaying of his client's first wife, and in rural Somerset County, murder was extremely rare.

Knowing someone facing a murder charge was unheard of. Plus, Michael George simply wasn't a problem client. He had a good reputation as an upstanding area businessman. Leventry, who began practicing law in 1982, had long been fascinated by Comics World, a quirky business that seemed to be thriving even in such a rural area, thanks to online sales worldwide.

"Michael was always a pretty upstanding guy who led a pretty normal life," Leventry said. "I don't know of anybody who has talked badly or seen a really negative side of Michael in this area."

Now, Michael stood before him uneasily. He wasn't quite crying, but he was clearly panicked. He was especially worried that the Michigan officers were going to arrest him and send him immediately to jail back in Macomb County. The idea was horrifying. He'd spent fifteen years building a life in Windber. His business and family were there. In Michigan, his mother would be close by, but that was it. Leventry spent about a half-hour talking to Michael, explaining that they could fight the extradition for a while to buy time for Leventry to help track down a competent Michigan lawyer and for Michael to get his business and family affairs in order before the inevitable move up north.

Michael and Renee George went to bed uneasy that night. Renee wasn't sure how dire the situation was. In her talk with police, they hadn't accused Michael of anything, but when he came home, he was visibly shaking, clearly upset. At minimum, they were accusing him of insurance fraud, and he was pretty sure they were going to accuse him of murder, he said.

Nearly two years later, Renee's eyes would well as she remembered the day. Windber, such a small town, was shocked by the news, and Michael was all over the television. Though Leventry had promised to help, Renee and Tracie still struggled to find a lawyer. They pulled out the phone book and began dialing at random. Reaching anyone on the weekend was proving impossible.

Renee said later that she realized this was no accident on the investigators' part. Just as they'd swooped in to conduct three interviews in two states simultaneously, she felt they knew what they were doing when they seemed poised to press charges so close to a weekend. Ultimately, she felt naïve. She thought she'd done the right thing by inviting the men into her home and answering their questions. When Michael came home panicked, she thought he was overreacting. Certainly they couldn't charge him based on a seventeen-year-old hunch. "I was just stupid," Renee said later. "I was naïve about the whole process."

Back in Michigan, Assistant Prosecutor Steve Kaplan was keeping abreast of the new interviews. When he learned Michael had admitted to having an affair with Renee, Kaplan was almost giddy.

"He'd never admitted it before. He'd denied it to Don Steckman in 1990," Kaplan later said. "He ceased communications around July 28, but between July 13 and July 28, he'd been interviewed several times saying, 'Great marriage, no affair.' Now we have him on tape admitting to the affair. Do we lose the case without that admission? I don't know, but it's important. It shows he misled the investigators initially."

The morning after the interviews, on Saturday, Kaplan drove into the office to help the warrant division's secretary type up the arrest warrant. He wanted to do it personally, Kaplan said. If Michael George had been in Michigan, the warrant wouldn't have been necessary; police had probable cause to arrest him, and they would've done so on the spot. But because Michael was in Pennsylvania, Clinton Township police needed them to make the actual arrest, and for that, they had to show a warrant.

The four investigators who'd interviewed the Georges stayed overnight in Windber. They'd already been in touch with Pennsylvania state troopers. As soon as the warrant was faxed to them, Michael George was arrested for the murder of his wife.

A week after the arrest, a story ran in the *Daily American*, a small-time paper in Somerset County, describing a sobbing Michael George being led from the courthouse after refusing to waive his right to an extradition hearing.

"I didn't do this!" Michael cried out as he walked, his hands and feet shackled. "My Lord knows I didn't do this. My family knows I didn't do this."

The *Tribune-Democrat* out of Johnstown interviewed neighbors who expressed the seemingly obligatory shock that all neighbors apparently possess: They were jolted by the news, saying George was an unassuming man who gave no indication of a troubled past.

"He kept pretty much to himself," one man said.

George refereed youth basketball and was known to let children hang out at his store, neighbors said.

Renee and Tracie were the only ones in town. Three of the children had moved to Vegas, and the others had flown out to visit them. The women decided to hold off on breaking the news to the kids—Michelle in particular—because they didn't want to ruin their trip when there was nothing anyone could do at that point anyway. That, Renee would say later, was a huge mistake. Michelle talked with her father nearly daily, and Renee backed herself into lies about his phone being broken to explain why he couldn't be reached. With Windber being such a small town, however, word got back to the kids through a friend, leaving Michelle and Joshua, who considered Michael a father even more than the other Kotula kids, extremely upset. That just added to the drama, Renee said.

The comic book store was closed while the women tried

to regroup and map out a game plan. Over the weekend, all they could do was sit huddled under blankets on the couch, watching the local news play and replay footage of Michael being hauled away in handcuffs.

"I remember they showed several suspects all in a row," Renee said. "It'd be one after another, covering their faces, not saying a word. Then there's my husband saying, 'I didn't do it!'"

Renee drove the thirty minutes southwest to Somerset, Pennsylvania, where Michael was lodged in the county jail, on Saturday night after his arrest. She'd been told she could visit him in the morning and was too antsy to wait to make the drive on Sunday, so she booked a room at a nearby hotel and made the drive. She visited the jail first thing Sunday, only to be told that visitation couldn't begin until 1:30 p.m. When she came back, there was more bad news: Michael couldn't see anyone, at all. Renee was devastated. She knew Michael was a wreck behind bars and wanted to let him see her strong face, to know that she was there for him. She headed home disheartened and plopped back on the couch with Tracie until the two decided they couldn't watch the news coverage any longer, for their own well-being.

When the felony charges were finally released, Michael faced five: first-degree murder, second-degree murder, using a firearm to commit a felony, insurance fraud, and obtaining money under false pretenses. The insurance crimes were basically throwaways in terms of sentencing, but prosecutors needed jurors to believe that Michael had lied about the theft of the comic books in order to believe that he, not a robber, killed his wife. The double murder charge, too, was standard. A jury would have to choose between first- and second-degree, but in such a circumstantial case, for them to decide it was murder at all basically guaranteed that Michael would be convicted of first—and that carried Michigan's heftiest sentence: life in prison without parole.

* * *

The news didn't hit metro Detroit until Monday. Smith's office was tight-lipped with the details. All that reporters learned was that Michael George had been arrested and was being held in Pennsylvania. Ben Liston, an assistant prosecutor under Smith, told reporters that investigators were still conducting interviews and that a ballistics test was under way. He refused to say more. Leventry, meanwhile, began making phone calls to Kaplan and investigators. What new information could they possibly have to warrant the arrest? It took a little haggling to get the information—Leventry not only wasn't licensed to practice in Michigan, but even in Pennsylvania, he handled business law, not criminal. But after a few phone calls and letters, he received a two-inch-thick case file that Leventry found anemic. There was no new smoking gun. Rather, he considered it page after page of speculation on possible motive and nothing more. The file didn't even include mention of Michael Renaud's July 13 phone call, making the evidence against Michael George seem ever the paltrier.

"When I reviewed that file, I saw nothing—and I still see nothing in the record to this day—that links Michael directly or indirectly to this murder," Leventry said. "He has always, ever since that first day, maintained he had nothing to do with it and that he was an innocent victim himself in the sense that he lost his wife to a murder."

Kaplan already was firming up his strategy, keeping his cards to his vest, so as not to make Michael's defense any easier for whomever he ended up retaining. And that became the big question around the office, Kaplan said: Who would represent Michael George? Metro Detroit has its share of high-profile, talented defense lawyers. Kaplan assumed that Michael, whose eight-bedroom home and regular trips to Las Vegas indicated he had some money stashed away, would hire a big gun.

Leventry didn't have strong connections in Michigan. He

turned to the Internet and began searching for a Macomb County lawyer. Soon, he stumbled on a man with deep roots in the community. He made a phone call and asked the lawyer if he'd be interested in talking about the case. The lawyer wasn't sure; first, he had to call Kaplan.

"It's Carl Marlinga," the lawyer told Kaplan. "I'm thinking of representing Mr. George."

Chapter 15

Carl Marlinga

Steve Kaplan was taken aback. Carl Marlinga had been his boss at the Macomb County Prosecutor's Office for nearly twenty years. Marlinga had even hired him in 1986 off a single phone call because the mutual respect was deep enough that they could skip the formality of an official interview process. He was a clean-cut, likeable man known to joke that he was born wearing a suit and tie—one of many chuckle-inducers he kept in his regular repertoire. Marlinga had overcome a speech impediment as a child and still had the occasional false-start remnants of a stutter.

When Leventry, the Pennsylvania lawyer, called Marlinga about the case, the former prosecutor said he didn't know if he believed Michael's claims of innocence, but as a defense lawyer, it didn't matter. He considered it his job to keep the system honest, to ensure that every person who lands behind bars deserves to be there based on the evidence. Marlinga knew what it was like to be targeted. He had made the ill-fated decision to throw his hat into the race for a U.S. Congressional seat in 2002. He ran as a Democrat and found himself under extreme pressure to raise hundreds of thousands of dollars for his campaign. It was new territory for him. When he'd first run to become county prosecutor in

1983, he was fighting for an empty seat. He had to raise money, sure, but it was a countywide post and there was no incumbent to topple, so the pressure was manageable. But to become a Congressman, he needed big bucks. He schmoozed the best he could, throwing fundraisers and making phone calls that he'd later say made his skin crawl. Along the way, he was courted by a couple of area lawyers who felt a man had been wrongly imprisoned on Marlinga's watch.

The man, Jeffrey Moldowan, was serving a sixty- to ninety-year prison sentence for brutally raping his girlfriend in 1990. It was an especially horrific case. The victim was not only beaten and sexually assaulted, but she'd been partially disemboweled when a foreign object—police figured a stick or pole—was jammed deep into her anus. Her body was covered with bite marks. She'd been left on the side of a Warren street to die. Somehow, she lived and identified her assailants as Moldowan and his friend. Both men were convicted. While in prison, Moldowan had drummed up some supporters. His sister worked for an area real-estate guru, Ralph Roberts, who took up the cause. He met Marlinga at a fundraising event, bent his ear about the case, agreed to donate some money to the Congressional bid and continued making phone calls to Marlinga insisting that the prosecutor look into the case. Another lawyer also had Marlinga's ear. He, too, donated money to Marlinga's campaign, while at the same time asking that the Moldowan case be re-examined.

Eventually, Marlinga relented. He looked at the case and realized that a chunk of the evidence against Moldowan and his co-defendant, Michael Cristini, was based on bite mark evidence that had been tossed out in other cases. The forensic odontologist who said the bite marks matched the men's teeth patterns had been flogged for assigning a degree of scientific certainty—something considered a no-no when weighing bite marks because, unlike DNA or fingerprints, matching tooth impressions was as much art as science, if not more so. Skin stretches, pinches, bruises, and heals, so taking a bite-mark impression and overlaying it atop a photograph of a bite mark offered strong evidence, but it was by no means conclusive on its own. Seeing this, Marlinga wrote a brief to the U.S. Supreme Court suggesting that they might want to allow Moldowan a retrial.

The higher court agreed to the new trial, and Moldowan was retried by Marlinga's own assistant prosecutors. They still argued his guilt, and they brought in a new forensic odontologist who testified that the bite marks were visibly consistent but stopped short of assigning them any scientific certainty. But Dennis Johnston, Moldowan's lawyer in the retrial, prevailed and, after more than a decade behind bars, the once-imprisoned man was acquitted and freed in 2003. In the months that followed, his co-defendant, Cristini, also got a new trial. He was acquitted in early 2004, though Marlinga never argued on his behalf.

Marlinga got similarly entangled for accepting $26,000 from a lawyer for James Hulet, a St. Clair Shores real-estate agent who raped and drugged a teenage girl. Hulet eventually pleaded guilty and was sentenced to prison.

Marlinga lost the Congressional bid and vowed never to run again. He didn't like the fundraising. It felt smarmy and cheap. He focused again on his job as prosecutor, but in late 2002, the *Detroit Free Press* broke the story that Marlinga was the target of a federal investigation. Journalist Nancy Youssef connected the dots, reporting that tens of thousands of dollars in campaign contributions Marlinga raised was somehow tied to the Moldowan and Hulet cases. Marlinga said he'd done nothing wrong, that his accepting money had nothing to do with any actions he'd taken as prosecutor, but he was indicted anyway on April 22, 2004, accused of taking $34,000 in campaign contributions to help the rape suspects in the separate cases. The feds also indicted Roberts, the real-estate broker who had lobbied on Moldowan's behalf and donated $8,000 to Marlinga's campaign—well over the $2,000-per-person limit set by Michigan finance laws—and

State Senator Jim Barcia, a Bay City Democrat, saying that the three were involved in a scheme to swap campaign contributions for prosecutorial favors. The indictment said that Marlinga suggested how Roberts, Hulet, and Hulet's lawyers could exceed the $2,000 individual cap on contributions. They also funneled $4,000 through a business Political Action Committee, $4,000 through Barcia's campaign and $12,000 through the Michigan Democratic party, and made the contributions in the names of other people, the feds charged. The indictment said the contributions "constituted a quid pro quo, that is, payment in exchange for defendant Marlinga taking official action as Macomb County prosecutor." Charges against Barcia and Roberts were dismissed before trial, but Marlinga was forced to face a jury.

Marlinga would later describe it as the darkest hour of his personal life and professional career. He'd been naïve, he conceded, but he insisted nothing he did was ever intentionally covert or sinister. He spoke regularly to reporters who called for comments during the ongoing investigation. And he took the unusual step of testifying in his own defense at his federal trial. By then, his career as prosecutor was over. He had been up for re-election in November 2004, but with the investigation looming, he withdrew his name, leaving the seat without an incumbent for the first time since he'd taken office twenty years prior.

Marlinga's testimony was effective. He said the timelines were muddled, that he had perhaps used bad judgment but that he had committed no crime. The jury agreed and acquitted him. The next day's *Free Press* story, co-written by David Ashenfelter, described the emotion that flooded the typically staid courtroom:

> With the first "not guilty," former Macomb County Prosecutor Carl Marlinga bent his head forward and began to cry softly.
>
> By the time the jury forewoman said those words for

the fifth time—acquitting Marlinga of all federal corruption charges that have dogged him for two years—he sobbed.

"I'm speechless for probably the first time in my life," Marlinga, still tearful, said after spectators left the courtroom.

But he wasn't.

"I want to thank God, my wife and two of the greatest lawyers and friends I could ever have in my life," Marlinga said, referring to defense lawyers Mark Kriger and N.C. Deday LaRene. "They just didn't stop working on the case."

It was a victorious day for the former prosecutor, but it also was an uncertain time. He wasn't ready to retire, and his life as a public servant seemed over. He figured he could never again lift a phone to raise money for a campaign. He decided he'd start his own law office and become a defense lawyer—a fitting next step, he thought, for a man who now knew well what it felt like to be targeted. It would be his job to ensure that those pointing fingers are held to high standards. He felt forever indebted to his own defense lawyers, Kriger and LaRene, and decided that he could play a similar role for others. Marlinga began slowly, taking smaller cases, most of which ended in plea deals. He hadn't taken on anything high-profile, much less a murder case, before Leventry called.

Leventry had made a few phone calls to area lawyers, but Marlinga stood out. Not only did the former prosecutor have experience working both sides, but he had strong ties to Macomb County.

"It wasn't like he was from two counties away and didn't know the parties," Leventry recalled. "He knew the system. He knew the people involved. He was familiar with that particular area."

And Marlinga seemed like an honest guy, personable and

easy to communicate with. Before Marlinga would even contemplate the case, he needed to know if there would be a perceived conflict of interest. He remembered the murder generally; he didn't recall ever making a decision as to whether or not charges should be filed. Kaplan, he knew, would remember.

"I'm thinking of representing Mr. George," he told his former employee on the phone. "Is there any reason I can't do it ethically?"

"I said, 'Carl, I assure you, you never saw the case,'" Kaplan later recalled. "It's not unethical at all."

Then Kaplan hung up the phone and, like a schoolgirl spreading gossip, rushed to tell his boss the strange news: Carl Marlinga would be representing Michael George.

Marlinga decided to fly to Pennsylvania to meet the man accused of murder. He flew into the small Somerset County Airport in Friedens about thirty miles north of the Georges' Windber home. The airport was so small, there was no missing his greeter: Renee George, petite and pale, smiled pleasantly and shook his hand. She was obviously shaken, but Marlinga had pictured her as a frail woman broken and devastated by the weekend's events. Instead, she was surprisingly collected. She helped Marlinga gather his case and loaded him into her minivan for a half-hour of getting-to-know-you talk, lawyer-style.

Renee was still shell-shocked by the Friday afternoon ambush-style interrogation in her home and business. She asked if the tactic was legal.

"Yeah, it's legal to do that," Marlinga responded. "If you were a police department, you'd do things the same way. You want to obey the law, you want to follow the Constitution, but you also want to catch the bad guys, so you're going to take every opportunity to see if there's a chink in the armor, a difference in the stories."

Then they inched toward the uncomfortable inevitable: the idea that Renee might be considered a suspect alongside her husband.

"Because you and Michael are married, there are some matters that never have to be disclosed, but the ground rules are I'm here to represent Michael," Marlinga said. "I'm not here to represent you. You should be careful talking to me because even though I'm Michael's attorney, if I find out any information that puts the spotlight on you rather than him, I'd have to go with that."

Renee paused a beat. "Oh," she said. "I understand."

She told Marlinga she had nothing to hide. For the rest of the car ride, Marlinga listened to more than her words. He listened to how she spoke, the cadence of her sentences, trying to see if she seemed more guarded than she had at first. She didn't. He believed she was telling him the truth.

After a night at his hotel, Marlinga readied the next morning to meet his client. He donned his suit and tie and met Renee outside, climbing back into her minivan to head to the Somerset County Jail. Michael greeted him in typical green-and-orange Somerset Jail garb. Unlike his wife, he looked as though he hadn't slept in weeks. His face had puffed from crying; dark semicircles hung beneath his eyes. He weakly shook Marlinga's hand and the two men sat down.

Marlinga went in empty-handed. He brought no notebooks or recorders. He explained to Michael that he simply wanted to chat, to form a first impression and to listen to his side of the story. In reality, he was scoping out his new client, wanting to pay close attention to any nonverbal clues that his body language or facial expression might convey—emotions or thoughts that perhaps he would not yet be comfortable articulating, if ever. Marlinga had discovered over the years that walking into a meeting ready to take notes can backfire in that way. By taking notes, you're hoping to chronicle every nuance, but by looking away from the client, you can miss the most important tidbits without ever realizing it.

"What the person keeps on going back to is important," Marlinga later said. "It's a subconscious reveal of where their mind is, and what their sense of guilt is."

After all, Marlinga had worked long enough with cops to know that they rarely levy charges without reason. Maybe Michael George wasn't guilty of murder, but that doesn't mean he was a genuinely innocent man.

So the lawyer sat down and examined his client's weary face. He seemed surprised at the charges and truly offended. He, like Renee, asked if the ambush-style interview tactic was legal. Marlinga repeated that it was. He asked what evidence they said they had after seventeen years—what possible clue might they have uncovered after all these years that pointed to him as the culprit. Marlinga said he didn't know.

"I've done a lot of bad things in my life," George said, sobbing, "but I did not do this."

Marlinga wasn't sure why, but he believed him. The meeting was brief, less than an hour. He told George that he'd begin the extradition process. It was silly to delay the inevitable any longer, he said. The next time the men would meet would be in Michigan.

Chapter 16

Tricky Case from the Start

As Marlinga delved into the case he had signed on to tackle, he quickly realized it would be unlike any he had tried before. Cold cases typically are challenging anyway—memories fade, documents get lost, witnesses move away or die. And this case wasn't just a few years old, or even just a decade. Witnesses' memories would have collected eighteen years of dust by the time a jury would be sworn in. The lawyers' jobs are easier when the witness was interviewed at the time of the crime—if someone didn't remember, the law was on his side to hand the witness a pertinent report and ask if it refreshed his memory. That usually did the trick. But if the witness hadn't been interviewed prior, things got hairy.

That was truer than ever for Marlinga. No one aside from Michael and his mother had been interviewed in depth at the time of Barb's death to establish his alibi, and in trial, the word of a mother and a suspect only go so far. Meanwhile, the prosecution had this new piece of evidence—the Michael Renaud phone call—that placed George inside the store closer to the time of death than he should have been. Because that Renaud phone call had slipped through the investigative cracks, no one had tried to firm up the phone call by tracking down records or other witnesses. Nor had anyone corroborated George and Janet's story with neighbors that he was asleep on the couch, meaning Marlinga wouldn't be able to turn to anyone and say, "Hey, remember what you told the cops way back when?" Instead, he would have to interview neighbors anew and pray that they remembered something useful.

That's how he stumbled upon Peggy Marantette, one of Janet's neighbors. Marinette said she got home from work between 5:45 and 6 p.m. every day around the time Barb died, and that on July 13, she saw Michael's van parked outside of Janet's house when she got home. She even saw Janet walking with the two girls from the park back to her house right around 6 p.m. While it wasn't the slam-dunk alibi witness for which he had hoped, Marlinga figured it was something—a nugget of potential reasonable doubt—for jurors to chew on come deliberation time.

Marlinga also tracked down Jim Vohs, the former police commissioner in Warren—Macomb County's largest and most crime-ridden city—to take a look at the crime scene photos with fresh eyes. Vohs had retired just six months prior and was readying to launch a private investigating firm; the George case would be his first high-profile endeavor. Vohs asked Clinton Township police for the investigative material, and the agency cooperated. He pored over the photos, analyzing the images captured in the hours after the shooting. Marlinga wanted to know if Vohs, based on his twenty-nine years of police experience, could definitively say whether the shooting looked like it had been a component of a robbery or if it was a straight-up execution, like the prosecution would argue.

Vohs noted the diamond ring still on Barb's left hand, the cash recovered from her pocket, the undisturbed cash registers, and told Marlinga that if it was a robbery, it wasn't a typical one. Still, he said, it could have started out as a robbery that somehow got thwarted, perhaps because the robber hadn't intended bloodshed and freaked out after pulling the trigger. Vohs told Marlinga that there just wasn't enough documented at the scene to say with certainty what had happened.

Marlinga turned back to Michael and pressed harder: Who might have had motive to kill your wife? Michael mentioned a onetime friend named Wally. He couldn't remember Wally's last name, he said, but the two men had been close until just days before Barb died, when they got in a fight over a CD player. Michael couldn't remember the specifics, and Marlinga didn't know if Wally would become a key to the defense, Still, the lawyer figured it was worth investigating.

After weeks of fighting extradition, Michael George finally agreed to come to Michigan. He had found his lawyer and gotten his affairs in as much order as possible, leaving a shaken but strong-willed Renee in charge of everything personal and professional. On October 1, he was arraigned in Clinton Township's 41-B District Court with newspaper photographers clicking and TV cameras rolling. The official charges: first-degree and second-degree murder, using a firearm to commit a felony, and insurance fraud. The latter charges were more or less for show. In Michigan, felony firearm charges are levied in any crime where guns and felonies collide. Unlike most sentences, felony firearm convictions are consecutive, not concurrent, meaning two years is tacked on to the end. The insurance fraud charge was to drive home the prosecution's belief that George had lied about the shooting being part of a robbery. Kaplan and Keith said they had discovered that two years before the murder, in 1988, George had reported a car stolen and had gotten money from his insurance company to cover the loss—and then told friends that the car was actually stored at his stepbrother's garage. Though jurors would never hear that tidbit because of a pretrial ruling forbidding its introduction as evidence, it helped solidify the investigators' belief that the stolen-comics claim was bogus.

Meanwhile, the duo of murder charges was standard.

First-degree murder indicated premeditation, while second-degree gave jurors the option of deciding that the evidence proved murder, but not planning. The former charge carries a mandatory sentence of life imprisonment in Michigan, while second-degree requires judges to evaluate a complicated formula of factors, from past convictions to crime severity, to hand down a punishment that falls within sentencing guidelines. In theory, someone could be sentenced to life in prison on a second-degree murder conviction, though that would be rare. Usually the sentence is more in the fifty-year range, with a few decades' wiggle room on each side.

At the arraignment, Marlinga did what every defense lawyer does: He asked his client be released on bond. Unlike many others, however, Marlinga was actually hopeful. George had been an upstanding citizen in the years since his wife's death, he argued, and the prosecution's case was too weak to assume his client would risk everything he had built—not to mention leave behind his wife and their combined seven children—to skip out on trial. Kaplan vehemently disagreed. George had everything to lose, he argued, and if he were to be convicted, he faced the possibility of never setting foot outdoors as a free man again. It was enough to deny bond, he said. The judge agreed, and Michael George was transported back to the Macomb County Jail to await his impending preliminary exam.

Chapter 17

Comic Fans

In the wake of George's emotional arrest, mainstream newspapers weren't the only ones reporting the latest development. News within the comic world spread rapidly, and a legion of Web-based gawkers kept tabs on the case from afar, emailing reporters and commenting on blogs. The reaction immediately was divided. Some had known George for years and didn't buy that he was the type to kill, no matter the supposed motive. Others damned him from the start and chastised anyone who still did business with the Georges.

Pittsburgh Comicon fans were aflutter: What would happen to the annual event? In the months after her husband's arrest, Renee had assured the event's repeat artists and vendors that the show would go on. It was what Michael wanted. He couldn't stomach the thought of the annual event disappearing, especially under such a cloud. Renee thought she was up to the challenge of becoming head organizer, at least briefly. Soon after the arrest, as Marlinga readied the Georges for the impending preliminary exam, Renee decided she would visit the Baltimore Comic-Con, an event she deemed on par with Pittsburgh's. She had convinced herself she was ready to show her face, promote the Pittsburgh show, and try to recruit artists.

"I was good, I got the badge, but then I had to go down the escalator to enter the convention by the riverfront," Renee later recalled. She could feel eyeballs on her, more pitying than judgmental, and her once-steeled jaw gave way to quivers. She took two steps at the bottom of the escalator and felt herself instinctively turn back around.

"What in the hell was I thinking," she muttered, heading back up the stairs and catching her breath alone on a couch. Soon, some friends met up with her and walked the convention halls at her side, making her feel as though she had bodyguards.

"I tried to go alone," she would reminisce, incredulous. "Stupid."

If the eyes that had trailed her had been hardened and cruel, she would have handled it better, she said. But these eyes were empathetic. "I could put up a strong front until somebody gave me those hound-dog eyes or tried to touch me. God forbid anyone wanted to hug me."

Renee ended up securing a solid lineup for the 2008 Comicon, which was scheduled for April. Surely Michael would be home in time, she thought.

Chapter 18

The Sparring Begins

On October 15, 2007, Carl Marlinga made his district court debut as a defense lawyer in a high-profile murder case. The time had come for Michael George's preliminary exam—a crucial date set for a district-level judge to decide whether there was enough probable cause to send Michael to trial at the county-level circuit court to face murder charges. As a prosecutor, Marlinga had been at many a preliminary hearing. Even during his twenty years as top dog, he occasionally handled big cases that came through his office. This time, however, he was seated on the other side of the courtroom, a suspect by his side whom he was fighting to free, not imprison. To top it off, the case had generated more than just local interest. *Dateline* had zeroed in on the case as potential fodder for an episode. Their camera stood alongside the local TV stations in the jury box, and a producer sat in the back row. All eyes were on the lawyers.

For Kaplan, it would be his first time squaring off against his former boss. It was the talk of the metro Detroit legal community. Marlinga had a solid reputation; he knew the law. He was generally seen as a good guy, if a bit verbose and scattered in his approach. Even before the federal indictment, he wasn't known as a lay-down-the-law kind of boss around the office. Some complained that certain assistant prosecutors were able to do less work than others because Marlinga seemed too timid to hold them accountable. Kaplan, on the other hand, was undeniably sharp and direct. In the courtroom, he could seem impatient with witnesses he felt were sidestepping questions. Critics would call him slippery, quick to use his encyclopedic memory of case law to shut down even legitimate objections. The first showdown between the men would prove somewhat of a spectacle; onlookers wanted to see how former boss and protégé, two men with such distinct courtroom styles, would match up.

Almost as a bonus, the presiding judge was Linda Davis, a woman who had worked under Marlinga and alongside Kaplan as an assistant prosecutor and had worked as a judge with both lawyers for years. Davis and Marlinga's past got even more complicated: While still working for Marlinga as an assistant prosecutor in 1996, Davis ran for county prosecutor against her then-boss. The race divided the office with half the employees backing Marlinga and the other half behind Davis. Marlinga handily won, and he never disciplined Davis or her followers for the attempted coup. Despite the obligatory barbs during the campaign, Davis continued working for Marlinga until she was appointed for the judgeship. The overlap was the first of many: Michael George couldn't have hired a more tuned-in defense attorney, and he'd stumbled on him out of sheer happenstance.

Kaplan usually didn't call many witnesses at the preliminary hearing. For starters, he didn't have to. The legal threshold at that level is lower than it is to secure a conviction; all he needed to do was convince Judge Davis that a crime had been committed and that it was reasonable to believe Michael George committed it. Few cases are tossed out at that level as most prosecutors are smart enough to avoid levying charges so weak they can't even make the cut to get to circuit court. Also, Kaplan, like most prosecutors, didn't want to give the defense a blueprint outlining his case, not to mention a dry run in cross-examining key witnesses on the stand prior to trial. Sure, Marlinga would see the witness list beforehand, and he would generally know what each witness was likely to say under oath, but allowing a lawyer to have full rein at a preliminary hearing was widely viewed as a bad tactical move. Each witness Kaplan called gave Marlinga the chance to basically vet his case before trial. If Kaplan had his way, he would prefer calling just a couple of cops as witnesses and be done with things.

In this case, however, getting Michael George bound over for trial wouldn't be as easy as with some others. Kaplan had eighteen people on his witness list, including the case's past and current lead investigators, and over the two-day exam, he called on friends, customers, and family members to describe the bad state of the marriage and George's bizarre reaction to his wife's death.

Eileen Kowynia, Barbara George's sister-in-law, who, like her husband, was a doctor, described pulling up to Comics World for the birthday party only to find chaos and police cars. She remembered her husband Peter going in to see Barb after doctors had worked on her; Michael refused to go. And when Peter came out and broke the definitive news that his sister had died, Michael heaved a sigh that, to Eileen, sounded like relief.

"Any tears or outpouring of emotion at that point by Michael George?" Kaplan asked.

"Not that I remember," she replied.

Other witnesses recalled George not only dry-eyed, but wearing sunglasses at the funeral. Maggie Bolos, who had worked at Nails Plus, another business in the Venice Square Shopping Center, testified by telephone in the afternoon. She had fallen ill and was hospitalized, but Kaplan didn't want to miss out on having her testify. She remembered seeing Michael and Barbara George fighting the day of Barbara's death. The couple had been standing near a Dumpster, their children playing nearby, loudly arguing about pizza. She'd heard them arguing before, but never so loudly.

Before Bolos hung up, she caught the judge off guard.

"I remember you, Linda," she said.

The judge laughed. "Oh, you do, OK. I used to get my nails done at Nails Plus."

A small town indeed.

Because the threshold is so low at preliminary hearings, many defense lawyers waive them altogether, partly as a tactical move, partly to spare their client the inevitable bad publicity that comes with a story spelling out witness statements, and partly to simply avoid prolonging the inevitable. Not Marlinga. Not only did he insist on the preliminary hearing, but he even called witnesses. He knew that the timeline would prove to be crucial, and if he could plant in the judge's mind early that it simply didn't make sense that Michael would be both at his mother's house and at the comic book store at the same time, perhaps he could avoid trial altogether. First up would be Peggy Marentette, the neighbor with whom Marlinga had spoken by phone the previous Friday.

Marentette repeated what she'd said over the phone: that she'd driven home from her job in Oakland County's Southfield and spotted Janet George at the playground with Michelle and Tracie sometime between 5:45 and 6 p.m.

"I just beeped the horn and waved at them and proceeded on home," Marentette testified.

Marlinga pressed her on the time: Did she look at her watch to notice the exact time? No, Marentette said.

"That was just based on the usual time and the fifteen-minute difference is depending on traffic that particular day," she said.

Marentette also noticed Michael's minivan parked in front of his mother's house, she said. She couldn't recall the make or model—a Ford or Chrysler, perhaps—but she recognized it as Michael's.

"And did you see Janet George later that evening?" Marlinga asked.

"Yeah," Marentette recalled. "She came over after she had received the news, you know, that Barbara had died."

Kaplan thought Marentette's testimony was ridiculous. Her memory was nearly eighteen years old. She hadn't been interviewed at the time of the slaying. She couldn't recall the exact date and was basing it instead on a potentially faulty recollection that it was the same day Janet George later stopped by to say that her daughter-in-law had been killed. Nor could she remember the type of van Michael drove, meaning that she could be mistaken in thinking it was his vehicle outside of his mother's house. Eyewitness testimony even immediately after a crime is generally deemed suspect at best; even rape victims were known to misidentify their assailants. Kaplan considered Marentette a Hail Mary offering on Marlinga's part, and he set about to highlight her potential shortcomings.

"The vehicle that you saw, you're not able to tell us the exact model?" he began.

"No, I only said it was a minivan," Marentette said.

"It could have been a Ford, it could have been a Chrysler, it could have been a GM?"

"Yes, that's true."

"You didn't record the license plate number?"

"No, sir, I did not."

"You're not able to tell us whose vehicle that was for certain, are you?"

Marentette paused. "Other than based on seeing what, you know, Michael and Barbara would drive over in, no."

Kaplan moved onto the time of day. Marentette had no benchmark to know what time she supposedly spotted Janet and the girls beyond remembering that she was coming home from work.

"Your job was such that you didn't punch a clock . . . because sometimes your responsibilities carry you beyond the time that you normally would leave?" Kaplan asked. "And you can't tell us whether on that particular day you had responsibilities that kept you beyond the time you would normally leave."

"That's correct," Marentette replied.

As for the vehicle, even if it was the same one Michael George drove, Marentette acknowledged she never saw the man himself. And she acknowledged that in the 204 months since Barbara George was killed, she never contacted authorities about seeing his vehicle outside of her neighbor's house. Kaplan asked when she'd learned Michael was arrested on murder charges. August, she said; she'd heard it on the radio.

"So then, of course, knowing that Michael George was charged with murder and you might have some information about this case, you immediately contacted the authorities to tell them what you knew, right?" Kaplan asked, tongue firmly in cheek.

Marlinga objected. He'd seen Kaplan like this before.

"There is no indication that she would have any facts relevant to the case from the police report—from the things that she heard on the radio," Marlinga said.

Kaplan shot back: "She's his witness, and I have the right to ask her when she informed the authorities."

Davis allowed it. Marentette never contacted authorities, she admitted. She only spoke with Marlinga a few days prior, and he had called her, not the other way around.

Marlinga next called Janet George, Michael's mother. She repeated much of what she had told Sergeant Kline and Detective Friedmann in August: Michael sprawled on the couch before she took the girls to the park, and he was still sleeping there when she got back some forty minutes later. Marlinga even presented photographs of her living room setup so she could describe exactly where her son had been. She remembered, too, that her son tried to call his wife to no avail, and that at some point he got a phone call that sent him rushing from the house. When Janet got word that Barb had been hurt, she gathered the girls, grabbed a neighbor for support and drove to the hospital. She did not recall breaking the news to Peggy before she left.

For Kaplan, having the chance to cross-examine Janet George before trial was gold. He didn't believe her story—not so much because he thought she was flat-out lying, but rather that he thought she was mistaken, that she wanted to believe so badly in her son's innocence that she'd accepted an alternate reality over the past eighteen years. He posed a question that would become a refrain throughout the resurrection of the aging case:

"You would agree that, from a general point of view, one's memory is better back when an incident occurred as opposed to seventeen years and four months later, right?"

Janet was slippery. "I don't know," she said.

"You don't—you don't agree with that," Kaplan asked, his voice incredulous.

"I don't know," she repeated.

Kaplan persisted: "No, I'm asking you in general about people's memories. Do you think people's memories improve over time?"

Marlinga objected: asked and answered.

"We know it's a stock question, but sometimes the answer is exactly the one that this witness gave, and that's her perception," he defended.

"I'd like her to answer my question," Kaplan said.

"She did," Marlinga retorted.

"The judge makes that ruling, not you, Mr. Marlinga."

And so began the tête-à-tête between Marlinga and his former employee.

* * *

Marlinga's style differed markedly from Kaplan's. His questions were less pointed, but also less argumentative. Kaplan had a tendency to word his questions as statements, to which Marlinga objected, calling it "more like a speech" than a cross-examination. After one statement, Marlinga couldn't keep quiet, adding an annoyed "weren't they?" to the end of Kaplan's statement to turn it into a question.

Kaplan bristled. "I don't need help with the question, judge," he complained.

Marlinga apologized.

"I withdraw, I withdraw," he said.

Two months before Janet George sat in Davis's courtroom, she had been interviewed by Kline and Friedmann during the last-minute blitzkrieg attempt to trip her son up into giving a damning statement. Back then, Janet George said her son had left her house about 5:30 p.m. That fit with police and prosecutors' timeline: It gave Michael just enough time to get to Comics World to shoot his wife. But on the stand, Janet George said she never told Kline her son left at that time.

"I'm not sure of the time," she now said.

"But would you concede that your son could have left the house while you walked around the block—" Kaplan began.

"No," Janet interrupted.

"—and take the girls to the park, play with the girls, walk slowly—"

"And made it back to my house, no way," Janet barked.

"—I'm asking you, ma'am, can you tell this court that Michael George stayed on that couch and never left?"

"Right," Janet said. She wouldn't budge.

"You know that," Kaplan said, growing annoyed, "because you were watching him the entire time while you were walking with the girls and playing at the park, right?"

"I wasn't watching him," Janet said. "I was taking care of the girls."

"So you didn't have binoculars to know where Michael George was the whole time you were gone?"

Janet sighed. "But he'd never have made it back."

Kaplan was growing frustrated. He felt that Janet George was dead set on clearing her son, no matter what questions he asked. He tried again to nail down the time frame. The walk to the park took ten to fifteen minutes, she said. She and the girls stayed maybe twenty-five minutes. Walking back took another ten to fifteen minutes.

"And do you remember telling Sergeant Kline that you don't know how long you were away from home?" Kaplan asked.

"I'm just saying that's what I think." Janet shifted. She looked around the courtroom and caught her son's eyes. Kaplan noticed.

"You don't have to look at that side, you can look at me, as homely as I might be," Kaplan said. "They can't help you."

Marlinga fumed.

"Oh, wait a minute now," he said. "That's just plain unfair, Your Honor.

"I move to strike and I don't like these questions, and I don't like all the argument, either, but I'm putting up with it. I'm just saying play by the rules."

Kaplan wouldn't back down. "If he has an objection, he can make it," he said. "I don't like the witness—it's the third time she looked to that side, and that is improper. And you have a right to direct her not to do that."

Marlinga conceded that Janet might have been looking at her son, but, he said, "There's no communication, there's no signals. Your Honor is in this courtroom, and I want to make this record perfectly clear that this witness is not getting any kind of signal or any information from either her son, myself or my associate—that's what I'm objecting to."

"I have seen her looking over at her son," Davis said, "and I have watched, and there are no gestures or anything being made." Within minutes, however, that changed, as Kaplan asked Janet George about comments overheard during the funeral—specifically Michael asking twice for his mother to call the life insurance company about Barb's policies.

Without prompting, Davis sternly interjected.

"Mr. Marlinga, now your client is making gestures and smiling," she said, then turned her attention to Michael George: "Every time a question is asked and an answer is given, you are making faces," she barked. "You stop it, or you'll be removed, do you understand that?"

Michael meekly nodded. "Yes, ma'am," he said.

Marlinga apologized. "He will remain totally silent," he promised.

Marlinga had one last witness to call. To reporters in the room, it was a surprise, one that would become the main thrust of the evening news and the next day's headlines. Tracie George, who was just four when her mother died, would take the stand in her father's defense. Marlinga knew Tracie's testimony wouldn't be weighed heavily. Her memory, more than most witnesses', would be called into question, but even at such a young age, some things about the day you learn your mother has died are bound to stick out.

"I remember my father sleeping on the couch at my grandma's house, and I remember rushing through stop lights to get to the hospital and getting to the hospital and playing under the chairs," she testified.

She didn't remember what she'd been doing before she saw her dad sleeping. She couldn't recall who drove her to the hospital. She just remembered her dad facedown on the couch.

Kaplan didn't spend much time on cross-examination. He didn't give Tracie's testimony much weight, didn't expect Judge Davis to, and certainly doubted a jury would if she were to testify again at trial.

"Do you remember playing by the Dumpsters that morning?" he asked.

"No," Tracie replied.

"Do you remember your mother and father having an argument?"

"No."

"Screaming at each other?"

"No."

"Do you know how long you were at the park?"

"No."

"Do you know how fast your sister walked?"

"No."

"Do you know how you got to the park?"

"No."

Kaplan was finished.

Just as in trials, the lawyers in preliminary exams sum up their cases in closing arguments. It all came down to the timeline. Kaplan summed it up thusly: "Unless the defendant is a magician and related to Houdini, he can't be in two places at one time."

Davis didn't surprise the courtroom by sending the case to trial. She did, however, acknowledge that it was far from a slam-dunk case.

"I will give Mr. Marlinga that this isn't an iron-clad case by any stretch of the imagination," she said.

Chapter 19

Attempts at Bond

As disappointed as Marlinga was in the judge's ruling, he was more downtrodden by another loss: Judge Davis still refused to release George on bond. "It is a huge jump to go from infidelity to murder," Marlinga had argued. Despite Davis's concession that the prosecution case was weak, she stuck to protocol. People charged with first-degree murder rarely were granted bond. The flight risk is just too high when the potential punishment is life imprisonment, she said.

Once the case hit circuit court, it was assigned randomly to Judge James Biernat, a grandfatherly man with a soft reputation and even softer smile who began his career as a lawyer after graduating from the University of Detroit in 1968. He had spent much of his adult life in private practice before being elected to the countywide seat.

Marlinga added another player to the case, too. In launching his private practice, the former prosecutor had set up shop across the street from the Macomb County Jail—a convenient location for a lawyer hoping to capitalize off the recently jailed walking outside and heading to the office of the closest defense lawyer. Marlinga had long known Joe Kosmala, a defense lawyer known for his bulldog approach and Panama Jack appearance (sans monocle). He was a broad man with a bulbous nose who liked his liquor on the rocks. Kosmala had offered friendly counsel while Marlinga faced federal indictment, once advising him over a lunch at Dimitri's Rendezvous in Clinton Township not to testify in his defense. ("Are you crazy? Don't talk to those people!" he had barked.) They had been friends for about a quarter of a century, and when Marlinga branched off to enter the world of defense lawyering, he wanted to somehow attach his name to Kosmala, whom he regarded as one of the best defense lawyers in the state, and certainly the best in Macomb County. At first, their tie was in proximity only: They decided to share office space. Soon, however, Kosmala's longtime law partner died, so he and Marlinga merged firms in January 2008.

It was a given that Kosmala would team up with Marlinga on the George case. Slowly, he got up to speed, reading through the case file and meeting with Vohs, the private detective Marlinga had hired. Finally, he joined Marlinga and Vohs for a meeting with Michael and Renee. He walked in with the same skepticism he has toward all new clients, he later recalled. After all, most defendants are guilty of something, he said. They're just not always guilty of exactly what they have been charged with.

"Cops aren't stupid," Kosmala said. "Most of the time, the defense attorney's job is to protect his client and ensure his constitutional rights are guaranteed. Most of the time, they've done something wrong. That's why we have so many plea deals: The guy is charged with A, and the defense lawyer says, 'Well, you'll never prove A, but he'll never get away with C, so let's talk about B.' "

With Michael, however, Kosmala said he grew to believe in his client's actual, uncompromising innocence.

"Things just didn't match up," he said.

A sticking point for Kosmala was a test drive Vohs had done to clock how long it took to drive from Janet George's Hazel Park home to the comic book shop in Clinton Township. Each time, it was more than thirty minutes. To believe that Michael made the trip in the time Janet was at the park with the girls was absurd, Kosmala said.

"It didn't match up," said Kosmala, his brow knitted and voice incredulous. "There are common-sense problems with it. If I'm in a hurry because I've gotta go kill my wife, am I gonna be speeding with a gun in the car and risk getting caught? It just doesn't make sense."

As his belief in George grew, Kosmala began squinting harder at Renee. If one had motive, so did the other, and if the timeline didn't allow for Michael to rush to the store and do the deed, perhaps Renee was the gunman. Soon, though, Kosmala shook that suspicion. Renee didn't seem calculating enough to pull off the crime without leaving behind telltale evidence. Besides, she was clearly family-focused, taking on George's two daughters and integrating them into her own brood.

"She just doesn't seem to be the type to do something like that," Kosmala thought.

Besides, he and Marlinga didn't believe that a marriage built on murder would survive nearly two decades.

"It's true that if you have had people doing bad things together, they can have some laughs in Vegas for a while, but trying to raise a family together in western Pennsylvania isn't in the cards," Marlinga said. "They would have been living a lie for nineteen years. If a homicide started this relationship, the odds are it would be over by now."

Michael George first appeared before Biernat on October 22, 2007, for a perfunctory circuit court arraignment. Marlinga again raised the issue of bond, prompting the judge to schedule a hearing to weigh out whether George indeed should be kept behind bars while he waited for his case to snake through the system. Biernat asked the lawyers to outline their arguments in briefs, which they then defended with oral arguments November 20. Biernat took ten days to weigh the arguments, but in the end, he filed some writing of his own, saying he had carefully weighed Marlinga's request but had to deny bond.

Renee made the four-hundred-mile trek to visit her husband each week and attended every court hearing. She had already been selling off her husband's collectibles to begin footing the bill for Marlinga, and she thought she could scrounge up enough in cash and collateral to pull off bond if Biernat granted it. Every time she visited an increasingly gaunt Michael, she became more adamant that he had to be released somehow. She had been hopeful when Biernat agreed to listen to Marlinga's argument that Michael might be allowed out so they could resume some sort of normalcy, but with the November 30 ruling, she lost hope. Marlinga promised to ask for another hearing—and when he did, Biernat again agreed to listen—but everyone told her not to expect much. People suspected of killing their spouses just aren't allowed to go home and leisurely await trial.

Meanwhile, other piddly court appearances came and went: a status update here, a discovery request there. On January 4, after Michael had been in jail for four months, Kaplan presented a motion spelling out his intention to introduce what is called "prior bad acts." He had previously told reporters that George had a history of filing fraudulent insurance claims, though he had not yet detailed what the circumstances of those allegations were. He also wanted to detail a history of adulterous behavior—evidence that Kaplan said provided George with motive to kill his wife. This all surfaced while Biernat also opened the door for Marlinga to again argue for George's release from jail.

As would prove to be the norm for the case, none of Biernat's decisions came quickly. The judge would schedule a hearing date, the date would come, and he would inevitably adjourn it until a few weeks later. Sometimes the delays were the fault of one or more of the lawyers; often, however, Biernat would be expected to rule on something, and then decide instead that he needed more time. It was maddening for reporters covering the high-profile case, but naturally worse for family members on both sides. Joe Kowynia, Barb's brother, had taken off countless afternoons from his job running an automotive dent-removal business. Renee, meanwhile, had to find someone to staff the Windber comic store every time she made the six-hour drive to Michigan.

On January 17, Biernat finally weighed Marlinga's request to reconsider bond and—in a move that surprised everyone—he granted it, saying that the circumstantial nature of the case, matched with George's spotless record in the intervening years, were enough to trust that he wouldn't skip town to avoid trial. Bond was set at $1 million on the condition that George stay under house arrest at his mother's in Hazel Park. He had to surrender his passport and was only to leave to go visit with his lawyers.

Renee thanked God. She had packed her husband's suitcase four or five times at that point in hopes of bringing him home, only to leave court with the suitcase in tow. Emotionally, she was drained. His release wasn't ideal in that he couldn't come home with her, but she figured that being with his mother would at least be an improvement. They could talk on the phone without the calls being timed and monitored. His mood would lighten. Maybe he'd even gain back some weight, she thought. She had to scrape to find the money, but on January 23, after working with Ability Bail Bonds in Clinton Township, Michael George walked out of the brick jailhouse he had called home since early September and headed to his mother's.

The defense got another break just before trial when Biernat ruled that the prosecution could not introduce evidence of alleged prior insurance fraud. George had never been convicted of fraud, Biernat reasoned, so the evidence had no merit in a murder case. But the prosecution was allowed to introduce evidence about other infidelities, so long as Kaplan first argued to the court why each witness could be construed as relevant to the case. Biernat also ruled that George's post-homicide behavior—the lack of tears and the dark sunglasses at his wife's funeral—was admissible, despite a defense motion that aimed to quash it.

Chapter 20

Opening Statements

It seemed the pretrial housekeeping was never-ending. Biernat was still ruling on motions the day that the lawyers began grilling a pool of about sixty summonsed Macomb County residents for the jury. At the last minute, Biernat set parameters on how much information about previous infidelities could be admitted. Kaplan argued that Michael George's adulterous past was more than a minor character flaw. The guy just couldn't seem to keep it in his pants, first having a torrid affair with Patrice Sartori, the coworker at the insurance company where he'd worked before opening Comics World. He'd been so infatuated with this woman that he threatened to make public a videotape of them having sex when she ended their affair, Sartori told investigators. The defense would want all of that evidence left out, Kaplan knew, and they would have legal precedent with which to argue. It would be up to Kaplan to convince Judge Biernat that the sordid details were more probative than prejudicial.

It would prove to be a difficult task. Biernat already had kicked out some of the adultery evidence. Kaplan argued that some should stay in. He laid it out: the Sartori affair and alleged videotape. Testimony from Dave Bareno, who said he'd seen Michael and Renee flirting before Barb's death. Testimony from Mike Benson, who said that in late 1989 or early 1990, George emerged from his shop's back room bragging that Renee had just performed oral sex on him while he was wearing a Santa Claus suit. Another witness who would say the same.

Defense lawyer Joe Kosmala said none of it was relevant. The relationship with Sartori ended some two years before Barb died, he said, and the notorious sex tape was but an urban legend, so far as he knew. As for the back room blowjob, "there is no indication, at least that we have or that has been provided by the prosecutor, as to the date," he said. "Are we talking about a week the Christmas before this murder, which occurred in July, or do we believe somebody was running around in July in a Santa Claus suit?" he asked.

Judge Biernat agreed that the time frame was ambiguous at best. He did not want this trial overturned based on his admitting evidence that had nothing to do with the murder but clearly painted Michael George as a filthy philanderer. He announced that he'd be reining Kaplan in, forbidding talk about the alleged Sartori sex tape, her accusations of him stalking her after their breakup, or descriptions of his flirtatious relationships with women before his wife's death. Details about the alleged oral sex incident, too, would never reach jurors' ears, he ruled.

"The court reiterates its apprehension that such proper salacious acts will serve no other purpose than to potentially predispose the jury to conclude that the defendant is, overall, not only a womanizer, but that he could also be a man capable of the crime of the murder," he said. "Such inferences paint a person of bad character and must certainly be avoided."

Kaplan felt slightly hamstrung, and he knew his case was thin from an evidentiary standpoint. That whole no-witnesses, no-murder-weapon thing would be a problem with jurors. Nowadays, the so-called "*CSI* Effect" made it tough to convince jurors of a defendant's guilt with anything short of a fingerprint on a murder weapon left in the victim's own blood. For police and prosecutors, shows like *CSI* proved downright detrimental. Still, he had worked with worse, he reasoned. Like the Pann murder case with no body. Kaplan had a history of pulling off the unlikely; this case was just another challenge to face.

Finally, at nearly 10 a.m. February 27, 2008—nearly seven months after detectives had made their surprise trip to Windber to confront George—the murder trial got under way with a jury selection that would take two full days. In the end, the pool of potential jurors was whittled to fourteen—twelve jurors and two alternates—composed of six men and eight women. It was showtime.

"In this case, the attorneys do agree on certain facts," began Kaplan, facing the fourteen jurors he and Marlinga had so carefully tried to vet. "We agree that on July 13, 1990, Barbara George died. We agree that she was murdered and that she was shot once in the head and that the shooting was not an accident and it was not a suicide. The issue is who did it.

"Now," Kaplan continued, "we claim that Michael George is the killer, and we claim so for many reasons."

Kaplan had readied his canvas. Now it was time to start painting.

"He was the husband from hell."

In Kaplan's description, Barb George was a sweet, likeable, slightly overweight woman who had no enemies. Like any person, she was not without fault, he said, but she had none of the habits or characteristics that typically made someone a likely murder target. She didn't do drugs, she wasn't an alcoholic, she didn't gamble, she didn't cheat on her husband, and she didn't suffer from a mental illness. Even Michael George said no one had reason to shoot his wife.

As Kaplan described Barb's last day alive, he painted with broad strokes: Customers arrived and couldn't find an employee. They got impatient and peeked in the back room, spotting Barb's body. They think she had a stroke or heart attack or maybe an aneurism because there was no blood, and it's uncovered "only at the hospital where a nurse discovers a small bullet hole and some blood that Barbara had been shot in the head."

Then, almost as an aside, Kaplan quickly added:

"Oh, in this case, we don't have direct evidence other than the defendant's statements," he said.

Because of the questions posed during the lawyers' *voir dire*, this didn't surprise jurors. They'd been peppered with questions about their TV viewing habits in such a way that they got the point: Evidence isn't always as clear-cut as *CSI* would have you believe.

"If you watch TV crime shows, current movies, they talk about circumstantial evidence and direct evidence," he said. "And sometimes you'll hear on a TV show, 'All they have is circumstantial evidence.' But in actuality, everything is circumstantial evidence other than an eyewitness to a crime, a videotape of the crime or statements of the person who did it. Everything else is circumstantial, such as hair found at the scene, property disturbed at a scene, money not taken during a fake robbery. All of those, all that type of evidence is circumstantial evidence. And that's what our case is based on."

Lawyers on both sides knew that was too generous: Kaplan would argue that property was not disturbed and money was not taken. He had no fingerprints, no hair, no telltale blood spatter evidence. Nothing.

He began describing the philandering, saying it illustrated "marital discord."

"Barb was unhappy in the marriage but wanted to make the marriage work for the sake of the children," Kaplan told the jury. "[The] defendant wasn't happy in the marriage and wanted out. His first way of seeking to disentangle himself from Barb George is a friendly, harmonious divorce, but she didn't want a divorce.

"The second way, the way he chose, is to kill her."

Defense lawyer Joe Kosmala, who would handle the opening statements, interrupted. It would be the first of many in-trial head-butts between Kaplan and him. He said Kaplan was overreaching, turning his opening statement instead into an argument, one meant to sway the jury rather than set up his case. Judge Biernat warned Kaplan to only present what he planned to prove.

Kaplan regained his footing.

"I mentioned the marital discord and before I was interrupted, I was saying what he gained by ending the marriage: Money. Money." That life insurance policy that was valued at $130,000 in 1990 likely would be worth some $250,000 today, he said.

That, and he wanted to trade Barb in for a younger, thinner model.

After Kaplan finished, Kosmala slowly stood up and walked to the podium. A religious man himself, Kosmala began by relating the story of Susanna in the Book of Daniel. As the story goes, a Hebrew wife is coveted by two voyeurs who watch her bathe in her garden. They accost her and threaten to claim that she was meeting a man in the garden unless she agrees to sleep with them. She refuses, and the men falsely accuse her of promiscuity—a crime for which she's sentenced to death. But Daniel interrupts, separates the two men and questions them about the details, specifically about what kind of tree under which Susanna had sex. One says a mastic; the other, an oak tree.

"Council, seeing their terrible mistake, released Susanna and condemned the elders," Kosmala said. "If it were not for the examination, were it not for the testing of their stories, she would have been wrongfully condemned. That is why we have cross-examination," he said.

He turned his attention to his client.

"So where does the truth lie in this case?" he asked. "Mr. Kaplan has given you a version of facts. We think the facts are different.

"Aside from all this infidelity business, aside from the alleged big cash accounts and all that other stuff, the basic line of offense is that this defendant was not there."

And therein began the point-counterpoint that would color much of the trial: Michael George said he wasn't at the comic book store, but one witness—Michael Renaud—said he spoke with George on the phone about an hour after he was supposed to have left. To counter Renaud's impending testimony, Kosmala said he and Marlinga would present other witnesses who backed up their theory that he was nowhere near the crime scene.

"To the living, we owe the facts; to the dead we owe the truth," Kosmala said. "And to the rest of us, the community at large, the citizens of Macomb County, we owe justice. Justice is not served by convicting the wrong man."

Chapter 21

Testimony Begins

Before Kaplan, the prosecutor, even had the chance to call his first witness, the case hit a snag. Juror No. 151, Steve Randall, had long known his wife's cousin worked for the government, but he had never asked any details about her job. After he landed on the jury, he found out: She worked at the Macomb County Prosecutor's Office—meaning the people who paid her salary were the same ones who wanted Michael George behind bars. Randall told the court and was called in before the lawyers and judges behind closed doors. He would try to be fair, he said, but he wasn't convincing. More than worried about being too gung-ho for prosecutors, he worried he might try too hard to overcompensate by being pro-defense.

"That's what a hundred percent I don't know," he told the lawyers and judge. "I'll try my hardest. I really would."

Kaplan didn't want Randall dismissed, but Marlinga said it was clear the man was struggling. Biernat agreed, and the pool of fourteen was whittled by one. There would be just one juror left who could be dismissed for an alternate post-testimony, pre-deliberation.

Finally, at 9 a.m. on February 28, 2008, the testimony could begin.

* * *

Christine Ball looked uncomfortable as she took the stand. She and her sister had been close—closer than her and her brothers before the shooting—and she'd long harbored the suspicion that her brother-in-law was responsible. Kaplan began his questioning the same way he would begin much of the direct examination over the next several weeks: How did you know Barbara George? When did you last talk to her? What happened July 13, 1990?

Christine was younger than Barb. She had last seen Barb on July 4. And July 13, she recalled, was a nightmare. She had been called out of work at her job as a grocery store cashier, rushed to the comic store, then was directed to go to the hospital. Her dad and brothers were already there, as was Eileen, her sister-in-law, Peter's wife.

Michael was there, too. The room was awkward, the air heavy with confusion and increasing despair. Christine turned to Michael.

"Do you think Renee's husband had anything to do with it?"

"And what did Michael George say?" Kaplan asked.

"No. He wouldn't be the one. He didn't do it, you know. I found it so odd that he would just say no. How would you know?"

He showed little emotion, she said. No tears, no anger.

And at the funeral: "He wore dark sunglasses. Again, no tears."

The strangest part of his demeanor, she said, was his reaction to running into her at the grocery store where she worked soon after the shooting. She went to hug him and he recoiled.

"And I said, 'Whoa,'" she testified. "And then I had to go back to the register and work, and then all of a sudden his demeanor changed."

People were around; now he was friendly.

Marlinga stood for cross-examination. The back-and-forth with witnesses officially was under way. Kaplan would pepper with questions about Michael, his pre-shooting philandering, his post-shooting oddball behavior. With Christine Ball, Marlinga began his own refrain.

"Now, at the funeral home you talked about dark sunglasses. Sometimes when people want to hide the fact that they've been crying or that their eyes are red, they wear dark sunglasses."

Christine looked at him blankly.

"Do you believe that could have been his reason or not?"

"My belief is no," she said, "because I didn't see no tears."

"Would you agree that, just in general, people sometimes can be very strong and not show emotion at the funeral home and then when they go home at night, that's when they break down and cry a river?"

"I guess it could be possible."

"Right," Marlinga said. "And also, you would agree with me that different people handle grief in various ways. Would you agree with that?"

"I agree with that." Christine hesitated. "But there was a calmness. You know, there was a—I don't know, no tears and no reaction, you know."

Marlinga took a different tack.

"You're probably too young to remember the assassination of Kennedy?"

Christine said she remembered learning about it on the radio.

"And do you remembering seeing the funeral and his wife Jacqueline that there were no tears?"

"She had to be strong there."

"Right," said Marlinga. She had made his point for him. He thanked her for her testimony.

Eileen Kowynia, the doctor married to Barb's brother, also a doctor, took the stand. She repeated much of what she had said in the earlier preliminary exam: She and husband Peter arrived at the store for the birthday party to find the parking

lot swarming with police. When Michael learned Barb was
dead at the hospital, he let out what to her sounded like a
relieved sigh. He never cried, so far as she saw.

At trial, however, Kaplan took her testimony further. He
asked if she had known Renee Kotula. Back then, no, she
said. But after Barb died, the girls told her they were living
with Michael's mistress. Daddy would tuck them in at night
and pick them up in the morning. That was within two months
of Barb's death, Eileen said.

Marlinga again focused on Michael's perceived lack of
emotion: As a doctor, hadn't she seen loved ones react in a
variety of ways to news that someone had died? She had, she
acknowledged. And that sigh of relief, might it have been
resignation, not satisfaction? Again, she acquiesced. And
though she didn't see him cry at the hospital or the funeral, "I
have seen him cry since then," she said.

Joyce Selke was married to Barb's cousin, and the two women
had become friends. Joyce used to swing by Barb's place for
haircuts. She and Michael often seemed at odds. Several
times, she'd shown up to find Barb bawling and Michael
fuming. Michael stormed out at least twice, she said.

Then there was the time Michael tried to sell Joyce and her
husband life insurance policies. She couldn't remember the
exact dollar figure, but it was so high that she and her husband
found it ludicrous that he would even suggest getting that big
an amount. Michael told them it was the same amount he had
on Barbara.

Kaplan called Anita Dukich for a simple reason: The
Georges' neighbor had told police—then later testified at
the preliminary hearing—that Michael did not act like much
of a grieving widower after Barb's death. She once offered
him condolences, to which he nonchalantly replied, "Those
things happened." That was two weeks after Barb died, she
said. Then, another two weeks later, she spotted him and a

dark-haired woman getting out of his car. She watched for a second from her mobile home into his and spied them in a steamy embrace. Michael kissed the woman. It made Dukich so uncomfortable that, feeling like a voyeur, she quickly looked away.

"When I saw that it wasn't like a brother or sister kiss, I immediately just shut my door," she said. "I was embarrassed."

Through the parade of customers who testified about finding Barb's body evolved an unsettling convergence of happenstance and habit that tied the disparate group together in tragedy. Nearly eighteen years later, they would be called forward to recount the bizarre evening that began, as they say, much like any other.

In July 1990, Kevin Biernacki was just sixteen going on seventeen years old. A comic book fan, he would swing by Comics World once or twice a week to peruse the new arrivals. It had been a ritual for some two years by the time he showed up at the store on the thirteenth at about 6 p.m. It had been a warm, sunny summer day. The sun had just begun to wane. A handful of customers milled about the store, but there was no employee on hand. It all happened really fast, he said, but he could recall the details even years later.

"It was a traumatic experience, and I remember a lot of it," he said.

He remembered a man and his wife—Tom and Lenora Ward, it would turn out—walking in. He thought, perhaps, a man and his son had shown up, too.

Peter Corrado was actually there with his younger brother, not his son, and the two simply wanted to kill some time while waiting to pick up a dry cleaning order. He had never been in the store before, but his brother liked comics, and it was one of the few open stores in the strip mall, so they went in. The other customers seemed perplexed that no one appeared to be working. After a few moments of confusion, the customers jointly decided to look for an employee in the back room. The door was partly ajar. Corrado stuck his head in. At first, he thought the arm he saw on the floor belonged to a mannequin. Quickly, he realized it was a woman—one whom the Wards recognized.

"I went to the front of the store by the cash register and I asked if somebody could call nine-one-one," Corrado said.

Tom Ward figured he had visited the store between thirty and fifty times. Usually he went with Lenora, to whom he still was married in 2007—they'd crossed the twenty-three-year threshold. This night, he and Lenora headed over about 5:30 p.m. He remembered someone calling for help after spotting Barb in the back room. Lenora had rushed back to put her nurse's training to work. Tom ran to call 911 and found it odd that the phone was off the hook, as though someone had set it aside with the intent of continuing a paused conversation. Tom hung up the phone, called 911, then rushed back to help his wife administer CPR.

"Our impression was that she might have stepped up on a crate to place a box higher on a shelf, and we thought [she] had possibly fallen backward and hit her head," Tom said.

After the first police officer showed up, Tom left his wife's side to run to the street and flag down the ambulance.

Kaplan peppered him with questions fitting for a regular customer: Had Tom seen anything out of place in the front of the store? Any broken glass from the showcases? Any cash registers tipped over or busted open? No, no and no, Tom answered.

But Tom did see that vehicle driving a bit too quickly away from the strip mall as he and Lenora drove in, and there was that slightly built person, seemingly male, in the Greek fishing cap Tom saw walking away from the store to the north. The man looked over his shoulder at the door to the comic book store.

"Do you know why the person might have been looking behind?" Kaplan asked.

Barbara George was born June 14, 1958, the oldest of four children raised in a 1,200-square-foot ranch in Warren, Michigan, a suburb north of Detroit.
Photo courtesy of Joseph Kowynia.

A tomboy in youth, Barb played volleyball and softball, bringing home tournament championships throughout high school.
Photo courtesy of Joseph Kowynia.

Barb continued playing softball as an adult on local teams.
Photo courtesy of Joseph Kowynia.

Barb met Michael George, left, when the two worked at Farmer Jack, a grocery store in Hazel Park, Michigan. The two got married Sept. 12, 1981. Before Michael, dating hadn't been a priority for Barb.

Photo courtesy of Joseph Kowynia.

Barb was eager to become a mother, said her friends and family. She gave birth to Tracie in September 1985, followed by Michelle, pictured, two years later.

Photo courtesy of Joseph Kowynia.

Barb and Michael raised their two girls in a mobile home in Macomb Township. Family members said Barb carefully balanced motherhood with helping Michael launch the couple's business, Comics World.
Photo courtesy of Joseph Kowynia.

When customers arrived on Friday, July 13, 1990, to Comics World in Clinton Township, no one was at the counter. They eventually found Barb sprawled on the floor in the business' back room. Her shoe is seen in the doorway.
Photo courtesy of the Clinton Township Police Department.

Among the ceiling-high crates stacked in the back room of Comics World hid a clue that officers didn't notice at first: a bullet hole on the far wall.

Photo courtesy of the Clinton Township Police Department.

The bullet hole, discovered after police realized Barb had been shot and was not the victim of a heart attack, pierced the left eye of a swimsuit-clad Kathy Ireland, pictured in a calendar hanging on a cork board. A private investigator hired for the defense theorized that Barb might have surprised a would-be robber.

Photo courtesy of the Clinton Township Police Department.

Macomb County Prosecutor Eric Smith launched the office's Cold Case Unit soon after winning his first election in 2004. His father, Robert Smith, had been police chief in Clinton Township when the shooting occurred and considered it the crime that got away. *Photo by Amber Hunt.*

After leaving Michigan two years after Barb's death, Michael and Renee George opened a new Comics World on Graham Avenue in Windber, Pennsylvania. After Michael's arrest, Renee rented out the front part of the shop to a computer repair business to help make ends meet.

Photo by Elijah Van Benschoten.

Michael George regularly conferred with his lawyer, Carl Marlinga, seen here as co-counsel Joseph Kosmala looked on during a pre-trial hearing at the Macomb County Circuit courthouse. *Photo courtesy of the* Detroit Free Press.

Renee George attended much of the trial with her son, Justin Kotula. *Photo courtesy of the* Detroit Free Press.

Macomb County Assistant Prosecutor Steve Kaplan had been hired by Marlinga and was surprised to learn that his former boss would be his courtroom adversary in the George case. *Photo courtesy of the* Detroit Free Press.

Renee and Michael George tearfully embraced after a day of testimony. Michael was prone to tears long before the trial, Renee said. "You know at graduations, you see some men quietly wiping away a few tears? Not my husband. He's sobbing, wiping away handfuls."

Photo courtesy of the Detroit Free Press.

Macomb County Circuit Judge James Biernat set aside the jury's verdict in September 2008.
Photo courtesy of the Detroit Free Press.

With her husband in jail awaiting trial, Renee George took over the 2009 Pittsburgh Comicon and secured comics legend Stan Lee as a special guest on Sept. 12, 2009. Though she kept her game face on during the event, she later acknowledged it wasn't the same without her husband. *Photo by Amber Hunt.*

Among the thousands of comics on sale at the 2009 Pittsburgh Comicon was *Action Comics* No. 81—one of the comics for which Barb was allegedly killed. In 2009, it was valued at only $280. *Photo by Elijah Van Benschoten.*

"No."

"What's the time sequence? Do you see the car traveling ten miles an hour to the parking lot first, or do you see the guy with the fisherman hat walking?"

"I cannot connect those two events together in my mind. I would say that they were two separate events: The car went by first, the person out of the store, second."

"Did either of those observations cause alarm for you such as contacting—calling nine-one-one?"

No, Tom said.

Both Lenora and Tom said they had likely knocked over quite a few things in that back room as they tried to breathe life back into Barb.

"I moved boxes so that the EMS unit could get a stretcher back there and bring their equipment back to continue to work on Barb," Tom said. "They were on the floor stacked up two and three high and the store was such that there was pretty much just an aisle to walk through in a lot of areas."

Lenora: "I moved those things that were in the general vicinity of Barb's body, moved things back and around. There was a baby blanket that was moved."

"Right," Kaplan prodded.

"And because she was so tight to the wall, I originally moved her out a foot from the wall, and then I asked my husband to move a number of different items, knowing that EMS was going to be there and that we were going to need more room."

Lenora moved Barb again another few feet when CPR proved too difficult in the confined space.

She described the haunting scene and giving CPR straightforward with clinical language, her nurse's training taking over.

"When I walked into the back storage area, Barb was on her right-hand side. Her arm was out. When I went, you know, 'Barb, are you OK?' I moved her onto her back and noticed that she was blue around her lips and mouth. She was still warm."

Barb's eyes were dilated and fixed, she said. She knew this was a bad sign.

"I was unable to find a pulse at that time and I knew that she was in a grave emergency medical situation. And at that time, I pulled her head back, made sure she wasn't breathing, and administered breath."

She again checked for a pulse and found none.

"I found my position on the chest to make sure I didn't crack any of her ribs—to make sure that my hands were in the middle of the sternum, and I did compressions."

Pause, two breaths, chest compressions, pause: The cycle seemed to last forever. In reality, it was seven to ten minutes, Lenora estimated.

Lenora never saw the person outside the store that her husband described, but she did see the person with the billed cap speeding away.

"I did not see a face," she said. "It is not someone I could pick out of a lineup, but [he] had a dark shirt on, had some type of a billed hat on, and the car itself was dark. So dark shirt, dark hat, male, it appeared."

Kaplan asked Lenora if she'd done anything besides talk to investigators before she left the store. She had, she said. She'd left her phone number on a piece of paper and placed it next to the cash register so that Michael George could call her and ask about their efforts to save his wife. Surely, he would want to hear the details, she figured.

"What type of information would you have given?" Kaplan asked. Marlinga objected, saying it was speculative. Biernat sustained.

"Were you surprised he didn't contact you?"

"Yes."

Lenora had answered before Marlinga could log his objection, which again was sustained. The jury was to ignore the response.

"Fine," Kaplan said, sounding impatient. "We're done."

Though Marlinga had objected to the question, he opted to revisit it on cross-examination.

"You don't have any idea of knowing whether or not Michael George ever received that note, do you?"

"No, but he had our information. We were customers."

But wouldn't police be the ones to talk about the case to Michael? he asked. Partly, Lenora answered.

Marlinga sounded flustered.

"Is there anything that makes you think that you were so special in Michael George's life that he would necessarily be wanting to call you?"

Lenora's eyes widened. She was special, she said, because she had put her mouth on his wife's bloodied mouth and tried to breathe life into her dead body.

"Right," Marlinga said. "And do you have any idea if he ever found that out? You don't know that, do you?"

"No, I don't."

The first day of testimony wrapped up at 2:40 p.m. Jurors got the usual rundown of instructions: Don't read the paper, don't talk to family members, don't do any independent research on the case. Be back 8:30 a.m.—sharp.

Chapter 22

Trial Day 2

Another day, another problem with a seated juror.

So began Day 2 of testimony. This time, Albert Lesniak—otherwise known as Juror No. 49—realized he and Michael George had both worked for John Hancock Insurance Co. He didn't know George, nor did he think they ever overlapped as employees, but he had grown to hate John Hancock employees so vehemently that he wanted to let the judge know he might not be able to be impartial while listening to testimony.

His story went like this, according to a transcribed meeting with the judge and lawyers: Lesniak was hired to sell insurance in the late '80s or early '90s. One day a lady told him she wanted to put $50,000 into an annuity. Lesniak said sure thing, went back to the office, and told his supervisor the plan. The supervisor instead insisted he not put it in an annuity but tell the customer he had. Lesniak thought this was bogus and quit.

"They came down on me big time, these guys," Lesniak told the judge. "You know, 'You ungrateful f'ing—' They just went off.

"I got out of there. . . . After all this time, I'm very upset."

"You're not suggesting anybody who had anything to do with Hancock is necessarily a crook?" Biernat asked.

Pretty much, Lesniak admitted. "I mean, like, to me, a lot of them are mean crooks," he said.

This prompted a half-hour of back-and-forth between Lesniak, Biernat, and the lawyers. At issue: Could Lesniak give George a fair shake even if he thought all John Hancock employees were inherently slimy?

"I can try," he said.

Lawyers on both sides were growing frustrated. Potential jurors often try to weasel out of jury duty, and a lot of times they succeed. After all, neither party benefits from having someone flat-out forced to listen to a case they don't care about—especially when it's a case where a man's life-long freedom hangs in the balance. But with George, the sides had carefully vetted the jury pool and picked fourteen men and women they really thought would be up for the job. On Day 1, they lost their first juror. Were they to lose another, there would be no more wiggle room. Every juror would need to sit through every day, and there would be no alternates. Kaplan especially felt like he was losing momentum.

Biernat asked what both sides felt was the most important question: Had Lesniak told the other jurors he thought all John Hancock employees were crooks?

No, he hadn't, Lesniak replied.

"And if you are retained on this jury, could you promise this court that you would not communicate that in any form or fashion?" Biernat asked.

"Yes," Lesniak answered. "Yes, yes, yes."

He stayed on the jury. Day 2 could finally start.

Ross Amicucci had worked as a Clinton Township police officer for just one year before he was called to the Comics World crime scene in July 1990. He arrived shortly after the 6:22 p.m. call to 911 was radioed out—woman down, a medical run—and was the first unit to arrive. When he got there, Tom and Lenora Ward were still performing CPR on Barb.

Amicucci took over the chest compressions and Lenora focused on mouth-to-mouth. Tom ran outside to try to flag down the ambulance in hopes of shaving off even a couple of seconds' response time. After the paramedics took over, Amicucci began collecting names and securing the store. No one at that point knew Barbara George had been shot, so the officer aimed to simply close up the shop.

"Basically, it was a heart attack," Amicucci recalled. "The lady fell, maybe possibly hit her head, and that was about it."

Kaplan began the rundown that he would pose to many law enforcement agents set to testify: Did anything appear to be disrupted? No, Amicucci said. Were the cash registers tipped over or glass cases busted? No again.

"I checked the back door," Amicucci said. "It appeared to be secured."

As the officer had only been at the store some fifteen minutes, his direct examination was correspondingly short. He'd arrived, helped with CPR, gathered some names, locked up, and left. Kaplan was done with his questions. Marlinga was slightly less succinct. He asked again what time the 911 call came in and whether the call would have been handled by the closest police station to where the call was being placed or not. Amicucci said he didn't know how the emergency calls were routed. Next, Marlinga moved on to the scene itself.

"Did you smell anything that you recognized as the left-over smell of a gun being discharged?" he asked.

The reply: "Not that I recall."

"Did you come to any opinion yourself as to what was the most likely result why the woman was down?"

The answer: "The nurse, the lady doing CPR, indicated that it was a heart attack. She's a medical professional. It didn't look like there was anything else, nothing out of the order, so it looked like a medical run. Whether it was a heart attack or something else at that time, I didn't know."

While Kaplan had questioned about the condition of the

front room, Marlinga wanted to know if the back room seemed disheveled. Amicucci said he hadn't really paid attention. He was focused on trying to revive Barb, he said. Marlinga whipped out some photographs taken by police after the shooting that showed some plastic bins downed in the back room.

"You see in this photograph a number of comic book bins . . . that had been tipped over. Did you push those over?" Marlinga asked.

"No, sir," Amicucci said.

More photos, the same question. Amicucci said he didn't knock the bins down. Kaplan objected: asked and answered. Overruled.

Kaplan shifted in his seat. He wasn't the most patient person in the world, especially when it came to questions he considered redundant. Each day, he began with a goal in mind—say, ten witnesses on this day, for example. With every redundancy, he felt himself slipping further from his goal. Marlinga, for him, could be a maddening opponent on that front. The former prosecutor was more verbose, and Biernat seemed to be erring on the side of redundancy over efficiency.

Marlinga showed Amicucci the calendar photo of Kathy Ireland, the swimsuit model who had taken a bullet to her eye while hanging on the corkboard in the back room. Amicucci said he had not seen the picture when he was trying to revive Barbara George, nor had he spotted the open safe on the floor beneath some overturned papers.

After Marlinga finished, Kaplan stood up and fired off questions in rapid form, almost as if to show his former boss how quickly it could be done.

"Detective, had you been in that store prior to July 13, 1990?"

"Not that I recall, sir, no."

"Had you ever been in the back room prior to July 13, 1990?"

"No, sir."

"Are you in a position to tell us the condition of that room on July 12, 1990?"

"No, sir."

"Or July 11, 1990?"

"No, sir."

"Or at any time prior to July 13, 1990, before six p.m.?"

"No, sir.

"Are you in a position to tell us whether that back room was generally tidy or not tidy?"

"No, sir."

"Are you in a position to tell us that the photographs of the back door that Mr. Marlinga featured on the screen is the way that door looked when you were there?"

"I don't recall, sir."

"Did you take any photographs of that door?"

"No, sir."

"Was there any reason to take photographs of the door?"

"No, sir, not at that time."

Kaplan barely missed a beat. The questions and answers hammered out, rat-tat-tat.

"You don't know whether boxes were tipped over or not tipped over before 6 p.m.?"

"No, sir."

"And if they were tipped over after 6 p.m., you don't know how that happened?"

"No, sir."

"Thank you, sir."

Marlinga asked one more time on recross-examination if Amicucci remembered knocking anything over himself. No, he replied. And he was dismissed.

Patrice Sartori had been a hot number at age twenty-three, back when she worked at John Hancock Insurance Co. In the nearly two decades since, she had aged well. Still slim and attractive, she took the stand and swore to God she would tell the truth.

Much of the more lurid details about her relationship with then-married Michael George would never reach jurors' ears, Biernat had already ruled, but Kaplan wanted Sartori on the stand to show jurors that George hadn't been happy in his marriage for years.

Sartori told the court she met George at the Troy branch, where some thirty employees worked. She knew he was married. She knew he had a daughter. She also knew his wife was pregnant with their second child. She dated him anyway.

"What do you mean by dating?" Kaplan prodded, then clarified: "I don't want details, you know what I'm saying? I don't want to know any specific types of acts, but what do you mean by dating?"

"We did have an intimate relationship," Sartori replied.

The two would meet at Michael's apartment on Mound Road between 14 and 15 Mile roads, she recalled. They carried on the relationship for maybe six months. She'd thought he was separated from Barb, whom she had met a few times at the Troy office.

"We didn't really talk about her," she testified. "I was under the impression when we were dating . . . that he was separated from his wife because he lived separately from her, or he was divorcing her."

Sartori realized that the Georges' marriage was far from over when he asked her to babysit Tracie while he brought Barb and baby Michelle home from the hospital. Sartori agreed.

"And that was the end of our relationship," she recalled on the stand. The two never had sex again. She told him multiple times that she wanted to end the relationship.

Kaplan wasn't allowed to prod further. Biernat already had ruled that planned testimony about George trying to keep the relationship alive by lording a sex tape over her was inadmissible. Kosmala asked for a sidebar to ensure the questions steered clear of the purported lurid tape. Instead, Kaplan went down another road.

"Did Michael George make any comment to you about his wife's appearance?"

Kosmala objected: leading. Overruled.

"In that case, I object as to relevance," Kosmala tried again. Overruled.

"I vaguely remember him saying one time that she was getting really fat because she was pregnant," Sartori said. Kaplan was done.

On cross-examination, Sartori said she didn't remember why she agreed to babysit for her lover and his wife. It wasn't to throw their relationship in Barb's face, she assured Kosmala. By then, she was done emotionally with Michael anyway.

"Were you interviewed by the police or anyone else in 1990 in connection with the incident at the comic book store?" Kosmala asked.

Answer: no.

"So the first time you became involved in this case is when? Last year?"

"About six months ago," Sartori said.

"Did you contact the police or did they contact you?"

"They contacted me."

Kaplan addressed that again on redirect. Sartori didn't learn about Barb George's death when it occurred, she elaborated. The rumor mill hadn't reached her. She learned about it the following summer, around the time her own sister died. She didn't call the police. She didn't see a reason to.

Next up was Michael Benson, who had worked at Comics World when he was twenty-two. He had since moved on and had been teaching elementary school for fourteen years. He remembered Michael and Barbara well, he testified. Michael was the boss man who gave out the orders; Barb carried out the demands.

"How did he treat her?" Kaplan asked.

"A majority of the time, kind of curt, straight to the point," Benson said. "I don't know what the word I'm looking for is, but not quite the loving husband type, I guess I'm trying to say. More like an employee."

While George was curt toward his wife, he was friendly to the store's female patrons, Benson said. Kaplan asked if Michael ever commented about his wife's appearance. Kosmala tried again with the relevancy objection. It again was overruled.

"I remember a comment about how she wears a night-gown down to her ankles, kind of in a dissatisfying tone," Benson recalled.

Benson went one night to view Barb's body, and he also attended the church service. The former worker didn't see his boss cry, but he recalled him sitting near the casket wearing sunglasses.

After the robbery, Michael passed out a list of the comic books that allegedly had been stolen. Benson hadn't seen any of them in the store prior to their disappearance. And Benson recalled a strange conversation he'd had with his boss a few weeks after Barb's death.

"I remember him saying he was getting some money," Benson testified. "He asked me, 'You know, Mike, should I get a new store or should I get a sports car?' I remember some sort of sports car—a Ferrari or something—and I remember thinking that was odd because I would want to get out of that store and get the new store."

Kaplan thanked Benson and sat down. Kosmala, on cross-examination, got straight to the point: "Do you remember being interviewed by the Clinton Township Police Department on or about March 13 of last year?" he asked. Benson remembered.

"Do you recall at one point telling them that 'my memory sucks'?"

A slight chuckle from the courtroom. Benson remembered that, too.

"Yes. Anybody's memory from eighteen years ago probably wouldn't be too sharp," he said.

"Exactly," Kosmala pounced. "You weren't interviewed eighteen years ago, were you?"

Benson agreed he wasn't.

"Even though you were a customer, and then an employee, of Comics World, the police did not seek you out seventeen and a half years ago to give any information?"

They had not, Benson said, nor had he sought police out himself.

"And the reason for that is?"

Benson paused. "I didn't think I had witnessed any criminal activity, I suppose. I didn't have a car or a person I saw so I didn't know anything of value I had."

Kosmala continued: "And you worked for some months at Comics World after the robbery and murder, is that correct?"

Before Benson could answer, Kaplan objected to the form of the question. Kosmala balked.

"What's wrong with the form of the question?"

"Because he said robbery and murder, and there's no evidence of robbery," said Kaplan, whose case hinged on there having not been a robbery at all. "We know it's a murder."

Kosmala scoffed. "Oh, I know what he objects. I'd object, too, if I had his—"

Kaplan cut him off before Kosmala criticized the case in front of jurors. "I don't understand this—"

"I'll strike that," Kosmala conceded with a cocked smile.

Biernat looked annoyed. Strike the question, he ordered, and keep the voices down: "As I grow older, my faculties, of course—like anyone else's—sort of dim, but one thing that hasn't dimmed is my hearing," he lectured. "There's no reason to raise your voices. Everybody can hear you."

Court watchers exchanged glances. Kosmala was living up to his bulldog reputation, and Kaplan was having none of it. It made for some testy exchanges.

Once the focus returned to Benson, he described how he essentially took over Barb's role after Michael reopened the store following the shooting. Benson was older than some other part-time workers. Michael viewed him as mature and intelligent, so he turned to him for help. Benson worked at the store for about four months. He wasn't afraid of Michael physically, but he did want to please his boss, so he fretted about doing a good job. But he was uneasy in the store after Barb's death. Whoever killed her was still loose, and one day a man came in who gave him the creeps. It wasn't his appearance but his odd behavior that he found unsettling, testified Benson, who quickly dismissed his earlier fear as paranoia.

"I was skittish of what had happened at the store, and I really didn't like being there by myself because it was just a murder scene, so my overactive imagination probably made everybody look very threatening when I was there by myself," he testified.

Kosmala latched on to the description Benson had given police: a man, slightly built, perhaps wearing a fake beard and mustache. Benson didn't remember the man that way now, he said, but if that's what he told police, it must have been true.

Kaplan next called Matt Baczewski, who was nineteen when he worked alongside the Georges as yet another customer-turned-employee. He remembered Barb as a nice lady with an "uppity attitude." George, however, seemed more interested in Barb's friend and the Georges' employee, Renee Kotula, whom Michael called a "very good-looking woman," Baczewski said.

The former employee remembered that expensive comics were kept in a front glass display case in the store. They usually weren't stored in the back room, except perhaps in the safe.

"I know he kept some in a storage room and maybe his house," he added.

Like Benson, Baczewski's memory was lacking, he admitted. He remembered that both Barb and Michael had worked the day she died, but he had trouble recalling the times each was there. Kaplan produced the police statement he'd given to police nearly twenty years prior to help jog his memory. And it did: Barb arrived around four, soon after which Michael left with kids in tow.

Baczewski stayed until about 5 p.m., then went home to eat, he testified. "I was told just to take my time, I could come back after, when we were going to throw the party and just pick up some party supplies."

But that testimony differed from what Baczewski told investigators a year prior to the trial. Then, he said he thought he'd left for lunch around noon and didn't return until after 6 p.m. He didn't remember if he'd helped organize for the party or if he saw Barb and Michael interact when Barb came to relieve Michael from work. He simply couldn't remember, he said: "It's kind of fuzzy."

Marlinga aimed to blow apart his testimony.

"I know that you gave your statement on July 14, 1990; then we know that you gave a statement to the Clinton Township police on February 1, 2007, in which you gave a completely different account that you weren't at the store at all in the afternoon. We're agreed on that, correct?"

"Yes," Baczewski said.

"And during the course of that interview, the Clinton Township police even said, 'Hey, wait a minute, you told us something different' . . . Correct?"

"Yes."

"Now, today is February 29, 2008. What happened between February 1, 2007, and February 29 of 2008 to refresh your recollection?"

Baczewski stammered. He said he didn't understand. Investigators had suggested he review his testimony before the trial, he said, and he prepared with Lieutenant Hrecho for a few minutes before he testified to make sure everything jibed. Marlinga prodded further: Had Kaplan helped shape his testimony? No, Baczewski insisted. No one had coached him. His memory was just more reliable in 1990 than it was in 2007, he said.

At 11:28 a.m., Baczewski stepped down. Because of a scheduling conflict, Biernat ended the day early. Mondays at the Macomb County Circuit Courthouse were set aside for judges to hear the slew of motions that accumulate over the weekend, so jurors were instructed to arrive back in court Tuesday morning.

Kaplan was not happy. He had expected to get through another witness that day. Kaplan wasn't anticipating such lengthy cross-examinations, nor had he expected to hit the roadblocks that Biernat seemed to be tossing in his path. On top of that, the judge had started late for the second day in a row.

Chapter 23

Trial Day 3

By all accounts, defense or prosecution, the case against
Michael George likely would hinge on the testimony of the
former customer Mike Renaud. The only person who seemed
oblivious to the weight of the testimony was Renaud himself. He arrived in court March 4 after the jurors had a four-
day hiatus and sensed something heavy in the hallway outside
of Biernat's courtroom. Marlinga, who had questioned him
during the preliminary exam, came up and petted Renaud's
service dog, a golden retriever named Bo, after legendary
University of Michigan football coach Bo Schembechler
Jr. As Marlinga made chitchat about his own dog, Lieutenant Keith walked up and stood beside Renaud, as if to say
"shoo."

"I didn't know what I had to say was important," Renaud
recalled. "I didn't know what else they had, and I was se-
questered, so I had no idea what was going on with anybody
else. The next thing I know, Lieutenant Keith is standing
there, eyeballing Marlinga. That's when I realized they considered what I had to say important."

After a four-day hiatus from the trial—from late morning Friday until after lunch Tuesday—jurors finally settled
in to listen to the man whose phone call to Comics World

placed George at the store long after he told police he had
left for the night.

Renaud's testimony was crucial, but you wouldn't have
known it. The long weekend made for an anticlimactic introduction of a star witness. Jurors get no refresher notes to bring
them back into the trial mindset. They didn't even know how
important both sides deemed Renaud, who was sworn in from
his wheelchair.

"Nice seeing you, Mr. Renaud. Good afternoon," Kaplan
said nonchalantly. "How do you spell your last name?"

It wasn't a sexy introduction, but it would do.

Renaud said he had been a member of the comic book
store, meaning he got his own numbered bin in the back
where the Georges would save the books he had requested.
He swung by every week, he said, and usually chatted with
Michael for a good half-hour. Occasionally, he would call
the store with questions. He had gotten to know Michael
pretty well, he testified.

On July 13, he was working at Crowley's, a department
store that by 2008 was long closed, and he had heard from
a coworker that *Captain America* No. 241 had gone up in
price. It struck him as odd, so he called Comics World to ask
what had happened. He knew the phone number by heart.
Michael George answered.

"He seemed like he was in a hurry," Renaud testified.

The men chatted for less than five minutes, he said. Renaud
wasn't sure what time precisely he had made the call, but he
believed it was between 5:15 and 5:45 p.m. Of course, that
wasn't the time he initially reported to police on July 14,
1990, the day after the murder. He initially said 6:15 p.m., but
then realized he was an hour off after he checked to see
when his coworker had clocked in. The coworker arrived at
4:53 p.m., the two had chatted for a few minutes, and then
Renaud called the comic store. When he realized his mistake, Renaud said, he called the police back to correct what
time he'd spoken to Michael.

"I heard she was killed that day around six o'clock," he said, "so I thought if I didn't speak to him at 6:15, it might be something the police would be interested in."

He felt the call was probably around 5:30 p.m., but estimated more generally that it was between 5:15 and 5:45.

Kaplan kept the inquiry short. To him, Renaud's testimony was important for one reason only: If Michael George claimed to have left the store at 4 p.m., he shouldn't have been there between 5:15 and 5:45 to answer the phone. And if that part of his story was false, so, too, was everything else.

Marlinga felt otherwise. He doubted that it really was George who answered the phone—assuming Renaud even made the phone call when he said he did. But Marlinga knew from having faced off with Renaud during the preliminary exam that the comic book aficionado's recollection seemed solid; that whatever the truth was, Renaud truly believed he talked with Michael George shortly before the shooting. Challenging it would elicit nothing more than insistence that Renaud was positive he knew with whom he was speaking. That wasn't the type of exchange Marlinga wanted to present to jurors. Instead, he hammered away at the timeline: How did Renaud know for sure his coworker punched in at 4:53 p.m.? Did police ever come by to check his or the coworker's timecards? Why did his estimate of the phone call shift from 6:15 to 5:30 when he'd called back to correct that he'd been an hour off in his estimate? Wouldn't 5:15 make more sense then?

Renaud said he'd tried to clarify for police back in 1990. He realized within fifteen minutes of his first call to investigators that he'd been an hour off in his time estimate, that he'd spoken with George prior to six. He talked to investigators twice on the fourteenth, a Saturday, and then called a third time to reconfirm the amended time after he spoke with the coworker whose timecard was at the heart of the matter. He even looked at the timecard himself. He felt

comfortable saying the call had come between 5:15 and
5:45—no earlier, no later.

To Marlinga, George being in the store at 5 p.m. wasn't
nearly as damning as him being there at 5:30 or 5:45 p.m.
He didn't feel like he could undercut Renaud's memory of
speaking to George, but he did want to explore the possibility
that the call could have come in a full hour before the shooting. Surely, Renaud's chat with the coworker wouldn't have
been very lengthy. The two were on the clock, working, after all; they weren't getting paid to chat comics.

Renaud dismissed that idea. "I was a college kid," he said.
"I wasn't too concerned about wasting Crowley's monies."

He didn't take an unpaid break to call the comic store,
either, he added. Still, he was conscientious enough to try to
help out police even seventeen years prior, he said. That's
why he called not once but three times.

"I didn't want to get Michael George in trouble if I was
off on my time," he explained.

Kaplan was already writing his closing arguments in his
head, though the trial was far from over.

Lieutenant Donald Brook of the Clinton Township Police
Department didn't know he had a murder on his hands when
he arrived at the Comics World store about 7:30 p.m. on July
13, 1990. He was off duty, but as part of the department's
investigative division, he got called in to help investigate the
suspicious death. By the time he arrived, word had gotten
back to the officers that an emergency room nurse had discovered the bullet hole. The suspicious death had turned
into murder. Within a half-hour of his arrival, Brook got the
dubious honor of being the first to interview Michael George,
he told Kaplan as the second witness in Day 3 of George's
trial.

He began with the basics: Where had George been? When
was he supposed to come back? Were he and his wife having
any trouble? Even though Brook didn't know how Barb died

yet, he knew it was suspicious—and suspicion always lands first on a spouse in such cases. Michael told him he'd left the store about 4 p.m. to go to his mom's house in Hazel Park.

"Did you inquire of him about the status of his marriage?" Kaplan asked. Brook said he asked "basic police questions, if there were any problems in the marriage, and he indicated, no, there was no discord."

He did not mention he was having an affair with Renee, the pretty employee, and he denied having any financial problems, Brook testified.

Michael said he'd left Barb with Joe Gray and Matt Baczewski, headed to his mom's, and planned to return to meet up with Barb to celebrate his birthday. He left Hazel Park about 7:30 p.m. planning to meet up at eight, but instead of being greeted by his wife, he found the store swarming with officers. Brook said he asked if the couple kept any money in the store safe. Michael said no, he and Barb hit the bank sporadically to deposit any cash they collected throughout the day. George said they didn't even bother locking the safe in the back room.

It wasn't until George was being chauffeured to the hospital that he made a comment that caught the lieutenant off-guard, Brook recalled. The men were in the squad car. Brook had paused from asking questions. Suddenly, George offered a theory as to how his wife had gotten hurt: Something must have fallen in the back room and hit her on the head.

Curious, Brook thought. He hadn't told George where in the store his wife had been found. Nor had he spelled out her injury—a bullet wound to the head—yet George's theory centered around something having happened to her head.

Kaplan rested. Kosmala slowly stood. He would be handling the cross. And because of the oversights of Brook and the other original investigators, he had plenty with which to play. Within a few minutes, he highlighted the case's flaws with a series of questions to which Brook could only reply, "No, sir."

Did he ask to look in George's car? Did he swab George's hands for gunshot residue? Did he ask for George's clothes so they could be tested for blowback gunshot residue or blood spatter?

No, no, no.

"Did you have any further connection with this investigation?" Kosmala asked.

"No, sir."

Kosmala had a police report that showed otherwise, however. The day after the slaying, Brook interviewed Baczewski, based on a report that bore the lieutenant's signature. It seemed another blow to Brook's credibility on the stand. He didn't recall the interview, he testified, nor did he remember canvassing homes in the neighborhood near the Venice Square strip mall. On redirect, he said it was simply because nothing useful was gleaned from the canvass.

Kaplan returned to that bizarre comment George made about something hitting his wife in the head. That's what he wanted jurors to remember from this witness's testimony.

"Regarding that statement, his comment in the car about how his wife might have been injured, was that in response to a question by you or was that offered by him on his own?" Kaplan asked.

"It was offered on his own."

Kosmala wouldn't let that be the last word.

"Isn't it likely that that spontaneous response would be as a result of him having heard something at the scene before you talked to him?"

"Objection," Kaplan barked. "It calls for speculation."

The objection was sustained; Brook stepped down.

By the time John Neal, then a detective lieutenant with the Clinton Township police, spoke with Michael George the night of the shooting, Barb's fate was well known. George already had been given, and turned down, the chance to see her one last time in the emergency room. Kaplan called Neal to the stand and got through the perfunctory background questions: Neal was among the department's original twenty-one members, joining the force in 1968; he retired in '93; he spelled his name with an *a*, not an *i*.

On July 13, 1990, he met George at 11 p.m. for an interview at the department. The men talked for about a half-hour. George's demeanor was "nothing out of the ordinary," Neal testified.

"While you're talking to him, did he break down sobbing or in hysterics?" Kaplan asked.

Neal managed a "no" before Kosmala lodged his objection for leading, which Biernat sustained. That gave Kaplan an excuse to re-ask the question.

"Can you describe it in terms of whether any evidence of sadness was manifested to you?"

"He was not sobbing," Neal said. "He was answering my questions."

George told Neal the same thing he had conveyed to Brook, though his timeline shifted slightly: He left the store between 4 and 4:30 p.m. for his mother's house. It took him about a half-hour to get there. Then he left his mom's between 7:15 and 7:30 to get back to the store about 8:10 p.m. He knew of nothing unusual happening at the store. Barb never said she'd seen anyone suspicious or felt uncomfortable. He had no idea what had happened to his wife, Neal testified.

For Kosmala, Neal's testimony allowed the same barrage of questions as Brook's to highlight what the department failed to do in 1990. No fingerprints, no hand swabs, no clothing examination.

After Neal's night of work on the case, he stayed on, interviewing multiple people in the days that followed, from Mike Renaud to Barb's brother Joe to Renee Kotula. Little was gleaned. Kosmala asked about Wally Last Name Unknown, but Neal said he didn't remember anyone mentioning a man by the name of Wally. Neal also didn't recall the conversation with the John Hancock insurance company, during which he allegedly said that George was not considered a suspect in his wife's death. A company investigator had called to determine whether Barb's life insurance money should be released to George. After speaking with Neal, the $130,000 was disbursed. Kosmala wanted jurors to be able to hear about that conversation, but as he started to read it aloud, Kaplan jumped.

"It's double hearsay," the prosecutor barked. "He has no memory of it; it's not his. It's somebody else's."

Biernat asked Kosmala for a court ruling that would deem the document's contents admissible; Kosmala had none. "It just seems it's a good thing for the jury to know," he said.

That didn't fly. After he acknowledged that police never had enough evidence to request a warrant in the case, Neal was dismissed.

Jurors were treated to some show-and-tell with the next witness, Douglas Mills, a police sergeant in 1990 who had advanced to captain before retiring in 2005. He had been the go-to guy when it came to all things electronic—especially videotaping and photographing crime scenes—and taught photography to evidence technicians. He also had an in with Macomb County Community College and borrowed some photographic equipment to document the scene.

Back then, video cameras weren't the slim and stealthy pieces of equipment they are now. Mills propped a two-pound RCA Pro Wonder on his shoulder. The device, his personal recorder, was big and bulky and slow to focus. It was about two feet long and a foot tall. Mills wasn't there to film evidence for trial so much as to record the scene well enough to give detectives something to turn to if they needed their memories refreshed, he told Kaplan after he took the stand. Mills videotaped first, then photographed the scene afterward. Then he helped evidence technicians lift foot-prints from the floor and fingerprints from near the safe and cash registers.

The videotape opened with a nine p.m. time stamp. Clearly, it was summer in Michigan because the sun was barely be-ginning to set. With the courtroom lights dimmed, jurors watched the VHS tape Mills had created nearly 20 years prior. It showed the unkempt store in its cluttered glory, the cardboard boxes filled with comics creating narrow aisles throughout the front room. An arcade-style videogame in-spired by the hit flick *Aliens* stood near the doorway. Through-out the store, dangling from the ceiling and hanging on the walls, were Batman T-shirts, no doubt the comic world's reac-tion to Tim Burton's movie released the summer prior.

As the video unfolded, Mills served as narrator, care-fully describing what direction he was showing. He high-lighted the cash register area, which appeared undisturbed. Behind the counter, the phone on the wall was back in its cradle, though Tom Ward had found the receiver off the hook, carefully placed across the base. Odds and ends were strewn along the wall on the floor—including a file box la-beled "Comics World memberships"—but the haphazardness appeared to be the result of pure messiness, not robbery-sparked chaos.

In the back room, Mills zoomed in on the stray cream-colored moccasin-style shoe that Barb had been wearing. It was visible from the doorway, sitting inches away from a pool of blood that darkened the already-red carpeting. As Mills explored the back room, he highlighted the plastic bins that reached the ceiling, some of which were knocked over, leaning in angular mini-towers from floor to wall. Barb's other shoe lay near another, smaller absorption in the car-peting that looked like more blood, and Mills zoomed in on a small dark speck that he deemed possible blood on the closing flap of a cardboard box.

The camera cut out occasionally, Mills explained on the

stand, so that he could step over items and reposition without worrying about tripping and undermining the integrity of the scene. An evidence technician opened the bathroom door with gloved hand. Nothing appeared amiss in that room, in which the Georges stored cleaners and WD-40 along with the expected toiletries.

Much of the video was shot around 9 p.m., but the footage stopped and, toward the end of its eighteen minutes, restarted at nearly 4 a.m. when investigators discovered the bullet hole in Kathy Ireland's left eye. The suggestive calendar hung on a corkboard in the back, near the phone and the small safe that sat on the floor near the furnace. Another pause, then Mills filmed again to show the corner of the corkboard removed, as well as the drywall behind it. The bullet had cleared both and apparently had reached the adjacent store, which was closed and locked and would have to be opened in the morning once investigators had a chance to track down the owner, Mills explained in his voice-over.

The video cut to an image of the tan-colored safe on the floor. The door was closed, and some Mylar bags in a nearby box protruded slightly in front of it. The bags seemed undisturbed.

As Mills was the first command officer on the stand who had spent real time investigating the scene, Kaplan directed questions about the investigation's shortcomings to him—namely, wasn't he familiar with gunshot residue tests?

"They were kind of unreliable," Mills testified. "We were getting a lot of false positives."

Because of that, the Michigan State Police, which handled the residue tests, had asked agencies to include a shell casing when departments submitted hand swabs. It helped weed out the false positives, Mills explained. He described getting on his hands and knees, searching for such a casing to no avail. No shell casing meant a greater chance of an unreliable test result, he said.

Again, Kosmala handled the cross-examination. A pattern

seemed to be unfolding: The gruffer of the defense lawyers squared off with the cops.

He immediately attacked the preservation of the crime scene. Too many people had walked through the back room before Mills got there and trying to lift footprints to identify the killer would have been useless, Mills conceded.

"So for evidentiary purposes, that room was pretty much a mess. Fair enough?" Kosmala asked. Mills agreed.

Mills had identified the two pools of possible blood on the videotape, but he admitted that he didn't know for sure whether the substance was indeed blood. He didn't test with Luminol, which, once sprayed and lit with a black light, glows in the presence of blood. Not only had those specific spots not been tested, but neither had the rest of the room, which could have shown whether there was more blowback blood than visible to the naked eye.

Basically, Mills conceded, the blood might not have been blood. Footprints were largely useless. Even the fingerprints lifted were not very helpful as a lot of people had access to the store both before and after the shooting. Investigators did track down the bullet that had pierced Kathy Ireland's eye—"It was mangled pretty good," Mills said—but they didn't use a probe to explore its path to see if anything had obstructed it, a move that might have been useless, but could have yielded some clues.

And as for that gunshot residue test, it *could* have been conducted even without the shell casing, Mills acknowledged. Apparently, no one bothered to try.

In a strange twist, the day's last witness wasn't able to appear. It was Maggie Bolus, the Nails Plus employee who had testified by phone during the preliminary examination because she had been in the hospital. Though Kaplan didn't feel he strongly needed her testimony during the prelim, he got her by phone anyway—a lucky move because Bolus's illness had proved fatal. As a last step in the third day of the trial, Kaplan read her testimony to jurors, in which she described hearing Barb and Michael argue about pizza in the alleyway behind the store. She saw them fighting as she took some trash to the nearby Dumpster. Her testimony was brief and concluded with Marlinga wishing her a speedy recovery.

With that, Day 3 was over.

Chapter 24

Trial Day 4

Some trial judges are notorious for tardy starts. If Biernat didn't have that reputation before, he was certainly developing it with the Michael George case. He had told jurors to return March 5 for a 1 p.m. start. At 1:30, the proceedings got under way. Already, his starts and stops had been in fits. Breaks consistently lasted longer than the ten minutes he typically announced. Family of both Michael and Barb George were starting to complain in the hallways. Christine Ball, Barb's sister, asked a reporter if all judges disregarded the clock so. Not all, the reporter replied, but many.

Witness 1 on Day 4 was Detective Tim Standfest, who had been an evidence technician in 1990. He helped Mills videotape the crime scene, lift trace evidence and photograph the store. His focus also was on the cash registers, which he had been instructed to open to see what, if anything, had been taken, he told Kaplan.

Both registers were secure when he arrived, he said. Neither appeared disturbed. One register had less than $30 inside, as well as some foreign currency, and the other had $715. Standfest helped lift prints from the area. From there, the prints were shipped to the state lab, where a special technician would do any comparisons. Standfest focused on the sales counter area, where the registers and phone sat.

"If I recall correctly, I spent probably an hour to an hour and a half attempting to lift prints," he recalled.

As much as Standfest remembered about the case, there were holes in his memory, he acknowledged. He remembered seeing a blue bank pouch but couldn't recall if he looked inside. Police reports showed that he had also been given a brown envelope by another evidence technician, but Standfest didn't remember it.

On cross-examination, Marlinga zeroed in on one main point: that no evidence collected at the scene linked Michael George to the murder of his wife.

Standfest agreed.

Theresa Danieluk had made an appearance at the preliminary exam, and here she was again at trial. She described taking her then-twelve-year-old son, Bart, to Comics World every Saturday. They had come to know Barb and Michael fairly well. Danieluk liked Barb; Michael was a bit too flirtatious. The Saturday before Barb's death, she and Bart went to the store, as usual. Michael was behind the counter, and when he spotted her, he stepped out to greet her. The two chatted as Bart perused the comics. Barb was there, too, Danieluk recalled.

"What, if anything, did Michael George say to you when he came out from behind the counter to where you were positioned?" Kaplan asked.

Kosmala balked. Objection: hearsay.

"The defendant enjoys the same protection from hearsay testimony, except for and limited to those statements against penal interest."

"That's not true," retorted Kaplan, whose expansive memory of state and federal statute was among his most valued courtroom assets. "MRE 801(s)(2)(a)—anything the defendant said could be used against. It can be in his favor or against his favor or benign."

Objection overruled. Kaplan returned to Danieluk.

"What did he say to you about Barbara George?" he asked.

"That she was unattractive and she was heavy, that he wouldn't have been with her if it wasn't for his two daughters," Danieluk replied.

"What did he say he would want to do if she weren't around?"

"He said he wanted to take the girls and move to Florida."

A week later, Danieluk read about Barb's death in the newspaper. She went to the funeral to pay her respects. She spotted Michael's back. When he turned to face her, she saw he was wearing sunglasses, she testified. He walked quickly to her and grabbed her in an embrace that made her uncomfortable.

"It was a hug that I would give my husband, not that I would give someone else," Danieluk recalled. "And I felt very uncomfortable and just said I was very sorry. . . . He thanked me for coming, but then also told me that I looked very nice that night and would I be back in the store."

"How far were you from Barbara George's coffin when he hugged you?" Kaplan asked.

"I was very close to her. When he hugged me, I could see her over his shoulder," she said.

Danieluk returned to the store with her son a few weeks later, after Michael had reopened it. She again said how sorry she was. Michael made chitchat, explaining that the medics at first thought his wife had had a heart attack but then noticed blood on the stretcher. Barb had been on her knees when she was shot, he had said. That was when Danieluk had asked if the store had been robbed in the shooting. Michael told her it had not.

"He said that there were expensive comic books in the store, but that nothing was taken," she said.

After Danieluk walked outside the store to leave, Michael

followed her, she testified. He handed her a schoolboy-type note, which she passed on to police. The note read: "You look very, very, very pretty today. Thanks for coming in. Sincerely, Michael." Beneath his name was a phone number.

In the weeks that followed, Michael called her house several times, she said. He never gave his name, but she recognized his voice.

"They came late at night," Danieluk said of the calls. "They were, 'I saw you today,' 'You looked pretty.' He knew where I lived, and I remember they were in August because my fiancé at the time, who is now my husband, was out of town."

On cross-examination, Kosmala prodded as to why Michael would confide his marital dissatisfaction with a woman who was allegedly engaged. Danieluk said she never invited the discussion.

"It was every conversation. When I went into the comic book store, it was the same thing," she said.

Kosmala wasn't satisfied. He returned to the hug at the funeral home. If Danieluk was so weirded out by the embrace that she turned to leave, why did she continue to visit the store afterward?

"As a matter of fact," he said, "that comic book store closed, the one on Garfield, and another one opened up on Hayes? . . . And you went to that one, too?"

Only a few times, Danieluk responded.

"But you went there a few times?"

"Yes."

"After this big, inappropriate hug?"

"Yes."

Kosmala's incredulity was obvious, and he wasn't finished. He needled as to why Danieluk waited seventeen years to tell police about Michael's claim there was nothing taken in the supposed robbery.

"Didn't you think that was significant—very significant—back in 1990?"

"In 1990, I was a divorced mother of two children. That was—"

Kosmala cut her off. "That isn't the question." He repeated: Why didn't she alert police to George's statement in 1990?

"Sir, I don't really recall. . . . I don't believe anybody spoke to me."

"But you recall it well enough to report it in 2007, is that correct?"

Kosmala paused a beat.

"I have no further questions, Your Honor."

The remaining witnesses of the day were crammed into 90 minutes of testimony. They were to illustrate specific points Kaplan wanted laid out for jurors. Buster Sunde, a childhood friend of George's, described offering to help raise a reward to find Barb's killer. Michael said no, that police didn't want to offer a reward. Gary Kwapisz backed up Sunde's recollection of the reward discussion, and recalled having dinner with Michael and Renee Kotula, his lover, before Barb died.

Next came Renee Balsick, the woman who worked at another Comics World franchise and had been on the phone with Barb minutes before the shooting. She recalled speaking to Barb for two or three minutes to talk about the surprise party that night. Barb put her on hold, she recalled—"She said she needed a second, she'd be right back, hold on"—with no panic in her voice. Barb never got back on the line. Balsick figured she'd forgotten she was on the phone, so after a few minutes, she hung up and called the Garfield store back. The line was busy.

Like many others, Balsick attended Barb's funeral and, like the others, recalled Michael wearing the dark glasses.

"I remember him speaking with me and my ex-husband and him sitting, just very unemotional," she testified.

Within a few months, she learned he had moved in with Renee Kotula.

David Barneo, another friend, recalled how different Michael was with his lover than with his wife.

With Barb, "he was more serious when he was with her. Seemed more businesslike," Barneo said. "With Renee, he was like a kid in a candy store. He was more jovial. He was more fun. He was flirtatious around her. He was just happier, it seemed."

None of the witnesses offered much for the defense except Barneo. He was the only one who remembered someone named Wally—a quiet man with a mustache who always wore a billed hat. It was the first time the defense got to explore Wally Last Name Unknown in any detail.

Chapter 25

Trial Day 5

In trial, "polygraph" might as well be a four-letter word for defense lawyers. The phrase "he failed a polygraph" is so fraught with negative connotation that upon hearing it, many instantly presume guilt. Never mind that polygraphs—devices that measure physiological changes in one's body, such as heart rate and respiration, when asked a series of questions to determine whether they're being truthful—are so notoriously imprecise that their results aren't even admissible in court.

Kaplan knew this and never intended to try to bring George's refusal to take a polygraph—a refusal that George had every right to invoke—into evidence. He did, however, want to explore witness Joe Gray's decision not to take a polygraph. Gray, one of the two men with whom George last saw his wife alive, told investigators that George instructed him not to take a polygraph when police asked him to. To Kaplan, this was consciousness of guilt; George was requesting that someone refuse, at least on some level, to cooperate with police. Perhaps the defense would be able to present a reason for that lack of cooperation, but Kaplan wanted jurors to have the chance to hear about it and decide for themselves.

Biernat faced a decision: Could Kaplan ask Joe Gray about the polygraph? Marlinga argued that the damage would be irreparable.

"Aside from the factual issue of what exactly was said and what implication can be drawn from that, just the word 'polygraph' is so pregnant with possible negative implications it can raise in the jury's mind that can never be taken out; you can't unring that bell," Marlinga said. "Once the word 'polygraph' comes in, there's so much of a prejudicial effect on the defendant that the minimal probative value is overwhelmed by the prejudice."

Biernat agreed, so Kaplan suggested another tack: He could have Gray simply state that George asked him not to cooperate with police. Kaplan would only use the "p" word if Marlinga or Kosmala opened the door on their cross-examination.

Biernat wasn't having it. Allowing any discussion of a polygraph would be unfair to George, he ruled, and if Kaplan's assertion that Gray was asked not to cooperate with police centered solely on the polygraph issue, he wasn't to raise it in front of jurors.

Kaplan decided that made Gray's testimony useless. He nixed him from the witness list.

Jurors returned promptly at 9 a.m. Thursday, March 6, 2008, as instructed. At 9:54 a.m., they were led into the courtroom. Biernat again got off to a late start, then had some housekeeping rulings to make to head off inevitable squabbling between Kaplan and the defense. The usually hushed courtroom chitchat had risen in decibel as the wait grew longer, until Biernat and jurors finally were seated and retired Clinton Township Detective Sergeant Donald Steckman took the stand.

Steckman, who spent twenty-six years with the township police, had left four years after Barb's death and had since become a senior investigator with the Macomb County

Medical Examiner's Office. Steckman was the detective on duty at 6 p.m. when the call came in about the shooting. At first he knew only that the death was suspicious; he was still en route around 7 p.m. when he got word it was homicide. Steckman was among those men milling about when George pulled up supposedly expecting to find a party.

Once Steckman identified George, he told him there had been a problem in the store, his wife was in the hospital and a detective would drive him to her.

"Did you mention to him what her injuries were?" Kaplan asked. Steckman said he had not.

"Did he offer any comment to you as to what might have happened to her?"

"He did," Steckman replied. "Something must have fallen on her head in the back room.

"He volunteered his statement," the former officer continued. "He was getting ready to leave the scene with Detective Brook, and that's when he said it. He said, 'Well, something must have fallen and hit her on the head in the back room.' "

Steckman found odd George's reaction to the news his wife was hurt. He asked if Barb was OK, and Steckman said she was not. But George didn't ask anything further—was she alive? How serious was it? How was she hurt? The only thing he said, Steckman testified, was this bizarre comment about getting hit in the head in the back of the store.

George initially seemed cooperative. He returned with police to the store after midnight July 14, 1990, in the hours after Barb's death to check the store and see if anything seemed amiss. Soon after, though, George got cagey, Steckman said. The officer asked repeatedly for a specific timetable explaining where he was and when, but it took George six days to comply. Nearly two decades later, Steckman needed to review the note George had scrawled to refresh his memory. The timeline was pretty simple: George woke up about 7 a.m., went to the store about 8:30, opened up at ten and was joined by Barb at 4 p.m. He took the children back to his mother's house soon after, fell asleep, then returned to the store about 8:10 p.m.

When George toured the store early July 14, he said that there had been money in the cash registers and the safe. The cash registers, it turned out, still contained cash; the safe was empty, short about $2,000, George had said. A few days later, he corrected himself, saying there hadn't been money in the safe after all. But something else was missing: the box of expensive comic books. Steckman said he had to harass George for that list, too.

"The longer the investigation went on, the less cooperative he became," Steckman said of George. "He would provide the information but we had to probe him to get the information."

After police got the list of comics, Steckman tried following up, he said. The list was circulated and investigators tried to track down the individual books. Steckman got a phone call from one of George's customers saying he believed George had sold him a Spider-Man comic that had been on the list.

"I called Mr. George," Steckman recalled on the stand. "And as soon as I mentioned it, it was 'No, no, that wasn't the one I sold. . . . That wasn't in the pile.'"

Kaplan's next step was to address those Luminol and AFIS questions that Kosmala had been lobbing at the other investigators. But before he could, Marlinga cried foul. The jury was excused so Marlinga could unleash.

Kaplan was readying to introduce lab reports that he had never provided the defense, Marlinga said in a rare flash of obvious anger. The report was dated July 17, 1990, and was on Michigan State Police stationary. It referred to fingernail scrapings and head hair samples. Marlinga and Kosmala had repeatedly asked for all discovery but, Marlinga fumed, this report was never turned over.

"It's just bothersome that this far into the trial, we get this document," he said. "It's not listed in any of the discovery material that we've ever received, and it is just a mystery how this suddenly appeared."

"Well," Biernat said, "let's find out."

Lieutenant Craig Keith wasn't supposed to take the stand for several days yet, but, outside the presence of the jury, he took the stand to explain the document. Like any witness, he raised his hand to God and swore to be truthful.

Kaplan seemed agitated. It was yet another delay. He quickly got to the point: In a meeting prior to trial, did he remember Marlinga asking about fingernail clippings? Keith said he did. Keith agreed to fax over the state police lab reports, he said, and sent them in January—more than two months before trial started.

"I've never received it," Marlinga protested. "I've never received it."

Kaplan bristled. He had been careful to quickly pass along all reports—even ones that didn't seem like they would be helpful to either the defense or the prosecution. He left them in short order for Ryan Machasic, one of Marlinga and Kosmala's assistants.

"I'm not hiding this report. It's not of any substance," Kaplan told Biernat, his voice bordering on shrill. "I wouldn't do that anyway because my character is important to me."

Maybe, Marlinga said, but all of the other discovery material was numbered, while the lab report in question was not.

Biernat spoke calmly.

"All right," he said. "Here's what I'm going to do."

He held the inquiry of Keith to uphold the integrity of the trial, and he explained: "We do not, and this court will not, tolerate a trial by ambush, period."

But, he noted, "Things happen. Sometimes matters are lost or misplaced or persons receive things and they don't remember them. . . . I do not find on this record that the intent was to deprive defense of this document."

Marlinga was given fifteen minutes to review the report. The jurors would wait in the jury room until he was finished.

In a first for the trial, the break was even briefer than planned. After 10 minutes, Biernat was back on the record. Marlinga had perused the report, as well as a copy of a fax that Keith found that was dated January 15, 2008. Marlinga stumbled through a semblance of an apology. Kaplan still hadn't furnished everything, he said, as some fingerprint cards and reports that would not be used in the trial hadn't been handed over until the break, but "it turns out there's an indication that it was faxed to us."

Keith's trial debut was over.

As the jury returned, so did Steckman. Kaplan returned to the topic of fingerprints and nail scrapings. The discussion was anticlimactic after the veiled accusations lobbed during the break. All Steckman had to say was that he had instructed an underling to send scrapings to the state police.

The bigger question, it turned out, centered around Mike Renaud, the customer whose phone call seemed to put George at the comic book store at the same time he claimed to be at his mother's house. Steckman never saw Renaud's statements from July 14 or July 17—the three times he phoned in to report he had spoken with George, then corrected the time he believed the conversation took place. Kaplan showed Steckman the written statement about Renaud's phone calls.

"Why is it that you did not know about this document, this report purportedly made on the fourteenth of July and then the seventeenth of July?"

"I have—I have no explanation," Steckman stuttered. "I had never seen that file."

"Did you interview Mr. Renaud?"

"I did not, no."

The question was pregnant with implication: Had Steckman gotten that tip and questioned Renaud in 1990, perhaps the case never would have gone cold. Kaplan was done with his questions.

For Marlinga, Steckman on the stand was another opportunity to highlight the shortcomings in '90.

"Is it fair to say there is absolutely no physical or forensic evidence linking Michael George to this crime?"

"Not that I'm aware of," Steckman replied.

Marlinga hit it again right away: "So whatever we're looking at, whether it be fingernail scrapings or fingerprints or anything, nothing would point to Michael George as being the perpetrator of this crime. Is that a true statement?"

Steckman was no dummy. "Would or would not," he said, to emphasize that nothing *excluded* George as the perpetrator either.

And when Marlinga came back to it yet again a few questions later—"As of July of 1990 there was no evidence to indicate any implication by Mr. George"—Steckman corrected: "No direct evidence. There was no direct evidence at that time."

"So would you say absolutely no evidence?" Marlinga pressed.

Steckman shook his head. "I can't say that."

"OK." Marlinga looked confused. "And so what evidence would you point to?"

"The lies that we found out that he told us."

Marlinga opened the door. "About the . . . ?"

"About the affair."

"Right." Marlinga nodded. Steckman wasn't finished.

"We were starting to have problems with the timelines of what time he left the store, what time he arrived at different places. And because he was not cooperating at that point, we weren't able to follow up on this."

Steckman perhaps wasn't announcing it overtly, but his tone was clear: He believed Michael George was guilty. He believed it in 1990, and he still believed it as he testified.

Courtroom onlookers exchanged glances. The side that had formed behind the prosecution—largely composed of Barb's family—shot satisfied looks at each other. The other side, seated behind George and the defense lawyers, looked exasperated. This man had an agenda, their eyes seemed to say. But based on what?

Marlinga tried to break down in what way George was not cooperating. He had provided fingerprints, had he not? He gave police a statement about his whereabouts, and he provided the list of stolen comics, yes? Steckman said he had. All came on the nineteenth, six days after the slaying.

"And in between those two dates there was the funeral, was there not?" Marlinga asked.

"Yes."

"And did you not indeed let him know that, you know, you can get back and talk to us after the funeral?"

"That's correct."

Marlinga launched into the SOD defense—some other dude did it. Other names came up during the investigation, yes? Steckman said they had. Name No. 1: Joe Caulman. His ex-girlfriend called police after the slaying and said she'd been with him a few times while he shoplifted comics.

"And also Joe Caulman had been convicted of second-degree murder, had he not?" Marlinga asked.

The courtroom stirred. Kaplan stood.

"Your Honor, we would object," he said firmly. "First of all, it wouldn't be admissible . . . but the jury's heard it, and therefore they should know the context—what type, what it involved. Otherwise, the jury's misled."

Caulman, it turned out, wasn't your typical killer, based on his rap sheet. Fifteen years prior to Barb George's death he had tracked down a man who had raped his then-girlfriend and shot him to death in a drug house. He was convicted of second-degree murder and by 1990 was out of prison. Steckman said Caulman was never considered a suspect despite him having been in the area around the time Barb was killed. Because of his prison record, his fingerprints in AFIS were compared with those lifted from the crime scene. None matched. Plus, there was nothing tying him specifically to Clinton Township or Comics World. Not that investigators had much of a chance to dig too deeply. They never could locate Caulman, Steckman conceded. They had tried; Steckman called the office of Caulman's parole officer and talked to the officer's partner. Caulman had absconded and was on the lam.

"You don't know what he was doing to get money in that time period, do you?" Marlinga asked. Steckman had no clue.

As for Wally LNU—Last Name Unknown—Steckman couldn't remember hearing about him at all.

"We received tips during this entire investigation," he said.

As for the reward that Buster Sunde and Gary Kwapisz said George dissuaded, Steckman acknowledged that some cops considered rewards a drag. They sometimes prompted more bogus tips than they were worth. Still, he said, he never would have told George not to offer a reward. He personally thought they were "fantastic."

Marlinga moved on. The photographs of the scene weren't complete, he pointed out. There were no photographs of the back door in the stack of 100-plus images investigators had shot and stored. That kept lawyers nearly eighteen years later from knowing whether the lock was a deadbolt style, a beveled lock, or a basic thumb-turn lock.

"I know that I remember specifically, and it's in my report, that [the suspect] had exited the back door," he said. "He would have—the person, I won't say 'he'—the person would have had to have a key to lock the door from the outside once he exited it. . . . That's the only thing I specifically remember is that he would have had to have a key to lock that back door when he exited it."

"And you didn't write that down in any report, did you?" Marlinga challenged.

Steckman said he couldn't recall, but Marlinga had a stack of police reports. Nowhere in them did it say a suspect would have needed to lock the door behind him.

"But I remember that very specifically," Steckman insisted. "That back door had to be locked when you exited it."

If Michael George had fabricated his story about a robbery, Steckman conceded that he overlooked the easiest way to do it. The night of the slaying, he said he thought $2,000 was missing from the safe, but he later corrected himself. Nothing was in the safe, he said.

Marlinga: "If a person were going to falsely allege that he had been robbed, money would be the easiest thing to say had been taken, correct?"

Correct, Steckman agreed.

"And so if a person was coming back and saying, 'No, money wasn't taken,' that would not be consistent with anybody who had previously tried to falsify anything. Would you agree to that?"

Kaplan stood to object. "I don't know reading into somebody's mind some amorphous theoretical murder or robbery—it just makes no sense at all. You know, what experience does he have to give that answer? It's pure speculation."

In a move that got chuckles from onlookers, Marlinga agreed: "And, Your Honor, I'd also agree I think it's argumentative, so I'm going to join Mr. Kaplan objecting to that last question."

Biernat's lips curled in a small smile. "That's a first."

Biernat broke for lunch. Clearly, Steckman's testimony was not close to wrapping up. Marlinga flipped through a few reports during the break as he prepped to continue.

"I promise I'll have you home by midnight, OK?" he laughed.

A moment of levity between the men. "That's fine," Steckman said.

"I actually tried to work on something over lunch to shorten this up," Marlinga said.

First, the photographs: Steckman agreed there was no significance to that stray bullet having pierced model Kathy Ireland's eye. The bullet had to go somewhere; that's just where it happened to land. That bullet, though, was likely the first one shot, Steckman said. If the killer had already shot the victim, why fire another round? Police had no idea where Barb might have been when that first bullet was fired, but when she was killed, she was either leaning forward or kneeling on the ground. Steckman had two theories as to what had happened: Someone shot at Barb and missed, prompting her to duck, which exposed the top of her head to the shooter. Or Barb was ordered to the floor and shot from above.

If that stray bullet had been fired second, Steckman didn't know why.

"I don't try to speculate on shooters' minds," he said. "I've seen so many strange things that happen that I don't try and would not offer a speculation as to why somebody would do something stupid."

Next, the trajectory of that stray bullet: Police never attempted any studies analyzing the bullet's angle because it was clear the bullet had hit something and was deflected, and when that happens, it's hard to find rhyme or reason to the bullet's path. Also, police could already tell that whoever shot Barb was standing in the back room with her. "It wasn't like we were dealing with a twenty-foot-wide room," he said. "With all of the stuff that was piled in there, the boxes and the cartons and the supplies and all that, there wasn't a very large walkway in there for anybody to be standing."

Onto the investigation: Marlinga highlighted a big hole in the investigation. "Did you ever do a canvass of the neighborhood to see if there were any neighbors or anybody else in the area who might have seen [George] between the hours roughly of five o'clock and seven o'clock?"

"No, sir," Steckman said.

The person Tom Ward spotted walking around the north side of the shopping center: Steckman never asked for a composite drawing of the man or pursued the mystery figure with any diligence.

Just shy of 2 p.m., Steckman was excused.

Because the trial was taking longer than expected, some witnesses felt out of place by the time they were called. Kimberly Koliba was one such witness. Like Maggie Bolus, she was a nail technician in Venice Square. And, like Bolus, she testified she had seen the Georges fight the day of the shooting. It was about 2:30 p.m., she recalled. "There was an extremely loud argument," she said. She had been outside on a smoke break when she spotted Michelle pounding on the front door to get inside.

"I had heard some loud screaming and Mike came out, pulled her in the door, and the arguing continued," she said. It wasn't the first time she had heard the couple arguing, but this one was "much angrier than the normal arguments. . . . It was more violent."

Kosmala, on cross-examination, spotted a discrepancy in the police report, however. The detective who took her statement reported that Koliba heard the fight July 12, not July 13. Koliba insisted the report was wrong.

"After I was done with work, I returned home with my husband and my children and we went back to the plaza . . . and we were going to have a dinner," Koliba recalled. "It was approximately six-thirty, seven o'clock and there was ambulance and police there."

* * *

Joseph Kowynia, Barb's brother, did not have a lot he could offer in terms of what happened the day of the slaying. He showed up for the birthday party earlier than most and discovered his sister had been hurt. But he recalled on the stand George's strange behavior at the scene and the sense that something was wrong in the couple's marriage. He didn't know about George's specific affairs, had never heard of Patrice Sartori, and knew nothing of an apartment his brother-in-law might have kept during an alleged separation while Barb was pregnant. He did, however, remember his sister saying that Michael wanted a divorce but she didn't.

Before Kaplan could explore the subject, Marlinga objected. The jury was excused. At issue: Whether Kowynia's memory of his sister's dissatisfaction would be presented to jurors. Marlinga, naturally, wanted it kept out. It would unfairly prejudice the jury, he said, and Kowynia only knew one side of the story. Just because Barb said Michael wanted a divorce didn't make it true. Kaplan argued vigorously that it showed marital discord. Barb wasn't there to testify herself, so her family and friends should be allowed to relay her side of things, he argued.

In another small blow to the prosecution, Biernat sided with the defense, which Kaplan realized threw his next witness in jeopardy, too. Kathy Treece, a friend of Barb's who had testified at the preliminary exam, was prepared to testify that Barb told her less than a month before her death that Michael had asked for a divorce and Barb said no. She wanted to save the marriage.

That, too, was inadmissible, Biernat decided.

When Kowynia returned to the stand, he was allowed to say only that Barb was worried about her marriage.

"She wanted to work on it. She didn't believe in divorce. She wanted to work on her marriage," he said.

* * *

Treece kept her recollection vague as well. She and Barb had been longtime friends, and Treece had even stood in the Georges' wedding. Within a month of Barb's death, Treece encountered Barb in tears. She was crying, Treece testified, saying she wanted her marriage to work.

"I know she did not want a divorce," she said.

Kaplan stopped her from elaborating.

Treece also told jurors about the strange question she had overheard Michael ask his mother at the funeral home—"'Mom, did you call the insurance company today?'"

After Barb's death, Michael wanted nothing to do with Treece, she said.

The afternoon seemed to be dragging. Much of the testimony was repetitive. Bob Reams, who ended up briefly partnering with Renee Kotula after Barb's death in opening a new Comics World store, simply described the same strange funeral-home behavior as many others had before him.

Then Mary Shamo took the stand. The feisty brunette had been Kowynia's girlfriend when Barb died. On direct examination, she described Michael after the shooting. She and Kowynia had gone to his house to be supportive. Michael grabbed the vacuum cleaner and embraced it emotionally. "This is Barb's vacuum," he said.

"He was hugging it and crying—pretending to cry. No tears were coming down his face," Shamo said. "And the second Joe walked out of the room, he took his glasses off, we were sitting at the table, and he threw his glasses on the table and he said, 'So what do you think of all this?'"

Shamo was taken aback, she recalled. And she was floored when her suspicions about Michael's relationship with pretty, dark-haired Renee Kotula were confirmed after the two moved in together soon after Barb's death.

The sleepy afternoon testimony got a jolt on cross-examination when Kosmala the Bulldog squared off with Shamo the Feisty. If Shamo was so concerned about this crime, why hadn't she gone to the police to report Michael's odd behavior? Shamo said she did—twice. Kosmala said there was no record of either visit.

"I don't know the detective's name," Shamo said. "It was so many years ago. But we went down there at least twice and we told them exactly how Mike was acting, exactly what we thought, and I definitely, still to this day, believe that he killed Barb."

Kosmala scoffed. "Oh, well, thank you very much, detective," he snarked. "I appreciate your conclusion."

Biernat issued a stern warning: No opining. Just answer the questions.

Even if Shamo had gone to the police just twice, Kosmala said, it was *just* twice.

"Did you go back again? Did you call [police] up once a year and say, 'Hey, what's happening with the George case?'"

"No."

"Matter of fact, you didn't do anything until you were contacted again in October of 2007, is that correct?"

"Was that my place?" she retorted.

"Sorry?"

"Was it my place to do that?"

Biernat stopped her: "Just answer the question, ma'am."

Kosmala played up Shamo's obvious disdain for George.

"If somebody other than Michael had been arrested, you wouldn't have been satisfied with that, would you?" The question seemed rhetorical.

"I don't know," Shamo shot back. "Do you know me that well?"

Kaplan objected: calls for speculation.

"Her testimony is obviously colored by her opinion," Kosmala said.

"He can argue that if he wants," Kaplan told the judge, "but the question is supposed to be proper."

"Well, my point has been made," Kosmala quipped.

Kaplan grew exasperated. "Well, we object to that. He's making a speech now."

"A short speech," Kosmala snidely corrected.

Biernat finally interjected: No speeches from anyone, ever.

Chapter 26

Trial Day 6

To piece together the last bit of what Kaplan considered a puzzle of circumstantial evidence, he needed to present more pieces, no matter how jagged and rough their edges seemed. What largely remained over the final two days of the prosecution's case was a series of witnesses who could largely speak only to George's behavior in the days and years after his wife's death, including Shawn Howard, who ran Cadillac Memorial Gardens East, the Clinton Township cemetery where Barb George was buried. Michael had bought two plots in the cemetery when his wife died. It took him nearly two years to pay off the second plot—the one that would be his when he passed—and after he paid, he never came in to sign the deed that proved his purchase, despite cemetery personnel calling him repeatedly, Howard testified.

"It is highly unusual," he said. "You spend that large amount of money, you need something to prove purchase."

"On a scale of one to one hundred, how often does that happen?" Kaplan asked.

"I would say maybe one percent of the time."

Howard also noted that in the nearly twenty years that had passed, George never once requested maintenance to the burial site. He never bought flowers or a grave blanket to

adorn the spot. And despite his claims to police that he visited the grave at least once a year—sometimes more—since
her death, George never signed in as a visitor, according to
the cemetery's records.

Kosmala, in cross, dismissed all this. By the time Michael
paid for the plot next to Barb, he was remarried, yet "he still
paid that money to be buried next to his wife," he said. And
as for not signing in to visit, there was no guard to insist
that people log their visits, Howard conceded, so George
and his children could have regularly visited the grave and
simply not signed in. Nor had anyone else from Barb's family tried to place decorations on the grave. If grief were measured in graveyard decorations, Michael wasn't the only one
bereft, Kosmala implied.

Kaplan thought that one of Michael George's most telling
moments after his wife died was his reaction to a priest who
came to speak to him at his mother's house. Michael, a devout
Catholic, ran from the holy man. On this last day of prosecution witnesses, he brought Patrice Schemansky, a friend of
Michael's mother, to describe the incident. She had barely set
the scene—describing that she brought food to Janet's house
when the priest arrived—when Kosmala objected to its relevancy. The jury was once again shooed from the courtroom.

Kaplan couldn't hide his annoyance. George ran from the
home at the sight of the priest, he told Biernat. "This is conduct after the fact reflecting consciousness of guilt," he said.

Kosmala argued otherwise. Avoiding a priest does not
make someone a killer, he said. Biernat agreed. The behavior
might be marginally relevant, but the description of the
scene would be so highly prejudicial that the jury should not
hear it, he decided.

Kaplan was visibly agitated.

"This witness was on the witness list," he said. "They knew
we were calling her. They have the same reports. . . . This
could have been resolved earlier."

Marlinga fought back. The defense didn't have to abide by any timeline the prosecutor wanted to set, he said, clearly offended.

"We certainly have the obligation and the right to make objections, and we're not going to be stifled because it somehow disagrees with the prosecutor's notion of what we should have done beforehand," he said, adding that not everything Kaplan had done sat well with the defense, either, but he saw no reason to lodge it as a complaint in open court, before *Dateline* and everyone else.

"We are not going to be stifled because we haven't followed his rules."

Schemansky was dismissed. Biernat instructed the jury to disregard everything she had said. Her testimony was not to be considered come deliberation time, he ordered.

Another piece to Kaplan's puzzle was the life insurance policy. To speak to that, he called Bradley Staeb of John Hancock Financial Services. Staeb explained that while Michael George had himself insured for just $30,000, he had Barb insured for $100,000 more than that. By the end of July 1990, just two weeks after Barb's death, he collected $29,545.24 in payment from one policy and $100,477.89 from another, Staeb testified.

In 2008 dollars, that was worth somewhere between $260,000 and $350,000, he said—a comment that was quickly stricken from the record after Marlinga began to battle Staeb's expertise on the matter.

Instead, Kaplan turned to the discrepancy between the policy amounts. Was the $100,000 difference typical or atypical? Atypical, Staeb replied. Usually, husbands are the breadwinners—or were more frequently in 1990.

"Mike should have had much more than what Barb had," he said.

Kosmala pointed out, however, that Michael initially had been insured for an additional $50,000 but had let that policy lapse. Though Michael had issued both policies to his wife, Barb was the one who actually signed the paperwork that kept hers active.

Another puzzle piece: the missing comic books. To speak about their value, Kaplan called Dennis Barger, a sixteen-year aficionado who owned a comic book store in Taylor, Michigan. In opening his own store, he researched safety concerns other owners had faced. In 1990, there were about twenty comic book stores in the Detroit area, and about a hundred across the state. Most buying and selling was done at trade shows and in stores. The Internet hadn't become a big player; eBay didn't even exist yet. Storeowners and collectors who had heard anything about the George slaying would have been on the lookout for the missing comics, making them easier to spot.

But as Kosmala pointed out, the books weren't numbered in 1990 like they were in later years. And the lawyer undercut Barger's purported expertise by asking him the off-the-cuff value of some big-ticket books, such as *Mickey Mouse* No. 1 or the first *Roy Rogers*. Barger said he would have to look at his Overstreet price guide to determine the books' value.

In most murder trials, the medical examiner's testimony is key. It provides the what, how, and when, though it is typically lacking the who. In Barb George's death, the autopsy was conducted by Macomb County Medical Examiner Werner Spitz, a since-retired, German-born pathologist who had handled nearly sixty thousand autopsies before his 2004 retirement.

Spitz was a character—blunt, matter-of-fact, hard to sway—and he knew his stuff. It ran in the family: Upon Spitz's retirement, his son, Daniel Spitz, took over the county post. The elder Spitz was no stranger to courtrooms, either. He had testified on the prosecution's behalf in the

O.J. Simpson civil trial, and he still used the case as an example in seminars he led—specifically photographs of crescent–moon–shaped marks on Simpson's hands that Spitz identified as defensive wounds left by Ron Goldman during the attack. As Macomb County's appointed medical examiner—not an elected coroner, as some counties have—Spitz helped law enforcement win thousands of cases in his years as head honcho. Kaplan hoped the Michael George case would be one of them.

His accent thick, Spitz spelled out his findings from the autopsy he conducted nearly eighteen years prior: The bullet entered the top of the skull, slightly to the left, and it seemed the gun was a few inches away from the head. The doctor couldn't determine the exact distance, but believed based on the wound characteristics that it was no more than five inches and no fewer than three inches from Barb's skull. The bullet passed through the vital centers of Barb's brain, immediately incapacitating her. Spitz couldn't determine what position Barb was in when she was shot; he could only say that the bullet went straight down into her skull.

When she got to the morgue for the autopsy, Barb was still wearing her wedding and engagement rings, as well as a bracelet. She had not suffered any injuries that indicated she might have been sexually assaulted. The only extraneous bruising was to her forehead where it looked as though she smacked her face against the floor, likely as she fell after being shot.

Kosmala and Marlinga had discussed who should handle the cross-examination of Spitz. While Marlinga knew Spitz well from his days as county prosecutor, Kosmala had more experience questioning the doctor. Thus, the duty went to the bulldog. His job was to highlight what the autopsy couldn't reveal.

"As you sit here today, you cannot tell this jury for certain how this shooting occurred other than that it had to occur, the gun somehow had to be above her head and the bullet entered—whether she was seated, kneeling down, lying on the floor, stretched across the countertop, that's all a matter of speculation?"

Right, Spitz replied—except that he also could say the gun was likely three to five inches from the skull. He knew that based on fifty-four years of experience, he said, and the lack of black smoke on the skin or burnt hair near the bullet wound. Nothing in his exam remotely revealed who might have been the shooter.

The jury next heard from Kris Kehoe, the emergency room nurse who began cleaning Barb's body to make her more presentable for her family members and discovered the bullet hole in Barb's head, thus changing the label from suspicious death to homicide.

Finally the tape of the August 3, 2007, interview of Michael George himself by Detective Hrecho was played. The jury heard the whole statement, save for a portion in which Michael acknowledged having videotaped himself having sex with Patrice Sartori, the pretty blonde coworker from John Hancock. Biernat had earlier ruled that talk of the tape wasn't admissible; he stuck by that even when the words came from George's mouth rather than Sartori's.

Jurors left for the weekend with George's own voice in their heads, finally admitting to investigators that he not only was a philanderer, but that he'd indeed been having an affair with Renee Kotula—something he had adamantly denied in the days after his wife's death.

Chapter 27

The Prosecution Rests

After weeks of listening to years-old recollections from witnesses and police officers, jurors finally would hear the details about what had breathed new life into the case during the last day of prosecution testimony. Kaplan's final two witnesses would be Detective James Hall, who had led the August 3, 2007, interrogation of Michael George at his Windber comic shop, and Lieutenant Craig Keith, the man whose idle hands led him to re-examine the case to begin with.

Hall described walking into Comics World with his partner, Detective Hrecho, and introducing themselves to George. They were immediately taken aback. The men said they were there to reopen his wife's murder case, but George didn't react how they felt an innocent man should.

"He was very stoic and when we told him, he kind of put his head down and didn't ask no questions whatsoever," Hall said.

The detectives had expected some excitement, and certainly a few questions. There was no "Did you find the guy who did it?" Instead, George looked nervous.

"When he answered us, he was kind of stumbling with his words," Hall said. "He kind of looked flush and pale."

Kaplan asked how the interrogation ended, and Marlinga

immediately objected. Anyone who had heard the tape knew it concluded with George calling the interview "bullshit," saying he needed a lawyer, and abruptly leaving. That was his constitutional right, Marlinga said after Biernat excused the jury. Kaplan disagreed.

"This was not custodial interrogation," he argued. "The fact is that's a lack of cooperation. That's his demeanor. That's his attitude during the interview, and the jury has the right to know that he concluded it and he wasn't happy about that interview."

Marlinga said the abrupt ending would unfairly taint the jury. "People have a right to walk away from any interview with the police at any time," he said. Besides, George didn't call off the chat until the detectives suggested he'd committed insurance fraud. "That's what caused the interview to end. There's an allegation of illegal conduct."

Biernat agreed; Hall couldn't testify about George calling the interview bullshit. Kaplan couldn't even ask who called off the interview.

After the jury returned, Kaplan quickly wrapped up his direct examination. Without those questions, keeping Hall on the stand any longer was unnecessary. Marlinga slowly stood to begin his cross-examination. He immediately went after Hall's subterfuge use of the tape recording, legal though it may have been.

"You didn't tell Mr. George that you were going to be taping this interview, did you?"

Hall looked blank. "I don't recall if we set the tape recorder out or if we kept it in our pocket, so I don't know if he was aware of that or not."

Reporters exchanged smirks. Anyone who had worked with a tape recorder could tell that the audio caught by Hall and Hrecho was too muffled to have been recorded from a tabletop. The recording quality was marred by subtle scratches and rustling. As Marlinga pointed out, Hall at one point even left the room when the tape stopped to switch sides. It seemed

a strange thing to avoid discussing on the stand; it wasn't illegal to covertly tape record the conversation, so why was Hall
hiding the tactic?

Marlinga asked if George seemed anxious. No, Hall said,
he had shown no emotion at all and seemed to elude the
detectives' questions.

"Well, how do you separate the issue of nervousness from
anticipation?" Marlinga challenged. "I mean, how do you
know as a human being that somebody is nervous because
they're anticipating information or nervous because you're
asking questions? How do you do that?"

Hall shrugged. "Basically, it was my observation," he
said. "He became flush, he became pale, he starts saying, 'I,
I, I' during our questioning, 'uh-uh,' those types of things. It
gives him a little time to think about what he's going to say
prior to saying it."

Marlinga shuffled some notes, glanced at George, then
looked back at Hall.

"Now, Detective," he said, "just as a general proposition,
isn't it true that when the year 2007 came around that your
investigation with regard to the seventeen-year-old homicide
focused from the very beginning on Mr. George?"

"That is incorrect, Mr. Marlinga," Hall retorted.

"You had other suspects?"

"We've had several other suspects, yes. And several other
motives."

"But in 2007, when this investigation was reopened, isn't
it true that you kind of put aside all serious investigation of
any other suspects to focus just exclusively on Mr. George?"

"No." Hall sounded offended.

In fact, he said, Hall had helped interview Joe Gray, the
store employee who had helped sneak party decorations to
Barb before Michael's planned birthday party, for about three
hours in February 2007. Another interview followed on
August 14—ten days after George was arrested in Pennsylvania. He, Lieutenant Keith, and Detective Hrecho also

conducted a phone interview with Fred Hodgson, Gray's friend, who described seeing a man in dark glasses with a fake beard who was so slightly built that Hodgson thought it might actually be a female in disguise. Gray didn't see the same person, but he helped Hodgson warn Barb and employees at the nearby pizza parlor that someone fishy was lurking in the parking lot. Hall didn't help interview Douglas Kenyon, however, another witness who reported seeing someone suspicious at the store, and Marlinga had a theory as to why.

"Isn't it true that you did not interview Mr. Kenyon face-to-face because he had information that was inconsistent with the possible guilt of Mr. George?"

"We object, Your Honor," Kaplan balked.

Hall had already started to answer. "No. We interviewed everybody that was relevant and pertinent to the case and we went in with an open mind to develop motives and suspects, and we talked to everybody."

George wasn't the only person of interest, either, he said. There was Wally Last Name Unknown—the elusive figure whose name had been raised without much explanation thus far in the trial. The man's name came up during the 1990 investigation, Hall said, but no one seemed to know who he was by 2007.

"Would it be fair to state that Wally has basically dropped out of sight since 1990?" Marlinga asked.

"I don't know even if he ever existed," Hall said.

Joe Caulman, the man who had served time on a second-degree murder conviction, was also a person of interest in the new investigation, largely because he had been accused of stealing comics in the past.

"He was eliminated as a suspect when the robbery theory was discarded, when it was eliminated as a motive," Hall explained.

Marlinga challenged the detective's decision to discard the robbery motive.

"Is it fair to say that not all robberies are successful? . . . That a person can come in, shoot somebody, panic, and then decide that he or she has to leave as fast as possible. Isn't that a fair statement?"

Hall agreed it was possible.

Marlinga's questions became reminiscent of those posed to the 1990 investigators, highlighting what Hall, Hrecho, and Keith neglected doing as the investigation unfolded: They didn't review gunshot residue or bloodstain evidence, nor did they canvass Janet George's neighborhood to find anyone who might corroborate Michael's alibi.

"That simply had to do with Michael George's alibi, and you weren't interested in Michael George's alibi, isn't that true?"

Kaplan objected: argumentative. Biernat sustained.

The entire trial, jurors had heard of Lieutenant Craig Keith and had seen him sitting at Kaplan's side, whispering in the lawyer's ear and fetching witnesses as it became their time to testify. Now, it was time to finally hear from the man himself. He described the early days of the investigation—how he had taken it upon himself to re-examine the file and how he, Hrecho, and Hall began meeting sporadically at first, then weekly as the investigation unfolded. He insisted he had an open mind when he launched the new investigation, and that George didn't become a strong suspect for a solid six months. It was when the team tossed out the robbery idea that the spotlight shined most brightly on George. It came back to Barb's jewelry and the registers.

"Based on my review of the photographs, based on my review of the videotape, there are inconsistencies with the armed robbery theory," he said. "Plus, Mr. George had made contradicting statements to the original detectives in 1990. Coupled with those facts, I don't think the robbery was a motive."

The investigators weighed other possible motives, too, such

as someone jealous of Michael and Renee's relationship, such as Renee's ex-husband. Keith said they examined whether sexual assault might have played a role in the slaying. Finally, all they were left with was Michael and Barb's rocky marriage and the husband's payout when his wife died.

"Did you discover any known enemies of Barbara George?" Kaplan asked.

"None whatsoever."

"Did you uncover any recent threats against Barbara George?"

"No, I did not."

"Did you look into the background of the murder victim to determine whether she has any human flaws, foibles that might cause a person to be a target?"

"Yes, I did."

"Such as what are some of those foibles or flaws?"

"Promiscuity, alcohol, narcotics, gambling, associating with unsavory-type people."

All of those were ruled out, the lieutenant said. Investigators also looked into whether Barb was cheating on Michael. They found nothing that seemed to put the young mother at risk.

Because Marlinga had opened the door during his cross-examination of Hall, Kaplan presented the incomplete-robbery theory to Keith. After more than twenty-two years as a police officer, Keith said he would estimate that 5 percent of armed robberies end in property not being taken by the robber. Even fewer, less than 1 percent, resulted in a fatality.

The court took a much-needed lunch break that gave Kosmala plenty of time to chew over what he wanted to ask Keith on cross-examination. After everyone got situated again, he dove in, asking Keith about the resurrection of the case. Kosmala was on the offensive. He quickly got Keith to acknowledge that he couldn't recall what all was inside the evidence room attached to George's case. He would need a

report to refresh his memory, he said—and then he admitted
that he hadn't created such a report.

"All right." Kosmala furrowed his brow. "Did you prepare
for this trial, Detective?"

"Yes, I did."

"Didn't you think that these questions would be asked of
you?"

Kaplan objected: argumentative. Biernat overruled, saying that cross-examination allowed for some argument.
Keith would have to answer.

"As it relates to the property, I sat down on one occasion
with Mr. Marlinga and . . . went over the property, so it was
my understanding you had a list of that property."

"Mr. Marlinga is not testifying today, sir," Kosmala
snorted. "You are."

That objection was sustained. Kosmala moved on to grill
on another subject.

"Good police work is ninety percent footwork, isn't it?"

Keith agreed it was.

"You knock on doors, you talk to people, you see where
it leads you, and this is what you're supposed to do, right?"

Case by case, indeed, Keith replied.

"It appears that this was not done in 1990. It didn't happen 'til 2006 or '07, fair statement?"

Keith shifted in the witness stand. "I don't know if it's a
fair statement, but—"

Kosmala corrected himself. "How about this, is it a true
statement?"

Keith had been put in the uncomfortable position of criticizing his predecessors' work. He said he couldn't speculate
what their thought process was back then. He could only start
the investigation where they had stopped, and the path his
went down did not begin or end with a robbery, he said. He
reached that conclusion in part because of what George had
told Theresa Danieluk, the woman he embraced near his
wife's casket and whom he told that "nothing was taken."

"So you eliminated robbery as a motive based on the testimony of that very angry and upset woman?" Kosmala asked.

"No, not solely." Keith also based it on the photographs, the video, and George's inconsistent statements to police.

When the questioning got to Renaud, the sole witness placing George at the scene of the crime within an hour of the shooting, Kosmala became critical: Why had Keith only interviewed Renaud over the phone? Why didn't he deem the witness important enough to interview face-to-face? Keith said it didn't matter whether he talked with Renaud in person or by phone. The witness's recollection of what happened stayed consistent from 1990 to 2007.

Police had looked into Joe Kotula, Renee's first husband, as a possible suspect in 1990, Keith said, and they interviewed him again in 2007. They found nothing suspicious. And while sexual assault was ruled out as a possible motive, investigators did discover—and preserve—a stray pubic hair from Barb's sweater that had been largely dismissed because her body was found on the floor near the bathroom in the back room, where, unseemly as it may have sounded, plenty of pubic hairs were subject to being found. In 2007, that pubic hair was finally sent for DNA testing, which determined it was from a Caucasian who was not Barbara George. However, Keith didn't send Michael's DNA profile along with it to attempt to make a match.

"Being that it was his store, I would expect his DNA to be at that store," Keith said.

"This was a stray pubic hair on the sweater," Kosmala barked. "The point of this is had you compared it and had it come back Michael, no problem, I mean, they were married. You might expect that. But wouldn't it be awfully inconvenient, Detective, had it come back not Michael?"

Biernat struck the question from the record.

Kaplan levied several more objections before the testimony was finished, mostly on the grounds that Kosmala was argumentative. The back-and-forth continued into Kosmala's questions about how much weight the lieutenant gave to Hodgson's description of the slightly built man with the fake beard. Hodgson had gone so far as to even help police create a composite sketch of the mystery lurker. The sketch, made at Keith's request, was forwarded to the Michigan State Police, but Keith never showed it to Douglas Kenyon or the Wards to see if they recognized the person as the mystery man they had separately spotted.

Kaplan finally rested. It looked as though the day would wrap up early, giving the defense time to map out its Wednesday-morning beginning, but a scheduling conflict forced Hodgson, the man who spotted the fake-bearded Some Other Dude, to take the stand as the defense's first witness. Hodgson had spotted someone walking along the building. The person caught his eye, he said, because he or she seemed to be "a younger person who obviously wouldn't have facial hair but [had a] big bushy fake beard and mustache."

"Joe, did you see that guy?" Hodgson recalled telling Joe Gray. "He's wearing a fake beard. It looks awfully weird."

Gray tried to catch a glimpse but couldn't. Still, the two were concerned enough that they went to alert Barb and other plaza employees to keep their eyes peeled. Barb took the warning seriously. She looked out the back with Gray and Hodgson, and then walked out the front door. No one spotted anything unusual, so they said their goodbyes.

Kaplan didn't spend much time on his cross-examination. Through his questioning, he made three major points: that whatever alarmed him about the person in the fake beard, it wasn't enough that he called police; that there were reasons other than murder that someone might be wearing a fake beard, such as being involved in a play or other theatrics; and that Hodgson's memory of the person had faded so much over time that he couldn't recall his or her hair style, color, or length.

Chapter 28

Directed Verdict Request

The prosecution had rested, leaving Marlinga and Kosmala ready to mount their defense. Behind the scenes, they had been gearing up to possibly put Michael George on the stand, running mock direct and cross-examinations with him. He stayed calm and cooperative throughout, though his behavior in front of the jury during the prosecution's case wasn't as controlled. As the still and video cameras had captured time and again, George regularly made faces, scoffing and laughing, especially as his lawyers questioned police about all they failed to do in 1990. Kosmala caught a reaction here and there from George and shook it off.

"If I were an innocent man being accused of this, I'd react the same way," Kosmala later said. But to court watchers, the head shaking and eye rolls risked coming across to jurors as indignant and arrogant.

Still, neither Marlinga nor Kosmala were sure when they prepared to begin their case whether they would put George on the stand or not. Most lawyers steer clear of having their client testify unless it's absolutely necessary. It's too risky.

Biernat entered the courtroom to hear the defense's seemingly obligatory request for a directed verdict. Such a verdict would mean that Biernat, in his role as presiding judge, would deem the evidence presented too flimsy for a jury to reasonably decide guilt or innocence and he would instruct the jury to find George not guilty. By law, judges have to view the evidence in the light most favorable to the prosecution. Thus, the request is typically perfunctory. Defense lawyers ask; judges deny. Marlinga began his request acknowledging it.

"Your Honor knows that oftentimes these motions for directed verdict are pro forma affairs where the defense is doing it merely to protect the record," he said. "In this case, we are not doing this as a mere pro forma matter."

Marlinga presented a case—People v. Fisher, a 1992 Michigan case—that also involved a murdered wife and marital discord. That case had stronger circumstantial evidence, with the defendant having previously beaten his wife and threatened to kill her as recently as three months before her disappearance. The Court of Appeals ultimately ruled it was an error not to grant the motion for directed verdict for the defendant.

"I think factually Your Honor can see that the evidence in this case is much weaker than what the Court of Appeals found was insufficient as a matter of law in the Fisher case," Marlinga said.

He laid out the prosecution's case. First, the timeline. Mike Renaud's phone call time estimate was shaky at best, Marlinga argued, and the prosecution was using Renaud's 5:15–5:45 estimate as leeway to decide that if George was at the store to answer the phone then, he must have been there between 6 and 6:15 when Barb was killed.

"Basically, the prosecution's argument is that, well, if he's lying about it, you can infer that he was there a much longer time. And that's kind of the lynchpin, the legal flaw in the prosecutor's argument."

Second came the premise that the case was not an armed robbery but an ambush. The only proof, Marlinga said, was store customer Therese Danieluk's statement that George told her nothing had been stolen. Finally, even if you bought that it was solely a murder, the prosecution then asks jurors to make the leap to decide that Michael George was the only person who could have killed his wife.

"The physical evidence is simply absent," Marlinga said. "It is not possible to say beyond a reasonable doubt that this was solely a murder as opposed to an armed robbery gone bad."

After more than seventeen years, memories fade, alter, he added. It's why statute of limitations exist, even though they don't apply in murder cases. And motive alone is legally not enough to convict someone of a crime.

Lieutenant Keith, who reopened the case, had good intentions, Marlinga said. He had a theory and found support for it, he said, but "when push comes to shove, we can't send a person to prison on the basis of this kind of speculation."

To Marlinga, this was about more than People v. Michael George. It was about how the legal system was supposed to work in the United States. There were other possible killers, he insisted, even if they weren't Joe Caulman or Wally Last Name Unknown.

"It could be and probably is somebody else that we don't even know," he said. "It's just an open question. People go in and try to commit robberies, people go in to do dastardly acts, and you never know what the real answer is. . . . That's why it's better to let a guilty person go than to take the chance of convicting an innocent person."

In the end, he said, the trial judge is obligated to weigh whether a jury should be allowed to decide the case based on the evidence presented by the prosecution.

"If for some reason this went to the jury and the jury came back with a guilty verdict, you know that we would have that sick feeling in the pit of our stomachs that this isn't really the way we should be convicting people in the United States," Marlinga said.

In most cases, the judge would have responded thoughtfully but immediately: motion respectfully denied. Not in

this case. Biernat thanked Marlinga and said he would
consider the motion. He called a recess: Be back at 1 p.m., he
instructed. "I'll either be ready to proceed at that time or
shortly thereafter, I'll address these motions."

Kaplan's eyes searched the courtroom and locked with
Joe Kowynia, Barb's brother. The lawyer marched over, assured Kowynia that nothing was out of the ordinary and
said he'd see him after lunch. Kowynia rolled his eyes. This
judge was something, he told a reporter. He drags everything out.

The media that had gathered for the day followed the lawyers into the hallway, notebooks in hand, to gather a few
quotes for the Web stories they would have to file to tide over
hungry editors. They'd write up quickie stories, slap them
online, grab some lunch, and be back for the ruling.

Virtually no one got back right at 1 p.m. Reporters and
family members had gotten used to Biernat's idea of prompt-
ness and straggled in ten and fifteen minutes late. They were
right; Biernat wasn't back on the record at 1 p.m. Two o'clock
came and went. Then 3 p.m. Reporters fielded frantic text
messages from editors wondering when they'd be freed from
court sitting. Detroit's two newspapers had largely been
covering the day-to-day proceedings with short stories and
briefs. Only the local paper, the *Macomb Daily*, had been
dedicating significant space to the case regularly. Editors
with the bigger metros didn't want their resources tied up
too long on a case that wasn't likely to land on the metro
front. The reporters faced a dilemma as the day dragged on:
The longer Biernat took, the more newsworthy the story, but
most editors considered topics such as directed verdicts too
"inside baseball" to be interesting to readers.

As 3:30 p.m. rolled around, rumors had circulated that
Biernat was going to dismiss the case. Behind the scenes, he
apparently was torn. He read the case law Marlinga provided
but found that neither case really matched the circumstances
presented in the George case. He told a county staffer that

he personally felt the evidence was too weak for a conviction, but he worried that he shouldn't preemptively take that decision away from the jury. Marlinga was hopeful. No one had ever experienced such a lengthy delay in weighing a directed verdict. Clearly, Biernat had taken his arguments to heart.

Just shy of 4 p.m., Biernat lumbered back onto the bench. He was ready to rule.

"The court has been reviewing this matter for approximately five hours, which as all seasoned counsel know is an extraordinary length of time to review any motion for directed verdict, which, as I believe Mr. Marlinga stated, is often perfunctorily denied," he began. This case called for more consideration than some others.

"I don't think there's any question that there's been ample evidence in support of the defendant having a motive," he said. "And there is arguably evidence of opportunity, albeit it could be argued that this evidence is marginal."

Onlookers looked confused. Reporters exchanged puzzled glances. It wasn't clear where Biernat was going with this. In one sentence, he seemed to be setting up for a directed not guilty verdict; in the next, it seemed no question that the trial would go on.

"This is in many ways a classic murder case, and so the time frame—where he was, if he lied, et cetera—those are all fact questions," the judge said.

The jury had heard evidence that George might have lied about where he was during a chunk of the night, he continued, and if jurors believed he lied, they might well believe he was covering up his activities that day.

Then, finally, came the clear English all sides were waiting to hear: "Directed verdict is denied."

Chapter 29

The Defense Begins

Jurors filed into the courtroom shortly after 4 p.m. They had spent a long five hours stuck in a stale room off a hallway behind Biernat's courtroom with no idea what was taking so long. All they knew is that there was a delay and they had to wait. Biernat seemed to sense their frustration.

"I'm not even going to thank you for your patience, because I suspect that your patience has worn thin," he said, "but I want you to know that the delay that has been occasioned this afternoon is again entirely the fault of the court."

He assured them the delay was necessary and implored that they not hold it against the lawyers on either side. With that, he introduced Marlinga, who would finally start presenting George's defense.

Several times during the prosecution's case, the defense tried to talk about the phone call Lieutenant Neal allegedly had with John Hancock insurance. Kaplan had objected each time. The documentation of the call was hearsay, he argued, and the lieutenant didn't remember the conversation he'd supposedly had with the company rep. The defense's efforts to get the document introduced hit another snag when the insurance representative, Jack Hopkins, couldn't be sprung in time from work to fly to Michigan and testify. Marlinga thought it was a lot to ask to have a guy take a flight to get on the stand for one minute to verify what he had jotted on a document nearly eighteen years prior. During one of the trial's delays, he and Kaplan reached a compromise: The document describing the phone call would be read into the record, but it would not be admitted as an exhibit.

Kosmala, in undramatic fashion, stood before the jury box and read it aloud: Contract No. 66068313, amount issued $100,000; contract No. VL61975, amount issued $29,000. "A telephone request was received . . . July 24, 1990, seeking immediate information pertaining to the possible implication of the named beneficiary, Michael R. George, the subject's husband in her homicide death. If Mr. George is not implicated, then no further inquiries need to be undertaken."

Kosmala looked up briefly.

"There's a double space and the next four words are in capitals and they are underlined," he said. "Those four words are Detective Lieutenant John Neal."

According to the document, a company representative called Neal July 26, less than two weeks after Barb was killed. The rep had written: "He states while he looked real hard at Mr. George as a suspect at first, he has found absolutely no evidence to indicate any implication by Mr. George whatsoever."

The defense's first witness was one the prosecution had planned to call but, because Biernat had ruled the man couldn't testify about George's suggestion that he refuse to take a polygraph, was scratched from the list. Now that Kaplan didn't want Joe Gray, Marlinga did. He had never met Gray before the heavyset man took the stand March 12, 2008, but in interviews after Barb's death, he had mentioned a man named Wally to police—the same Wally with whom George said he'd had a falling-out just days before Barb's murder.

The details on Wally were sketchy. Wally was about five-foot-eight with black hair and a thick black mustache, and he always wore a baseball cap, Gray said. "Kind of normal build, maybe," he said. "Didn't look too thin, too heavy." He seemed like a comic collector and carried some valuable books around in a briefcase. Gray didn't know Wally's last name and didn't know the man well personally, but he knew that Wally was friends with George and, after some prodding by Marlinga, he recalled that the men had an argument about a CD player around the time Barb was killed.

But that's all jurors could hear. Gray never saw the spat himself, so Kaplan objected to him testifying about it because everything he knew was based on what he'd heard from others. In a word, it was hearsay. Otherwise, Gray said, Mike and Wally "seemed like normal friends." Maybe he could remember them being cold toward each other once or twice, but he couldn't recall the particulars. Marlinga was quick to remind him that he had told police "Mike treated him like shit once because they got into a fight." Gray remembered saying that, but he still couldn't remember what sparked the fight.

The testimony seemed to drag, especially after the morning's excruciatingly slow start. Gray's memory was lacking. There was no moment of "aha" for either side. A reporter sitting in the back row yawned.

Gray had worked for George years before the trial, but first he was a Comics World franchise owner and ran a store in Madison Heights. He and his partner eventually sold the store to George, and Gray took a job under him for a few months.

Still, though he hadn't worked at the Clinton Township store on Garfield, Gray had been there often enough to remember its layout. George kept comics ranging from $30 to a few thousand in the store, Gray testified. The expensive books were kept in a glass display case. Some, he recalled, were stored in the safe in the book room.

Switching gears to July 13, 1990, Gray said he was working

from 11 a.m. to 4 p.m. at a Domino's Pizza at 18 Mile and
Hayes. After work, he went to Comics World, where he was
going to help Barb prepare for Michael's surprise birthday
party. His job was to take the party supplies from Barb's van
and hide them because Michael would be taking the van to
drop the girls off at his mother's house. After George left,
Gray passed the supplies back to Barb, who was going to use
them to decorate the store for the party. More than seventeen years later, Gray estimated he left the store with the
supplies between 4:30 and 5 p.m. to pick up a friend, Fred
Hodgson, but en route, Barb had called and left a message
for him that he still had something in his car she needed. He
and Fred headed back to Comics World and got there about
6 p.m. Outside the store, they noticed someone walking by.

Fred said the slightly built man seemed to be wearing a
fake beard. Gray did a double take to spot the man, but he
was gone. It was enough of an oddity that Hodgson and
Gray felt inclined to warn some of the storeowners that a
strange-looking fellow was hanging out in the strip mall.
They warned Barb first, then Hodgson and Gray headed to
Hungry Howie's. The pizza store seemed the more likely
target, especially on a busy, cash-heavy Friday night. The
men's civic duty done, they took a final lap around the parking lot as they drove away and still spotted nothing. The bizarre man with the fake beard had disappeared. Hodgson and
Gray finally left the parking lot for good sometime between 6
and 6:15 p.m., enough time to get to a wedding rehearsal in
Burville.

After the rehearsal, Hodgson and Gray went to a Ram's
Horn restaurant for a late dinner, then Gray took Hodgson to
the pizza parlor where the latter worked and had left his car.
The manager there came out and said she'd heard some bi-
zarre news: Barbara George had been killed. Gray rushed
back to Comics World and saw the gaggle of police officer.
About twenty minutes after he got there, he spotted Michael
George. The men hugged and cried together.

"I was very upset," Gray recalled. "Nervous and like—like, 'cause I remember seeing somebody I felt—feel a little guilt."

"A little guilty why?" Marlinga asked.

"Because I didn't think we did enough maybe to warn her."

Marlinga tried to better pin down the time frame—the dead horse of the trial that had been beaten beyond recognition. Seventeen years later, Gray said he couldn't be sure. He left the store about 5:30 p.m., and Michael George had headed to his mother's house with the children maybe an hour and a half prior. That didn't jibe with the time frame he had given earlier when he said he unloaded party supplies from the minivan Barb was driving—the same one Michael would take to drive to his mother's—between 4:30 and five.

The discrepancy fueled a tit-for-tat between prosecution and defense.

"Didn't you already tell us that the loading of the items from the white minivan to your car occurred sometime between four-thirty and five o'clock? Is that correct?" Marlinga asked.

Kaplan: "Objection. That's not what he said. It's improper—"

"Let him answer the question," Biernat barked.

"I don't recall saying that," Gray stuttered.

"OK, and Michael George left after that stuff was unloaded from the white minivan into your car, isn't that correct?"

Kaplan: "The questions are leading."

"It's cross-examination," Marlinga shot back.

"It's *not* cross-examination." Kaplan looked at Biernat. "It's his witness. I could not do that in my case. The same rules should apply."

Biernat tried to defuse.

"That's an improper objection. What I rule previous has nothing to do with this. I'm going to rule on this question.

My response, Mr. Marlinga, is you cannot cross-examine witnesses. You can impeach this witness if you wish."

Marlinga wrapped up, and Kaplan set about to cross-examine. Heads butted again.

"Although I might not be able to use cross-examination, I believe it's unfair for the prosecution to use cross-examination as well," Marlinga said, after Kaplan's initial questions highlighted the fluidity of Gray's timeline.

"That is incorrect," said Kaplan, his voice rising with impatience. "He's misinterpreted the rule. He called this witness, I can cross-examine him.

"I'm saying because of the extraordinary circumstances in this case where this person was a government witness prepared by the state. . . . I can live with the fact that I can't cross-examine him, but I think it is highly prejudicial to this defendant's right to allow this to occur as a result of them not calling this person in their case."

Kaplan, careful in front of the jury not to spell out why he hadn't called Gray after Biernat's polygraph ruling, said that because Marlinga called him, the prosecutor could cross-examine.

"You can't prevent me from doing this," he said. "There's no case that says so; there's no rule that says so."

Biernat agreed: Kaplan could continue. He reminded Gray that he had told police he seemed more distraught over Barb's death than Michael did.

"You weren't married to her, were you?" asked Kaplan in the first of a barrage of borderline-rhetorical questions designed to drive home his point.

"No."

"And you and her, you weren't romantic with her?"

"No."

"You didn't have any children with her?"

"No."

"You didn't own a store with her?"

"No."

As for Wally, Gray remembered that Wally Last Name Unknown had been a pallbearer at the funeral. Another barrage:

"And generally pallbearers are people who are close to the family?"

"I assume so, yes."

"You weren't asked to be pallbearer?"

"No."

"But Wally's closer to the defendant than you are?"

"I don't know for sure, but—"

"Does the defendant know your last name?"

"You have to ask him. I don't know."

"Would he know Wally's last name?"

"I assume they would; they were friends."

"They were buddies, he's a pallbearer, they do contracts together, correct? . . . For Wally Last Name Unknown, somebody might know the last name of Wally, correct?"

"They might, yeah."

Like other witnesses, Gray said George's behavior after his wife's death seemed off. George didn't seem overly concerned about figuring out who killed his wife, either.

After Gray stepped down, murmurs rose in the courtroom. Word was spreading that George's daughters were going to testify. Court watchers exchanged puzzled looks. Tracie, the older daughter, was just four when her mother was killed. Michelle was two. What could they possibly be able to offer his defense?

After a brief pause, the speculation was confirmed: Tracie George stepped forward, raised her right hand and swore she would be truthful. She was now twenty-two, an adult and accomplished athlete. With light brown hair reaching past her shoulders, she had grown into an attractive young woman.

Kosmala handled the direct examination. He wanted to know what Tracie remembered about the day her mother died. It wasn't detailed.

"I remember being at my grandma's house, and my father was sleeping on the couch," she said. "And we had raced through the stoplights to get to the hospital."

"Who are you referring to?" Kosmala asked.

"Whoever was driving. I don't remember who was driving. I was in the car."

The image of young Tracie, just a toddler, sitting in the car with street lights whizzing by, quieted the courtroom. It was sobering to think of the little girl learning that Mommy wasn't coming home.

"Do you remember anything about going to your mom's funeral?" Kosmala asked.

"I remember seeing my mom. She was very cold," Tracie said steadily. "We were playing around a lot, and I remember my dad picking me up, telling me that it probably would be the last time I would see my mom. And she was wearing a blue cross around her neck and he had asked me if I had wanted it, and I said no, because it's my mom's."

Since her mother's death, Tracie lived continuously with her dad and, soon after, with Renee. The family moved to Windber, Pennsylvania, in time for Tracie to start second grade. They returned to visit Michael's mother at least once a year, and nearly every time, they stopped by the Clinton Township cemetery where her mother was buried. And yes, Tracie said, her father did cry.

Kaplan had the undesirable job of cross-examining the dead woman's daughter. He set out to quickly highlight everything from the day that Tracie couldn't remember: what she did that morning, the loud fight the nail technicians had reported hearing about 9 a.m., playing near a Dumpster outside of the store.

"Fair to say you don't remember anything about what you did that day before you claim to have seen your dad sleeping?"

"Fair to say." There was a hint of defiance in her voice.

The cross-examination was brief. It was time for the defense to call Barb's other daughter.

Michelle George didn't remember anything about the day her mother died, but she told Kosmala that she, her sister, and her father did visit the grave when they were in town, no matter what the cemetery records said.

"First when we find it, we say a prayer, and then normally there's grass covering it because it's a flat stone, so we clean the grave off and then we just take our time and leave."

"Does your dad get emotional at the gravesite?" Kosmala asked gently.

"Yes."

Kaplan took his turn.

"Are you saying that the gravesite is very tidy and well maintained?"

"Not every time we go," Michelle said. "Like, we clean it. We have to clean it ourselves."

"If I told you in August of 2007, it was not in good condition, would you quarrel with that?"

"I could not tell you. I was not there August 2007."

The tedious day drew to a close. Biernat instructed everyone to be back by 8:15 a.m.; the last day of testimony would begin promptly at 8:30.

Chapter 30

Last Day of Witnesses

At nine o'clock, the final hurrah of witnesses finally got under way. Prosecutors had spent days laying out the reasons Michael George was the only person who possibly could have killed his wife; George's lawyers now needed to needle into jurors' brains that someone else could have just as easily gotten away with murder.

The case laid out by Kaplan had nothing resembling a smoking gun. There wasn't a gun at all. But there was plenty of motive and, as Judge Biernat had said when he denied the directed verdict, at least the argument of opportunity. Still, defendants walk into court as innocent people, and as Marlinga and Kosmala set about to wrap up the trial, they focused on the two most important words jurors must weigh: reasonable doubt.

Entering into the last day, it wasn't clear if they were going to call George to testify. The *Dateline* cameras were poised and ready, as were the still photographers for the daily newspapers. They had captured the array of emotions George had so readily worn on his face throughout the trial. Onlookers were antsy to learn if they would hear Michael's words to back up those non-verbal reactions. With Marlinga as his lawyer, it seemed more plausible than in most cases.

Marlinga, after all, had testified in his own trial over the protests of many peers. Defendants are innocent going in, and testifying is typically more than just risky. Usually, it's downright stupid.

The lawyers had already begun zeroing in on the two characters in the Venice Square Shopping Center parking lot that had caught visitors' attention July 13, 1990—the man who sped away from the parking lot, and the slightly built person who appeared to be wearing a fake beard and a Greek fisherman's cap in front of the comic book store shortly before Barb was killed. Now they hoped to hit the point home.

Robert Pavlock owned a picture frame and art gallery in the shopping center a few stores away from Comics World. About 2 p.m. the day Barb was killed, he had noticed a beat-up car, light in color, turning toward his business front.

"It caught my eye because it was in bad shape," he recalled.

The car turned left in front of Pavlock's store, and he caught a look at the man inside—forty-something, white, dark beard, dark hair, and wearing a Greek fisherman's cap. Pavlock watched as the car followed the building row out of the parking lot. The guy inside looked "very unkempt, a rough, rough John."

Pavlock had never seen the man before, but, he said, he believed he had seen him once since.

"I would say it was about ten years later," he told Kosmala. "Similar circumstances, just passing toward my window, and at that point in time it just stuck out in my mind that I think it was the man who I had described to the police [in 1990]."

"Did you report this second sighting to the police?"

Pavlock had not.

Kosmala showed Pavlock some pictures of hats and asked him which most closely looked like the hat on the man he had seen driving away. The cap he chose was classic Greek

fisherman: short-billed, with braided detail, tough-guy mas-
culine.

"The shape of the hat is exactly as I remember and I believe it was black," Pavlock said, pointing. "This one here is
very close to it."

The car, he remembered, was a station wagon, possibly
a General Motors product. He couldn't remember anything
more specific.

Kaplan considered testimony such as Pavlock's to be in the
red herring family. He began his cross-examination in a tone
that seemed to say, "So what if you saw a random car?"

"You called the police that day as soon as you learned
that Barbara George had been murdered?" Kaplan asked.

Pavlock looked confused. "Did I call the police? No, I did
not call the police," he said.

Kaplan's brow knit in faux confusion.

"Well, when you waited, you waited a day or two to call
the police?"

"No, I never called the police," Pavlock said. "They came
to my store."

"So after you heard Barbara George had been murdered
and you remember the day before at two o'clock seeing a
vehicle in the parking lot, you did not call the police?"

"No, sir."

In fact, the police came to him, Pavlock explained. The
cops had been canvassing the nearby business owners and
employees, asking if they had seen anything out of the ordinary that might lead them to answers.

"And when they talked to you, did they rush you?" asked
Kaplan, his voice tinged with sarcasm. "Did they say, 'Look,
we need to know if you know anything, here's our stopwatch,
you have one minute to start talking'?"

"No."

"They gave you as much time as you needed to share
with them anything you knew from the day before?"

"That's correct."

That opened the door for Kaplan to highlight the portions of Pavlock's testimony that, based on police reports, he didn't tell officers the day after the slaying. He showed Pavlock the police report. The witness acknowledged that he reportedly told police seventeen years before that the man was in his late twenties or early thirties and had a mustache, not a beard. And the report said the car was dark and rusted, not light-colored. There was no mention of a Greek fisherman's cap.

None of that jibed with Pavlock's memory on the stand, however.

"I don't believe I ever gave that description," he said.

Barbee Hancock-Kalbfleisch was twice as old as she had been when, at age eighteen, she stopped by Comics World to chat with Barb about her recent breakup and her pregnancy. She was there about a half-hour, between 5 and 5:30 p.m. Barb was killed less than an hour after she left.

Now a married woman, Hancock-Kalbfleisch took the stand and tried to recall those last few moments she spent with the shopkeeper. They chatted mostly about her pregnancy, Hancock-Kalbfleisch recalled, before the phone rang. Barb answered.

"I remember her saying—"

Kaplan objected: hearsay.

"If she wants to characterize the conversation, fine, but it is a hearsay statement, which I would not be allowed to introduce myself." He argued that she should not continue.

Marlinga shook his head, as if to steel himself for a face-off. What Hancock-Kalbfleisch overheard could be admitted, he said, as an exception to the hearsay rule that allows a statement describing or explaining an event to be made.

"It's not the purpose of the ruling," Kaplan argued. "The purpose of the rule is when a person observes an event, like a speeding car or some hail— Excuse me, you're in my way, Mr. Marlinga," he said. Marlinga had drifted between

Biernat and Kaplan and, seemingly oblivious, stayed put. Kaplan shifted back into Biernat's line of sight and, like a perturbed child, said, "I'll just move."

Marlinga shrugged. "OK."

"Because otherwise every conversation would be present-sense impression," Kaplan continued, "whether it's a telephone conversation or in the presence of somebody else."

No dice. Biernat allowed the testimony. Hancock-Kalbfleisch could continue.

"She stated that she would not discuss this over the phone, that they needed to come into the store," the witness recalled.

She didn't know the specifics, but she gathered the conversation was about expensive comic books, and that Barb was uncomfortable.

"It made her uneasy," Hancock-Kalbfleisch testified. "Tense, nervous and scared."

It was Kaplan's turn for cross. He skipped the pleasantries altogether.

"Were you able to hear the voice of the other person?"

"No, I was not."

"Do you know whether it was female or male?"

"No, I did not."

"Were you able to hear the words of the other person?"

"No."

"Were you able to tell whether the other person was angry or upset?"

"No."

Nor could Hancock-Kalbfleisch remember details about her visit. She forgot briefly that she hadn't been able to walk into the store at first because the door was locked. Barb had left to order sub sandwiches for the party. Hancock-Kalbfleisch couldn't recall how long she waited outside.

"I wouldn't have waited long," she told Kaplan. "I was a teenager. I would probably have just left. She probably came out pretty soon after I walked up to the door."

Hancock-Kalbfleisch had attended Barb's funeral all those years ago. She saw Michael there. With some prodding by Kaplan—and the review of yet another police report taken nearly two decades prior—she acknowledged reluctantly that she never saw him cry. "Does that mean he never did? No," she said.

Kaplan sounded as though he were ready to wrap things up when another thought popped to mind: The store had a phone, right? Of course, Hancock-Kalbfleisch said; she had seen Barb talking on it.

"Now, if somebody calls the store about 5:30 p.m. while Barb was at the Hungry Howie's ordering food, she can't answer the phone, can she?"

Hancock-Kalbfleisch responded as though she were talking to a toddler: "If she's not there, no, she cannot answer the phone."

"But if somebody else is at the store, that person can answer the phone?"

"That is correct."

"Were you ever on the back room?"

"No."

"Do you know whether Michael George was in the back room at five-thirty?"

"No, I do not."

Nothing further.

In the days after Barb's murder, then-sixteen-year-old Douglas Kenyon and his mother were freaked. They had been at the store between 5:15 and 5:30 looking for a comic the teenager had wanted to grab before the weekend. The store was holding it for him even though he wasn't an official store member, and reserving comics usually was a privilege only for members. When the Kenyons learned of the shooting, they realized they could have been there, and Douglas recalled seeing a man that gave him the willies as he left the store. The man was in the back of the store wearing a sweat-shirt and jeans and a dark baseball cap. He had a mustache, Douglas remembered.

"He was looking more or less evasive in terms of making sure we didn't see his presence," he recalled.

The man was flipping through comics stacked in racks in the back of the store. He was about five-foot-ten or five-foot-eleven, between 160 and 175 pounds, and wore sunglasses.

On direct examination, Douglas had remembered he got to the store in the 5:15–5:30 range because he wanted to get there before it closed. On cross, Kaplan asked if he realized the store didn't close until 9 p.m. on Fridays. Douglas seemed taken aback.

"That I didn't know . . . Then it wasn't before closing."

"I wasn't there," Kaplan said.

"So maybe—I could have misestimated the time," Douglas said. "I could have misestimated the time frame in terms of the hours. I was sixteen at the time, so believe me, I wasn't concerned about the time. I was concerned about getting the comic book. But thank you for recalling that."

"Oh, I'm not criticizing you," Kaplan said.

"I know you're not," Douglas said, smiling, then explained his strangely worded gratitude: "I'm an analyst. I'm sorry."

"I need one," Kaplan quipped.

Douglas conceded that the man might not have stood out in his memory as seeming out of place if he hadn't learned later of his close proximity to Barb's death. The man could have shied from showing his face because he had acne or scars or a cleft chin or other defect, he said. The man could have been absorbed in a comic book, or, as Kaplan proposed, he could have recognized Douglas's mother and not wanted to say hello. Or, in one of the more entertaining scenarios Kaplan proposed, the man could have been looking at items from the Georges' "adults only" comics section.

"That could be a true statement."

Douglas smiled.

It was time for a morning break, Biernat decided. At 10:15
a.m., the court recessed for a planned twenty minutes. Forty-
five minutes later, court actually resumed.

Janet George, Michael's mother, was a key witness, but
not necessarily a star witness. What mother wouldn't testify
for her son, after all? Still, she was the only adult who could
attest to her son being at her home during the time of Barb's
shooting. She was his alibi.

The years hadn't been kind to her memory, but at 74,
she was nothing if not feisty, as investigators had learned
when they surprised her with an interview the summer before. Most people are retired by that age, but Janet worked
in the sauce room at a Big Boy restaurant. She had worked
there 17 years earlier, too. After she got off work, she chatted with her daughter-in-law to arrange the drop-off of
Michelle and Tracie. Barb gave Janet a mission: Keep Michael
busy as long as possible so she could get the store ready for
the birthday party. The call came sometime around 5 p.m.—or,
after Marlinga had her look more closely at the statement
Janet gave police at the time—possibly closer to 5:30 p.m.
Michael arrived soon after.

"He stayed a while, we talked," Janet recalled. "He said
he was tired. I told him to lay down and take a nap for a
while."

He did, resting on the couch in her living room. Marlinga
entered into evidence photographs taken in 2007 of Janet
George's living room. Like her job, her furniture hadn't
changed in the nearly twenty years since: She still had the
same love seat and couch. The only difference, she testified,
was that she had flipped their positions in her living room.
The love seat now sat where the couch had once been, and
vice versa.

While her son napped, Janet said she took the girls for a

walk down the street to the park. They played on the swing, then headed back. As they walked home, they spotted neighbor Margaret Marentette and waved. Michael was still on the couch asleep when they returned.

Marlinga's direct examination was quick, painless. As Kaplan approached her, Janet seemed to bristle.

"Do you remember being interviewed by Sergeant Donald Steckman in 1990?"

She did not.

"Do you remember being interviewed by a police officer in 1990?"

She did not.

"Do you remember telling a police officer in 1990 that you walked around the block first before—"

"No, I did not walk around the block, sir," Janet interrupted.

"Please listen to my question. Look, I'm not trying to argue with you," Kaplan said. Both sides seemed poised for battle. Janet was adamant that she never told Steckman that she and the girls walked around the block before going to the park.

"Now when you took the girls for a walk, they were both in strollers, correct?"

"No."

"Only one was in a stroller?"

"No."

"Neither one was in a stroller?"

Kaplan knew the answer to that before he asked. His point: It takes a while to walk anywhere with young children, especially if the kids aren't in a stroller.

"While you were at the park, are you involved in walkie-talkie discussions with your son?"

"He wasn't with me." Janet sounded irritated.

"Did you have any binoculars that enabled you to see through your house into the room where the couch is situated?"

An aggravated glare. "No," Janet said.

Over the years, Janet's timeline varied. In her interview in August 2007—the surprise chat she'd had with Sergeant Kline as other detectives caught Renee and Michael off-guard in Pennsylvania—she said she didn't know what time Barb's party would be, but she remembered that Michael left her house at 5:30 p.m. because she warned him about the traffic. Now, she remembered with certainty that he left after 6 p.m., she said. His arrival time shifted, too. As recently as the preliminary exam, she said he'd gotten to her house not long after 4 p.m. According to police reports, she'd also once estimated that she could have been away from her house for as much as ninety minutes when she left Michael behind and took the girls to the park, but on the stand, she estimated she was gone less than thirty minutes.

"Now tell us about Barbara and Michael's marriage," Kaplan asked. "As far as you're concerned, how was it?"

"Good."

"Did you know he was having an affair with Renee?"

"No."

"He didn't tell you that?"

"No."

"Do you remember about three or four days after Barbara's death, you found something in Michael's house that alarmed you? Found some panties of Renee's at Michael's house?"

Marlinga objected; Biernat sustained. Jurors heard nothing more about the panties that Janet George allegedly discovered and deduced belonged to Michael's lover just days after his wife's death.

Police never interviewed Margaret Marentette in 1990—or any of Janet George's other neighbors, for that matter. In October 2007, as the defense was gearing up for the preliminary exam, Marlinga contacted Marentette because Janet recalled waving to her the day Barb died. Fast-forward to the trial, and Marentette—known as Peggy to friends—was on the stand to verify the all-important wave. She was on her way home from work, she told Kosmala on direct examination, which put it at between 5:45 and 6 p.m.—right around the time Barb was being shot to death about a half-hour's drive away. Marentette noticed Michael's white minivan outside Janet's house, and then she spotted Janet and the girls waving from the sidewalk.

"I just beeped the horn to them and waved and went down our street and went home," she recalled.

Later that night, Janet knocked on her door. Barbara had been shot. Marentette cried.

In a not-so-subtly-veiled condemnation of the initial police investigation, Kosmala asked if anyone had ever interviewed Marentette in person. They hadn't, she said. The only time she spoke with a detective was near the time she was to testify at preliminary exam. She told the detective the same thing she said on the stand—that she indeed saw Janet and the girls heading home from the park about 6 p.m.—and the cop never called her back to follow up.

Marentette was close enough with the Georges that she attended both the visitation and the funeral service. Her memory of Michael's demeanor was nothing like the prosecution witnesses'. He was crying inconsolably, she recalled. Nothing anyone said seemed to calm him in the slightest.

"I can truly say that I've never before or after seen anyone as distraught as Michael was," she said.

"Never before or after," Kosmala echoed.

Kaplan objected: "He's repeating the answer."

Kosmala smiled slyly. "I guess I was, and I'm sorry, Judge."

Kaplan's cross began with his typical "gotcha"-style rundown: Did you punch a clock when you left work that day to document the time you left? Do you remember if there was construction or a traffic jam on the expressway? Do you remember if you stopped and chatted with someone in the parking lot on your way out? Marantette answered with straight "no"s.

Jeffrey Mandziuk had handled countless grieving loved ones in his years as a funeral director. He entered the family business a few years before Barb's death, but had grown up in the environment; his family had run the Warren-based E.J. Mandziuk & Son Funeral Directors, Inc., for fifty years.

He remembered helping George make the arrangements. The widower was "quite broken up," he recalled, especially at the beginning of the process. During the visitation itself, he seemed more preoccupied talking to family and friends in attendance. His behavior, Mandziuk said, was typical.

He told Kaplan he didn't remember seeing Michael wearing the damning sunglasses that others had recalled him wearing.

"That's something you would remember," Kaplan said. "That's rather unusual, isn't it?"

"No, sir," Mandziuk said. "A lot of people wear sunglasses."

Regardless, Mandziuk didn't see any.

"Now, do you remember at the funeral about three feet from Barbara George's open casket when the defendant approached a woman named Theresa Danieluk and gave her a very long hug—not a grieving type of hug? Did you see that?"

Mandziuk had not.

"Now, what is your view as a funeral director when a man's wife is in the casket and he's three or four feet from her, and he approaches a woman and hugs her in a way which is romantic? How do you feel about that?"

Kosmala was already on his feet.

"I must rise to object," he said. "This is beyond speculation. It's beyond guesswork."

And it was sustained. The question was stricken. Kaplan was finished.

After an hour's break for lunch, during which jurors traveled as a pack into downtown Mt. Clemens with bright red "juror" badges on their chests, court was back in session. Marlinga and Kosmala had at least two more witnesses left to testify: the private investigator they had hired and his son and sometimes partner.

Daniel Vohs, the younger of the two, went first. He had been recruited by his private detective father to drive the route from Janet George's Hazel Park home to the Venice Square plaza. Daniel drove it three times over the winter, he told Kosmala. On Feb. 19, it took him thirty-nine minutes. The next day, it took thirty-six minutes. On Feb. 22, thirty-four minutes. Each trip was between 5:15 and 5:30 p.m., and each time he made the trip back from the store to Janet's. Those trips clocked thirty-two minutes, thirty-two minutes and thirty-three minutes.

He also walked from Janet's home to the swing set about one-quarter of a mile away. He videotaped the walk for good measure. It took about eleven minutes round trip, he said. As Kaplan was quick to point out, he did not have two young children in tow when he made the trek.

"Would you agree it would take more time?"

Vohs agreed.

"Did you try the experiment with a two-year-old and a four-year-old?"

"No, I didn't."

"Or with just a two-year-old?"

"No, sir."

"Or just a four-year-old?"

"No, sir."

As for the trip from Janet's to Comics World, Daniel Vohs acknowledged he didn't make the trip on July 13, 1990, for a fair travel comparison—or, as Kaplan pointed out, even on July 13 of 2008. Traffic patterns could vary with the seasons, he acknowledged. But he disputed Kaplan's claim that

Lieutenant Craig Keith, the officer in charge of the case, had made the trip, using a slightly different route, in just 29 minutes.

"So you're saying he's not being truthful?" Kaplan asked.

"Um, yes, sir," Daniel stumbled.

Daniel Vohs' father had retired from the police department in Warren, Michigan, the state's third-largest city with a hefty crime rate. The elder Vohs had worked his way up from cadet in 1978 to chief in 1998. Six years later, he was appointed police commissioner, from which he retired in March 2007. Six months later, he launched Relentless Investigations, a private eye firm, where he could put his years of police training to work in the private sector.

Marlinga had worked with Vohs for years. When the George case came up, he asked the former commissioner to look at the evidence and the reports in the case. Vohs asked Clinton Township police for access to some of the materials, and the agency cooperated.

Vohs had investigated numerous armed robberies and homicides in his day. Warren's murder rate was nowhere near Detroit's, but in Vohs' last two years as head of police, the city saw ten homicides, and it sported one of the state's highest violent crime rates overall. Based on that experience, Marlinga asked him on the stand to say whether Barbara George's death seemed like part of an armed robbery or solely a murder.

"I can't make a conclusion either way," he said. "There's just not enough evidence there to say why she was shot."

It appeared two shots were fired—though that stray bullet in Kathy Ireland's eye could have been from another shooting, however unlikely. He agreed with the township investigators in guessing that the shot to Ireland came first. Given the medical examiner's testimony, there would have been no reason to fire another round if Barbara George indeed had fallen to the ground, immediately incapacitated by the bullet in her brain.

Kaplan, on cross, played up the unknowns: It's not clear what gun was used, when both bullets were shot, why the bullet entered the top of Barb's head, whether she had tried to duck at the sight of someone with a gun. Vohs agreed: There were a lot of things investigators would apparently never know.

Kaplan was done. Marlinga uttered the long-awaited words: "Nothing further."

Court watchers shifted in their seats. This was the moment they would learn whether Michael George would take the stand to defend himself.

"You may call your next witness," Biernat said.

Marlinga glanced at Kosmala.

"The defense rests, but I would like to have a brief sidebar with Mr. Kaplan before I put a period on that sentence," he said.

The air in the room seemed to lighten.

"Or exclamation point," Kaplan joked.

The two lawyers exchanged a couple of hushed whispers before Marlinga spoke up.

"Your Honor, let me say that the defense rests with a period and exclamation point, as Mr. Kaplan has suggested."

Chapter 31

Deflating Kaplan

After nearly every one of George's days in trial, Kaplan left the case behind in the courtroom. Like Marlinga, he had long had his sights set on other posts, running in 1996 for Oakland County prosecutor and briefly being declared the winner until a clerical error put his Republican opponent ahead by just 7,000 votes. Kaplan also lost a bid for Oakland County Circuit Court. By 2000, however, the losing streak ended when Kaplan won a seat as a trustee in West Bloomfield Township. As the George case was winding down, Kaplan was gearing up for re-election while also campaigning for a long-shot challenger, Michele Ureste, to take over as township supervisor. To keep his various gigs clearly defined, Kaplan rarely dwelled on his cases after work hours, and with the George case in particular, he felt confident he would win.

Until a TV producer called him on his drive home.

He said, "Steve, you're not gonna win this one," Kaplan later recalled. The seasoned journalist complimented Kaplan's effort but said there was no way a jury would come back with a guilty verdict.

"He's stroking me, telling me, 'You did a great job,' but he says there's just too much doubt," Kaplan said.

The assistant prosecutor was disconsolate. The conversation consumed him much of the night. He told his wife about the talk and she tried to cheer him up. "It's just one man's opinion," she assured. "He doesn't know; he hasn't been to court *every* day."

Kaplan decided he needed to buckle down and spend some extra time pondering his closing argument. Maybe the jury was as on the fence as that producer.

Chapter 32

Closing Statements

The thirteen remaining jurors filed into their seats. It had been a grueling few weeks, full of late-morning starts, delayed rulings and seemingly never-ending "excuse the jury" breaks, especially when Kosmala and Kaplan began butting heads. They didn't know the behind-the-scenes details—the reason for that five-hour break during which Judge Biernat agonized over the directed verdict, for example, or the heated arguments about whether sordid proof of Michael George's infidelities would be allowed into the trial. All they knew was that no matter how interesting this case might be to chat about later at dinner parties, it was hellish to hear now. But it was nearing an end.

The defense had rested. Today, they knew, would be for closing arguments. Thank God.

"Good morning," began Kaplan, wearing one of his trademark three-piece suits. He was clearly focused, barely waiting for the obligatory "good morning" response before launching into his argument.

"We all know Barbara George died and one has to conclude who did it, obviously, and there are three possibilities," he said. "Now Sherlock Holmes was fond of saying that when

you eliminate the improbable and you're left with the probable, that's the solution."

The three possibilities? Robbery turned murder, grudge
murder, or spousal murder, he said.

"Let's examine those three very quickly," he said. "You've
heard that Barbara George had no enemies. In fact, the only
person who disliked her as far as you know is her husband."

Marlinga shifted in his chair.

"You heard about the robber claim—we'll talk about that
later—but if it's not a robbery, then she wasn't killed by a
robber. And then the other possibility would be some third
person who had something against her and there's no one in
this world. And if there had been, the defense would have
presented that to you."

Marlinga finally interrupted: "Sidebar, Your Honor, please."

Few lawyers like interrupting in closing arguments, not
even as a strategic move to throw the opposition off his game.
It's frowned upon, looked at as an open door for tit-for-tat, an
invitation for the other lawyer to object during your closing,
thus ruining the flow of your narrative. But Marlinga couldn't
wait any longer. Kaplan's argument ran counter to the whole
setup of the judicial system, he thought. It's not the defense
lawyer's job to prove innocence, he whispered to Judge Biernat; it's the prosecution's job to prove guilt.

Biernat quietly nodded and sent the lawyers back to their
seats.

"Ladies and gentlemen," he said to the jury, choosing his
words carefully so as not to call Kaplan out too strongly. "I
want you to fully understand that irrespective of what either
of these attorneys say, the burden of proof remains always
with the prosecution. If something is said here that implies
to you that the burden is shifted to the defense to present
evidence, you're to remember my instructions."

Jurors nodded that they understood. It was Kaplan's turn
to talk again.

"Greed, sex, and power," he began, his voice forceful as he tried to regain momentum. "Those are your defendant's—this defendant's—motivation. The greed is the money that we'll discuss later, and then the power—the power being he takes over the business alone, he has the children, Barb's out of the way."

The juror didn't need much explanation when it came to the sex. They'd already heard about the disparaging comments Michael had made about his wife, the snide remarks about her weight and the way she wore ankle-length nightgowns. They remembered how he creeped out his brother-in-law's girlfriend and intimately hugged a woman just feet from his wife's dead body at the funeral. And while they never heard Renee Kotula speak, they knew damn well that she was the woman with the dark hair who'd sat behind Michael throughout the trial—the same woman with whom he'd had an affair, been spotted kissing just weeks after his wife died, and married within two years.

Michael George had motive. Jurors had decided that within the first day of the case. But they'd listened to Judge Biernat and seen enough court shows on TV to know that motive wasn't enough. This case, based entirely on circumstantial evidence, came down to the timeline more than anything. And that was the element Kaplan intended to drive home. Michael George had said he left the store sometime around 4:15 p.m. Matt Baczewski had testified that Barbara George arrived just before then, around 4 p.m., with her daughters, tag-teamed with her husband, and Michael left with the kids soon after. That seemed undisputed. But then there was Michael Renaud's testimony.

He was the man in the wheelchair, the one whose calls to police went ignored for nearly twenty years. So much depended on Michael Renaud.

"Both attorneys examined Mike Renaud for a long time and it was obvious to the thirteen of you why that was occurring," Kaplan said. "Because his testimony is important placing the defendant at the store at a time when defendant claims not to be at the store, because when defendant was interviewed by the police, he says, 'I left and I came back at 8:10.' Doesn't say anything about returning a second time and then going home again.

"What time did Mike Renaud place that phone call? You know there are no phone records—phone records were not available then and are not available now for a call from Sterling Heights here in Clinton Township. But consider what Mike Renaud did initially. He calls the police on the fourteenth of July because to him this was important, he had some information considering somebody he likes. He's not an adversary of Mike George. He's not a nemesis. He has no axes to grind, and he calls and he says, 'I talked to him between six and six-fifteen and he seemed to be in a hurry.'

"Mike Renaud then calls back a few minutes later. He says, 'I thought about it and it was closer to five-thirty,' and that's what his view was on July the fourteenth."

Eighteen years later, testifying at trial, Renaud held tight to that second time estimate. He'd spent time, back in 1990, to double-check what he'd originally told police by looking at his coworker's time card. He was sure he called sometime between 5:15 and 5:45 p.m., with 5:30 being as close to accurate as he thinks he can get, Kaplan said.

"The next time that's important is when was Barbara murdered," the lawyer continued. "Do we know for sure? No, but we can eliminate some times. We know that nine-one-one was called at six twenty-two p.m. We know that the youngsters had been in the store about ten minutes before her body was found. We know that Barb George is on the phone with Renee Smith Balsick at about six o'clock. So when was she murdered? Sometime after she's off the phone with Renee Smith Balsick and when the youngsters arrive at the store. But it has to be before the youngsters arrive at the store because they would have heard gunshots, and they didn't. So the best time that she was shot, most accurate time, is 6:05 but it could be 6:03, it could be 6:07."

The point, Kaplan said: Michael George should not have been at the store at 5:30. He'd left about 4:15 and told police he didn't return until eight-ish, when he pulled up and saw the police tape, the squad cars, the crime scene. If he was being honest, how could Mike Renaud talk to him some thirty to forty-five minutes after he said he'd left? And if Michael George was lying about that, what else was he lying about?

"There could be only one explanation as to why he was at that store at five-thirty," Kaplan said. "Because he came back to the store after dropping the children off at his mother's house, deciding to kill Barbara George, and laying for the right moment."

That moment came at about 6:05, Kaplan said.

Renee George shook her head. What about the man in the fisherman's cap? she thought. Where's the murder weapon? How could a jury convict her husband without any physical evidence?

Kaplan acknowledged this: "There's no eyewitness to this crime. There's no video cameras to the crime. There's no physical evidence left by the killer," he said. "That means the killer was careful enough to dispose of the gun and not leave physical evidence behind."

Kaplan predicted the defense's arguments and preemptively dismissed them as garbage. A man in a fisherman's cap? Someone wearing a fake beard and mustache? None of it made sense, he said. Then there was this business of so-called Wally Last Name Unknown.

"Is his last name really unknown? He's a pallbearer at the funeral," he scoffed. "Who knows him? Is there any evidence in this case that Wally, last name unknown, had some resentment against Barbara George? In fact, the testimony in the case is that he's a friend of the defendant and he and the defendant engaged in transactions together, so how he becomes the killer one doesn't know."

Robbery-homicide? More garbage, Kaplan said. Why would a robber leave behind Barb's jewelry, including a $2,500 ring, and $420 in her pockets? And the robber didn't disturb anything in the front of the store, so far as anyone could testify to. It didn't help, either, that Michael George supposedly told Theresa Danieluk—the woman to whom he passed a flirty note saying how pretty she looked shortly after the murder—that nothing was taken from the store.

"Those were his words," Kaplan said. "It's not a robbery because the defendant says it's not a robbery."

Then there was the life insurance policy. Michael George in 1990 cleared $130,000, tax-free. "And $130,000 in 1990 obviously is worth much more now. . . . That's ready cash."

Kaplan brought forth a poster board as a visual aid, which he propped on an easel in front of jurors. Marlinga craned his neck to get a glimpse but couldn't. The back of the poster board faced Judge Biernat. Kaplan explained that individually, the circumstantial evidence was simply individual chunks of random information, the edges of each piece jagged and nonsensical. But when brought together, he said, the information became pieces of a puzzle—a puzzle with twenty pieces.

He began to count them down: the affairs, the insurance money, the constant flirting, the strange comment he made to cops about something falling on Barb in the back room. He refused to look at his wife's body to identify her for doctors. He too quickly dismissed the idea that his lover Renee's husband could have been the killer. He wore sunglasses to the funeral.

With each piece of information, Kaplan uncovered a piece of the puzzle. Slowly, beneath the irregular pieces, a picture of Michael George wearing a black shirt began to appear. He reached evidentiary piece thirteen: the lack of cooperation in the investigation.

"One of the first questions posed to him by Sergeant Steckman is, 'How is your marriage? Were you having an affair?' 'No, not me, no affair.' Why does he lie to the police? Now, he was pretty open at the store about his affection for Renee, but a sergeant investigating a murder wants to know about his marital status and what does he say? 'Oh, no affair.' Why does he lie?"

Just then, the puzzle fell off the easel. Judge Biernat caught his first glimpse of the photograph of Michael George that had begun to appear. He beckoned the lawyers to the bench, quietly admonished Kaplan, again not wanting to distract jurors too much by calling his use of the picture into question in open court. The damage already had been done: That picture had not been entered into evidence and Marlinga had immediately regarded it as a mug shot. All those days of making sure that jurors never saw his client in jail garb were tossed out the window. The point had been to ensure they didn't automatically view him as a criminal, that they saw him as a person first.

On the record, Judge Biernat simply said: "Please put that to the side. Let's carry on."

Kaplan didn't argue. The visual aid had perhaps been a little hokey anyway. No need to push further. Kaplan continued at the point where he'd left off, asking again why an innocent man would lie about having an affair.

"Because if the police know he's having an affair, they're going to look at him harder," he said.

"Is that evidence consistent with a non-murdering spouse?"

Kaplan rested. Marlinga, still upset by the puzzle-piece photograph, geared up to make his own argument. But first he had to get something off his chest and on the record.

For seventeen minutes, Marlinga stewed over the photograph. When the judge returned to the bench, he asked to speak before jurors were allowed back into the courtroom.

"Mr. Kaplan in his closing argument used a photograph of Michael George very dramatically," he said. "However, I believe that it was in error. This photograph was not marked into evidence. It shows Mr. Michael George in a mug shot in jail garb, highly contrary to the law. I believe we have grounds for a mistrial."

Kaplan stayed seated. Did he deserve admonishment? Maybe. He knew it was a questionable move to bring the photo in, but he also didn't think it was an improper one. Judge Biernat was prepared for Marlinga's comments. The court was partly to blame, he said, because one of his own bailiffs was requested to help with the visual aid.

"I had no idea what was being put up until it became evident at the very end," Biernat said. "Let me see that."

He eyed the photograph.

"I'm not sure that that's a mug shot, although it looks like a mug shot."

Marlinga acknowledged he didn't know for sure whether it was a mug shot, but, he added, "Normally, attorneys can bring in demonstrative evidence, but the picture of the defendant is in a non-flattering light when it's a mug shot. I think it crossed the line."

Kaplan asked to respond.

"This is what attorneys can do in closing argument," he said. "I can create a puzzle of a photograph of Mike George, which was relatively recent in time. . . . I'm not the first attorney in the world to use a puzzle in closing arguments. I wish I could say I created the idea."

Biernat was not impressed. Kaplan should have shown him the photo, he said. He might not have precluded it—but, then again, he might have. Whatever damage had been done would be impossible to fix. But he wasn't going to order a mistrial. Instead, he ordered the photograph not be shown again. "That would just aggravate the situation, and it would be unnecessary," he concluded.

Marlinga wasn't satisfied, but he thanked the judge anyway. Now it was time to focus on his own closing argument. He skipped the Sherlock Holmes reference and hopped instead to the board game Clue, which, he said, he finds "God-awful."

"Murder should not be entertainment. It is not fun. It is not a game," he said.

But with games like Clue, it all comes down to motive, he acknowledged, and that's what most people look at when trying to decide who committed a crime. It's a dangerous game based on process of elimination that has little to do with actual evidence, he said.

"That is no way to try to solve a crime."

His point was simple: Michael George might have been a cheater, but that didn't automatically make him a killer. And if it did, it could be assumed that tons of men—from former President Bill Clinton to Prince Charles to Michigan Attorney General Mike Cox—are just as likely to kill their wives.

"The common thread, of course, is that all of these people had a history of infidelity and adultery. While immoral and the cause of a lot of heartbreak, it does not incline a person to violence," Marlinga said. "So in terms of motive, this is meant to be inflammatory, it's meant to get you upset with him, it's meant to make you want to hate him and condemn him, but the fact of the matter is that when all is said and done, you can condemn what he did, but you cannot use that as an inferential leaping—a stepping stone—to say that he would be guilty of murder. Because if he were, if that really is a motive for murder, there would be a lot more dead people in this world."

Marlinga faulted Kaplan's arguments further. Michael George didn't cry at the funeral? "Everybody reacts differently to grief," he said, then added that funeral director Jeff Mandziuk, who had seen his share of grieving people did see George crying and shaking as he made funeral arrangements.

Michael George and his family didn't buy grave blankets for the cemetery? "Maybe they don't pay the outrageous rates that the cemetery charges to try to buy to put a grave blanket on, but they visit that grave," he said. "You can't measure grief by what somebody does at a cemetery grave afterwards."

But all of those arguments were lightweight in Marlinga's

mind. The real component he needed to undermine was the timeline—especially that phone call that Mike Renaud said he placed around 5:30 p.m. That was the one element in Kaplan's case that he knew would likely give jurors pause. Why was Michael George at the store answering the phone during the time frame he told police he was at his mother's house some 30 minutes away?

His response: Mike Renaud's time was imprecise. He'd called once to recant and fix it. He'd supposedly based his qualified time estimate on a coworker's time card, but police had never bothered to retrieve the card or interview that coworker. It was shoddy police work, he argued, and with Renaud unable to provide concrete proof that he called when he said he did, it wasn't enough to convict a man of murder.

Besides, he added, Kaplan's theory was absurd in another way: Why would a man supposedly lying in wait for his wife answer the phone anyway?

"This is mind-boggling," Marlinga said. "According to the prosecution's theory, he's back there lying in wait, not wanting to be discovered and so suddenly the phone rings and he says, 'Oh, this might be a comic book sale, I better answer the phone.'"

Marlinga scoffed at Kaplan's premise.

"He's talking about him lying there, nervous and sweating, and the phone rings and suddenly he decides to answer it to show that he's at the store, to be out in a visible area so that if Barb comes back at any time, he will be seen. It's so illogically connected, it is so contrary to the rest of the prosecution's theory, that it is not plausible."

As for Renaud, he might believe he made the phone call when he did, but that doesn't mean he's right, said Marlinga. And because the burden of proof lies with the prosecution, "that really doesn't bother me that much," he added. Still, Renaud could have remembered that all-too-important 4:53 p.m. time-card punch incorrectly. "It could be 3:53, it could be 2:53, it could be a different day," he said. But "going with

4:53, I'm going to suggest to you that 4:59, give or take a couple of minutes, is the most likely time for the Michael Renaud call to come in."

He based that, he said, on the benchmark Renaud used and on the length of time a quick chat with a coworker would likely take. And after 5 p.m., defense witnesses' testimony created their own puzzle pointing away from Michael George: Joe Gray leaves Comics World at 5:30 p.m., having not seen George there. Janet George gets a phone call about the same time from Barbara George warning of Michael's imminent arrival with the children. Peggy Marentette sees the girls walking with Grandma, as well as Michael George's van in the Hazel Park driveway, at nearly 6 p.m. About the same time, Renee Balsick Smith speaks with Barb on the phone and doesn't hear a voice that she recognizes as Michael's. Fred Hodgson and Joe Gray see a person at 6 to 6:05 p.m. that strikes them as so suspicious, they go to employees at the Hungry Howie's pizza joint and warn them that someone might be planning a holdup. Then, at about 6:10 p.m., Barb George is shot dead.

Next are those two mystery people—the slight man or woman in the fake beard and Wally Last Name Unknown. Maybe they killed Barb, maybe they didn't, Marlinga said. But they should be considered more likely murder suspects than Michael George, who had an alibi.

This led to Marlinga's final point: Police investigating Barb George's murder did a half-assed job, failing to test Michael George's hands for gunpowder, to check his car or home for a weapon, to identify and question this Wally person. Nor did police canvass Janet George's neighborhood or pull Secretary of State records to find who owned what type of car in 1990—a tidbit that would prove useful in matching up testimony about a suspicious-looking Monte Carlo. Kaplan's evidence about knowledge of where Barb was when she was hurt—in Clue terms, in the back room with a fallen box—was useless, Marlinga continued. There's no way that eighteen years later someone can positively say they didn't murmur that she'd been found in the back, unconscious. And if it truly had seemed so suspicious back in 1990, why didn't police work harder to prove their suspicion then?

"There's no physical evidence that alone could be looked at as reasonable doubt," said Marlinga, prompting Kaplan to interrupt. It was slippery for a lawyer to try to tell jurors what reasonable doubt actually means. That's usually left up to judges, Kaplan argued.

The judge reminded jurors to listen to his instructions, not Marlinga's interpretation, so the defense lawyer continued.

"After you listen to the judge's definition of reasonable doubt, this is what I would ask you to keep in mind as my argument of how to apply that," he said. "If you believe that Michael George is innocent, then your verdict of course must be, it should be, not guilty. But if you think that maybe Michael George is guilty, your verdict is still not guilty. If you think that he is possibly guilty, your verdict is still not guilty. If you think that he is probably guilty, your verdict is not guilty. If you are almost certain but still hesitant that he is guilty, your verdict is not guilty."

"Objection," Kaplan barked. "That's not the standard. It's incorrect law."

Judge Biernat nodded: "And I remind the jury of that then."

Marlinga wrapped up, thanking jurors for their attention.

"Nothing will probably be ever more important again in your entire life, at least in terms of what you will do for other persons," he said. "I don't envy the hard work that you have to put in now. Thank you very much."

Kaplan's rebuttal largely was repetitive. He'd made his point and, he felt, had Marlinga on the run. But he got to get a personally satisfying jab in against George:

"A comment was made about why would he be stupid enough to answer the phone," Kaplan said. "Well, the prisons are full of people who do stupid things."

Beyond that, he merely hammered away at the timeline defense. Arguing Renaud's timeline was "very good lawyering on the other side," he said. "If counsel can move that back to five o'clock, it helps his case immeasurably because it means another thirty minutes is added onto the window of opportunity for the defendant to commit the crime. Who knows best when Mike Renaud made that phone call? Mike Renaud."

And then Kaplan moved on to another rebuttal, paraphrasing Sergeant Steckman's testimony.

"Remember, Sergeant Steckman contacts the defendant soon after the murder: 'Good news. One of the comics that you reported to be stolen, we've recovered it but we recovered it at a place where it wasn't stolen. It was some guy selling it and he had the right to sell it.' And what does the defendant say? 'Oh, oh, I made a mistake. I made a mistake. That's not one of the comics that was stolen.'"

Marlinga took note. He didn't think that's what Steckman had said in his testimony, but, without transcripts to thumb through, he couldn't know for sure.

Kaplan's tone was flip. The whole stolen comics story had holes, he said. The bottom line? "Divorce could be ugly. It's cheaper to kill the wife."

Chapter 33

The Verdict

Jurors listened patiently as Biernat read them instructions. Then, they filed into the back room, where they would begin the daunting task of deciding a man's fate. Because Michael was out on bond, he had a luxury not afforded to most murder suspects: He could sit with his family, hold his wife's hand and get supportive hugs from his daughters while he waited to learn the jury's decision.

Kaplan, completely deflated the night before, got a new jolt post-closing: The producer who had filled him with doubt approached again, this time to apologize.

"Steve, you turned it," he said.

But Kosmala and Marlinga were equally confident. They had been bolstered by Biernat's five-hour delay in deciding whether to issue a directed verdict after the prosecution rested. That kind of delay could only bode well for the defense, they figured, because it meant that the judge had agonized over determining whether the evidence was too flimsy to even move forward. Surely, that meant there was plenty of room for reasonable doubt.

Marlinga and his wife, Barbara, had longstanding plans to go to the Caribbean that weekend. The deposits had been made and the plans were solid—the couple was even meeting up with other couples for a relaxing, beach-filled retreat—so Marlinga decided that if the deliberations went past the weekend, he would leave Kosmala in charge. It wasn't ideal, but Marlinga had peace to keep on the home front, not to mention his own sanity to hold together.

The most seasoned lawyers always say it's useless to try to read the jurors' minds—and then they try to anyway. It's inevitable: Every time the jury makes a request to see more evidence or to read transcripts from a witness's testimony, the legal minds involved weigh out what that request might mean. In the George case, jurors wanted to rehear testimony of three witnesses: Matt Baczewski, who said Michael left the store soon after 4 p.m.; Sergeant Donald Steckman, the original officer in charge; and Lieutenant Donald Brook, who had testified about that odd comment Michael allegedly made about a box falling on his wife's head in the back room. They also wanted to listen again to the August 3, 2007, interview with George that investigators had conducted in Windber.

Kaplan told Lieutenant Keith they had won the case. Keith wasn't reassured. He didn't even put the odds at a true 50/50.

Friday evening hit and, not surprisingly, the jurors hadn't reached a decision. It would be a long weekend for everyone involved. Marlinga clasped George's hand as he said good-bye and assured him Kosmala would be by his side after the weekend.

The jurors returned Monday morning and reconvened in the stuffy jury room down the hall from Biernat's chambers. No one knew what was happening behind the closed doors. Reporters milled in and out of the courtroom, checking in with Kosmala and Kaplan and making friendly chitchat with secretaries in hopes of getting the all-important heads-up when the jury announced it was ready. Everyone had seemed to have given up hope for a Day 2 verdict around 5 p.m. when word began to spread: The jury had decided.

Family members from both sides rushed into the courtroom, followed by reporters. Michael George sat next to Kosmala and shot a smile back at Renee, who sat next to Michelle a few rows behind him. Renee nervously smiled back. Daughter Tracie had decided not to sit in on the verdict. If the jury found her father guilty, she didn't want to land in jail herself with her reaction, she had told her stepmother.

Biernat entered the courtroom, prompting the seated crowd to rise. He knew the case was as emotional as they come, he told the court, but he warned against any emotional outbursts. A minute later, the jury followed, taking their seats in the jury box to Biernat's left. A man who appeared to be in his forties identified himself as the foreperson.

Peter and Joe Kowynia exchanged nervous looks. "Is your heart beating fast?" Peter asked his brother. Joe nodded. "Yeah, it is," he said. "This is it."

"Have you reached a verdict?" the judge asked.

The jury nodded and the foreman, his voice steady, read the verdict:

"Count number one, first-degree murder, we find the defendant guilty."

Christine Ball, Barb's sister, started in shock. Renee George bowed her head. Michelle immediately slumped forward, face buried in her hands, sobbing. But no one reacted more visibly than Michael George himself, who immediately collapsed into Kosmala's arms as he wailed.

"I didn't do this!" he sobbed, his face on Kosmala's shoulder. The grizzled lawyer looked dumbfounded. He helped George walk to the podium to receive his sentencing date, still bawling.

Lieutenant Keith watched George's breakdown without sympathy. To him, it was too little, too late: George had been untouchable, detached when his wife died. Now that her murder was pinned on him, he finally had tears to shed. Eric Smith wasn't there for the verdict, leaving the matter in Kaplan's hands. From the courtroom, a reporter shot Smith a text message that read simply: George guilty 1st. The shocked prosecutor read the news and began to holler in his office.

Often, lawyers from both sides meet with jurors to discuss what worked and what didn't during trial. Kosmala couldn't stomach the prospect. He walked out of the courtroom and angrily faced reporters.

"I've never second-guessed a jury, but I'm doing it today," he said. "There was zero, zip, nada evidence. It's outrageous."

Renee gently placed a hand on Michelle's back as her stepdaughter shook with tears. She had barely even contemplated that as a possible outcome. She'd been anxious, but still certain the jury would acquit Michael. She was so sure that she'd had a neighborhood business back in Windber make a sign she could put on her van. "Innocent," it read. She planned to circle the courthouse with Michael in the passenger seat, the sign serving as a triumphant "I told you so."

Now, she thought of the sign and it seemed to mock her from the back seat of her van. There would be no victory lap. Michael had been convicted of murder. Worse yet, he was convicted on their sixteenth wedding anniversary—March 17, 2008.

"I woke up thinking it was going to be a lucky day for us," Renee said later. "I never use the word 'luck' anymore."

Michael's reaction was haunting. She could still hear him wailing down the hallway, crying and proclaiming his innocence. She held it together for his sake and for Michelle's. The family somberly piled into the van and Renee started making the obligatory phone calls to family and friends. She wanted them to hear the news from her, not the media.

"The jury did not get it," she said to each, matter-of-factly. "They found him guilty. We are going for an appeal. It could take two more years."

Marlinga and Kosmala had told her that the likelihood of him getting a new trial was slim. Judge Biernat had already shot down one attempt for a directed verdict. Clearly, he'd thought the jury had enough evidence to make up their own minds, and they'd come back with a guilty verdict. People don't tend to get second chances when it comes to trials. They might win an appeal, but rarely are they afforded a new trial straight out.

Renee felt like she was being held under water. Everything moved in slow motion, and she found it hard to breathe. She kept a strong front for Tracie and Michelle, and told them each time they spoke that they were still fighting, that it wasn't over, that they'd win in the end. She didn't give herself the option of questioning whether what she said was actually true. It just had to be that way.

Justin Kotula, her poker-dealing son who attended much of the trial, met with Carl alone to discuss what he thought were the pros and cons of the case. Justin had invested himself as though he were Michael's biological son. At just 26, he was protective of the girls and the family as a whole, even kiboshing *Dateline*'s efforts to interview Michael during the trial for the news piece they were planning. Michael and Marlinga had OK'd the interview; Justin was concerned his stepfather's words would get twisted. The interview was nixed.

Marlinga and Kosmala had asked for another directed verdict after they rested their case, a decision Biernat held off making for several weeks. Finally, on Friday, May 23, he denied the request. The *Detroit Free Press* ran an explainer story the next day:

It came down to a phone call.

Michael George hurriedly answered the phone in his Clinton Township comic book store sometime between 5:15 and 5:45 p.m. the night his wife was killed 18 years ago—and that, a judge ruled Friday, means he lied about his alibi, an indication George had a guilty conscience.

That was part of the rationale behind Macomb

County Circuit Judge James Biernat's ruling to uphold
a jury's first-degree murder conviction in the case
against George, 47.

George was convicted in March of shooting his wife,
32-year-old Barbara George, in the head in the back of
their comic book store.

Assistant Prosecutor Steve Kaplan's case was circumstantial. There were no eyewitnesses to the crime
and the murder weapon was never found. But friends
and family members testified that Michael George
was a philanderer who wanted out of his marriage and
walked away with $130,000 in life insurance money.

George was having an affair with one of his employees, whom he later married.

George has maintained he went to his mother's
house at about 4:30 p.m. and didn't return to the store
until after 8 p.m. A neighbor testified that she saw his
car outside the Hazel Park home about the time Barbara George was shot.

But, Biernat said, a customer's testimony that Michael George answered the phone an hour after he said
he had left "demonstrates the alibi to be false."

George's stepson began shaking his head halfway
through the judge's comments—about the same time
defense lawyer Carl Marlinga leaned over to his client
and whispered: "It's over."

"I simply think his decision was wrong based on
the law," a clearly disappointed Marlinga said after the
ruling. "We disagree."

Cocounsel Joe Kosmala added: "Respectfully, but
strongly."

Marlinga and Kosmala asked the judge to overturn the
jury's conviction before George received a mandatory life
sentence. Such rulings are rare.

The two said they will file a motion for a new trial. George is to be sentenced June 20.

Biernat said he made his ruling with misgivings. Because of the time lapse, some evidence was no longer available.

"The court has no other choice but to do its duty and deny this request," Biernat said.

Barbara George's family celebrated after the decision.

"Justice has restored my life," her sister Christine Ball said in a shaky voice.

The only dark side to the conviction, she said, was the rift it has caused with her nieces. The Georges have two daughters, both of whom testified in their father's defense.

"I'm sure their life has been torn apart," Ball said. "I'm going to give them time."

Chapter 34

Dateline *Episode*

George's case had made national headlines in smatterings, but come Friday, May 9, it reached a far broader audience when *Dateline* dedicated a two-hour special to the case. They labeled it a real-life mystery in a comic book store. Host Ann Curry said the case ended with the discovery of a long-lost clue: "If you lose something, say like your car keys, maybe the worst thing that happens is you need to walk. But what happens when police lose track of a critical clue in a murder investigation?" The episode had been long in the making; producer Fred Rothenberg first staked out District Judge Linda Davis's courtroom during the preliminary exam in October. Most of the interviews for the show had been conducted post-trial, however, and—thanks to Biernat's approval of cameras in the courtroom—*Dateline* used footage from the trial to flesh out the story.

Dennis Murphy was the reporter, playing up the visuals that the comic book setting lent: "In the front of the mom-and-pop comic book shop were bins of the fantasies, Spidey, Hulk, X-Men. In the storage space in back was the ugly reality. One of the shop owners, the woman on the floor, ominously still. No superhero had come to her aid, just some customers, regulars."

Tom and Lenora Ward found themselves key players in the show, describing the fateful July night when they stopped by to peruse some comics. The amateur sleuthing efforts of Joe Kowynia and his former girlfriend, Mary Shamo, were also highlighted. Kowynia described his early suspicions, and, with the finality of a conviction lending credibility to his certainty of Michael's guilt, he spoke publicly with more certainty than he ever had before. "I believe he planned out the whole thing," he told Murphy. He also admitted that vigilante justice had crossed his mind. "There was times I felt, you know, that I should do something. But, you know, I'm a Catholic, I couldn't live with it. I don't know how he does it."

Few people spoke to *Dateline* on George's behalf. Renee had warned friends and family back in Windber that the TV show would be in town, and she sent word that she and Michael didn't want to cooperate. Still, the crew found Jeff Lively, who ran an electrical supply shop three blocks from the Georges' store, to offer a positive take on George as a man now known for his philanthropy, not his philandering.

"His life was for the kids," Lively said, "and I'd have to say his life was for Renee. He treated her like gold."

Like Kowynia, Eric Smith felt more comfortable being candid with the verdict rendered. He described his relationship with his late father to Murphy and acknowledged that although he never pushed for the George case to be reopened, he had hoped Clinton Township would tackle the case when they learned of the prosecutor's new cold case unit.

"I did it with Michael George in mind," he said. "There's no question in my mind that at the time, while I was hoping that we'd get a lot of cases, I was hoping Clinton Township would pick this case up."

"And maybe resolve one for the old man?" Murphy asked.

Eric laughed. "That's it. That's it. That was the case that was unsolved for my old man, for my dad."

Those familiar with the case watched the *Dateline* episode

intently. Macomb County crime had been featured in a few national programs in recent years—including another *Dateline* episode just a few months prior that highlighted a case in which police discovered a missing woman's torso in the home she shared with her husband and two children—but overall, it still was a rarity.

Of course, not everyone was happy with the episode. The *Dateline* cameras captured foggy images of a sleepy Windber, calling it a "played-out coal mining town with more in common with Appalachia than greater Pittsburgh." Windber residents winced at the backwoods portrayal. Murphy interviewed jurors, too, and they openly slammed the 1990 police work. "Clinton Township should be just totally ashamed of what they did," jury foreman Garry Kuzikoski said.

While Marlinga had interviewed with Murphy, offering the defense's take on the case, he shuddered at the thought of the piece airing and re-airing as he prepared to ask Biernat to set aside the jury's verdict. If Biernat turned down that request, there were still years of appellate limbo that inevitably lay ahead.

"I'm hoping for a sequel," Marlinga later said.

Chapter 35

"My Dad Is My Life"

Michael George appeared for sentencing June 20, 2008. In first-degree murder convictions, there is no wiggle room, no cause for shocked headlines at the judge's imposed sentencing in Michigan. The punishment is mandated: life behind bars, period. But sentencings prove newsworthy for another reason: It's often the first chance the victims have to put their thoughts on the record, as well as the last chance for the defendant to either proclaim his innocence or, in cases so rare you figure there must be a chill breeze wafting through hell, 'fess up and apologize.

Michael's daughters, Tracie and Michelle, decided to speak out. They were walking a tightrope, balancing between their love and respect for their mother and their belief that their father, whom they adored, was innocent. Aside from testifying, they'd been quiet since his arrest. They wrote their statements privately, intentionally not sharing them with Renee and Justin before reading them to the court. They wanted the words and thoughts to be their own, uninfluenced by the side of the family that some felt had brainwashed them.

Tracie approached the podium, standing before Biernat and a hushed courtroom packed with family and media. She thanked the court for letting her speak, then began.

"I think it's a fair thing to say that nobody in this room or building has to go through what my sister and I have to, and if you want to look at victims, I think we're definitely the prime ones here," she said. "When people think of family, a lot of people think of a group, but in our case, to my sister and I, our father is our family. We have not really had a lot of contact with our other family members and, you know, I'm not here to challenge that integrity. However, it has given our father more ability to shine not only as a father, an uncle, an aunt, a grandma, a grandpa—and not only to my sister and I, but to five other siblings—and my dad's accomplished many things. . . .

"I recently graduated with two degrees," she continued, "and my sister is going to graduate with two degrees, and multiple siblings are all-state sports players and I know without my father's support, none of this could have happened."

Everything her father had ever done was for his girls, she said.

"It's not about choosing sides, because it's my mother and my father and she's fifty percent of me, and I've never forgotten that," Tracie said. "My mother died physically, but I feel that she has always lived in my father."

Awkwardly, Tracie finished: "That's all I want to say, and I support my dad a hundred percent."

She sat down, and Michelle stood up. The younger of the two, Michelle looked the most like Barb with her rounded face and red hair. She couldn't remember her mother, but she cherished her pictures and loved her nonetheless, she told Biernat. What she did remember, however, was her father constantly at her side, cheering her at basketball games and supporting her through college.

"Being the proud father that he is, he never once doubted that I could do something," she told the court. "He would tell me, 'If that's what you really want to do, you know all the hard work you have to do to accomplish it, but I know you can do it,' and he hugged me every time. He never put limits on my dreams," she said.

It was his dream, in turn, to see his two girls graduate from college, but the trial denied him that, she said. Tracie graduated that year, and Michelle was in her last year, too, so her father would be imprisoned, unable to attend the ceremony, to watch her snap up the diploma in black robe and cap. It was tough already when he missed Tracie's graduation, she said. It marked the first major event that Michael didn't attend in either girl's life.

"My dad is my life," Michelle said. "I never wanted to think what I would do without him. I would talk to my dad at least every other day, whether it was just seeing how class went today or asking how practice went the other night or even just to say, 'Hi, honey, I miss you and love you.' Now I only get to talk to my dad once or twice a week. It is something so little that I will never get used to.

"First, my mother was taken away from me as a child, and now my father is being taken away from me."

The gravity of the statement hit the quiet courtroom. Here were two girls, essentially orphaned, regardless of how it came to be. Either Michael deprived them of both parents by killing their mother and putting himself at risk for a lifetime behind bars, or a cruel system piled onto an already cruel twist of fate, stealing their father after some other killer stole their mother. Michelle and Tracie were convinced it was the latter, and not only because he'd been supportive and loving through the years.

"He hated weapons, period," she said. "He has always hated guns. He would never hold or shoot one at a place."

She recalled that as a child, her grandfather, a hunter, had visited one year, excited to hit the Pennsylvania forests for game. Michael wouldn't allow him to keep his hunting gun in the house.

"He truly hates guns," Michelle said. "There is no way my dad could have committed this crime."

Michael always instilled in his daughters a never-quit attitude, and so she wouldn't, Michelle promised. The girls would fight until his release.

Almost as a rebuttal, Barb's sister Christine Ball and brother, Joe Kowynia, stood to speak next. They had waited eighteen long years to see Michael convicted of killing their sister. They blamed him not only for her death, but also for driving a wedge between them and the girls. They were never comfortable talking with him before, and their relationship with their nieces was a casualty of the nausea and fury they felt whenever they considered picking up the phone to check in and say hi. Now, any hope they had to rekindle that relationship was dead. The girls believed he was innocent; how could they ever embrace a family that helped send him to prison?

"Mike, you cheated my sister, myself, and my family, and most of all—*but* most of all," she corrected, "you cheated Barb's girls. You could never replace a mother's love. . . . The way you destroyed our lives is just brutal, brutal. Through the trial I learned you were looking for something new and different. I believe you found it."

Joe asked the question that haunts every family member of every murder victim: Why?

"You should have walked away," he said. "You were thirty years old, you should have walked away. You could have started a new life. Instead, you chose to cheat on my sister, have affairs, and do things your way. Well, it didn't work."

He accused Michael of turning the girls against him. They never once tried to speak to their maternal family, he said, even though they'd sat just feet away in the courtroom during the weeks-long trial.

"Why, Mike?" he asked. "You have turned this blame on us. For some reason, you have made them feel that it's our fault. Why? I have no idea. Now they know the truth. They know what kind of bad father you are. Look what they're going through. I hope that burns in your head."

Joe had long been the unofficial family spokesman, and he hated it. His voice thick with sarcasm, he thanked Michael for the post.

"I have to be on the news because of you for something like this. . . . Our nieces have no mom and now they lost their dad. Thank you. I appreciate what you've done and I'm sure they appreciate that, too, and maybe some day they can come to us and have some kind of family life. You take them away for seventeen years. We see them maybe once a year. You wouldn't even come by. Why? Why were you so scared? I think we found out why."

Before Biernat imposed the mandatory sentence, he asked if Michael George had anything to say.

"Yes, Your Honor."

"You may proceed."

Reporters put pens to pad and began furiously scribbling. The TV cameramen that had largely been on autopilot sprung to life, their eyes pressed firmly against their viewfinders. The *click-click-click* of still photographers' cameras filled the courtroom. Michael George had been plenty animated during the trial—shaking his head, scoffing at questions, at times even laughing—but he had never before spoken. He began by playing to the judge, complimenting him for giving him as fair a trial as possible—"In the middle of a media storm I know how difficult it is for you"—then saying he empathized with someone bound to send an innocent man to prison.

"Please don't let it waver on your heart," he said sympathetically. "You're only following the laws of this state."

Then he set about declaring his innocence.

"Eighteen years ago, my daughters lost a mother, I lost a wife and, eighteen years later, my daughters will have no father, not because of the truth, but because of the exact opposite," he said, his voice heavy. "I have from day one—from day one, Your Honor—said the Lord knows I could never, ever do this to anyone, much less my wife. . . . I've read the more trials and tribulations the Lord puts you through, the more he loves you. Your Honor, he loves me a great deal."

To his family, he sent love and thanks. To his lawyers, he sent undying gratitude. To his supporters, he sent out hope.

"I received a letter last night, Your Honor," he said. "The envelope is dated the 17th from a man I don't remember. . . . 'Mike, I'm not sure if you will remember me. I was a member of your comic club back in the late '80s and early '90s when I was in high school,'" the letter read. "'I used to come in the store and buy everything you had with Bo Jackson on it. He was my idol. I also used to sell comics to you from time to time. I often wondered what happened to you after you closed the store on Hayes. I got my answer after reading the *Macomb Daily* article about Smith bringing charges against you. I have been following your case ever since. I prayed for you and your family from the time I first read of the charges through the announcement of the verdict. I was deeply shocked and saddened to read that the jury returned a guilty verdict. I do not believe the jury got it right. I do not believe, nor did I ever believe, that you did it. I really wanted you to know this.'"

After Michael finished the letter, he paused, and then looked back at the judge.

"Your Honor, I receive letters like this every week. Sometimes I don't even know the people. The people that have known me all my life know I could never do this."

Finally, Michael directed his attention to whoever did kill his wife.

"I will be going to prison for the rest of my life for your crime," he said, "but no one—and I repeat, no one—will ever take my heart, soul, or mind from the Lord and Savior

Jesus Christ. Your Honor, I want to thank you for your indulgence."

The rest of the sentencing was routine: sign this, do you understand that, a new date set for the obligatory motion for a new trial. Bottom line: Michael would spend the rest of his life in prison. Court was adjourned.

Chapter 36

Verdict Reconsidered

Michael George shuffled into the courtroom, his hands and feet shackled and his eyes cast to the floor. He had reverted to the jail-issued jumpsuit that he'd been able to leave behind throughout his trial, during which he sported the suit and tie that allowed jurors to see him as a man first and a criminal defendant second.

But the clothing wasn't all that had changed. Gone were the smirks, the defiant head shakes, the eye rolls and the questionable tears that George had shown during the trial. This time, he walked into the courtroom as a man convicted of first-degree murder, and he wore his new label—"convicted killer"—across his face. His eyes met briefly with his wife, Renee, and she forced a hopeful smile. This hearing would decide whether Judge Biernat's obvious misgivings during the trial would lead him to grant the defense's last-ditch effort to spare George the life sentence and face trial again. The judge already had turned down two requests for directed verdicts, and judges rarely grant new trials once a jury has spoken. This hearing largely was perfunctory, Renee knew. Still, she smiled at her husband.

The hearing was supposed to begin at 8:30 a.m. Biernat was late again. The courtroom slowly filled with family

members and friends from both sides—Barbara's brothers
and sister, Michael's mother and Renee. Tracie and Michelle
sat alongside their stepmother in the wooden pews behind
their father. Michelle rocked slightly, her hands on the seat
in front of her, her face marked with worry. Her father had
lost so much weight since being jailed six months earlier.
His spirits were down. The whole family felt it.

Finally, at 9:30, Biernat took the bench. His face was
pensive, just as it had been time and again during the trial.
This case had clearly troubled him more than most.

After the case was called and the lawyers read their appearances into the record, Biernat softly spoke.

"Ladies and gentlemen, I'm instructing those persons
seated in the benches to maintain themselves with the demeanor that is appropriate to this court," he said. "You're not
to speak out loud in this court while these proceedings are
going on, you're not to make any expression, verbal or otherwise, during the course of these proceedings. If you're found
to be making a demonstration of any kind or emotions or the
like, I will instruct the court deputy to escort you from the
courthouse."

He flipped through the pages of the court file, then asked
if the defense was ready to argue for a new trial.

Carl Marlinga said he was ready. He, too, addressed the
tension in the room.

"I understand there's a lot of passion in this matter, and I
understand that the beliefs are firm on both sides," he said.
"But ultimately we are here because the law believes, and I
think it is right over a couple of thousand years, that everything eventually yields to reason."

Marlinga's trademark stutter had softened. He stood at a
podium before the judges, his shoulders slightly hunched forward as he seemed to desperately try to get his point across.

"A couple of years ago, I was reading Barry Scheck's book
Presumed Innocence, and I read the portion where a man is
convicted of a rape-murder in Manhattan, and after he is

convicted, he is allowed to speak at the time of sentencing," Marlinga said. "And this poor, illiterate soul—all he could do is say, 'I don't even know how to drive a car in downtown.'"

Marlinga paused. He had made a mistake. The book was called *Actual Innocence,* but a lawyer's job is as much presentation as it is content, so he pushed forward with his point.

"It was the only thing he could think of in his defense. He could drive a car, but he just couldn't drive it downtown and it was the only little bit of fact that he could hold onto to try to explain to a disbelieving world that he was truly innocent."

Marlinga began outlining what he believed should prove Michael's innocence to a disbelieving world. He began with Kaplan's controversial closing arguments. At one point, Kaplan had summarized testimony from the officer-in-charge, Sergeant Donald Steckman, by saying that the sergeant had called Michael after the slaying with good news—that one of his stolen comic books had been found. Kaplan characterized Michael's response as backtracking: "Oh, oh, I made a mistake. That's not one of the comics that was stolen." Marlinga said that called into question whether any comics were stolen at all.

The trial transcripts recalled Steckman's testimony differently: Michael asked if police had learned anything of his stolen comics, and the sergeant replied, "No." Steckman asked specifically about one comic book—he recalled it as being a *Spider-Man*—and Michael said that no, *Spider-Man* hadn't been stolen.

"And it gives a completely different cant to the testimony because in the prosecution's version, it sounds like he listed a comic and then it was discovered that he had it all along because he sold it," Marlinga said.

Marlinga moved on, this time to seven documents that were recovered after the trial. They had literally fallen through the cracks of the cold-case shelves in the police department's archive room, and they were the beginning of Marlinga's argument of prosecutorial misconduct—not because the omission was intentional, he said, but because Sarah v. Michigan Department of Corrections finds that "the touchstone of the due process analysis is the fairness of the trial and not the culpability of the prosecutor."

"So it matters not that Lieutenant Keith innocently came upon these things," Marlinga said. "It matters not that they innocently failed to turn these things over. If it affects the outcome of the trial, if it affects the course of the trial, it's a violation of due process."

Josh Abbott, an appellate lawyer for the prosecutor's office, shifted in his chair. Kaplan sat back in his seat, a hand to his chin. The lawyers had already examined the documents and felt they never would have been allowed in trial anyway.

One was a single-page police report dated July 14, 1990, a day after the murder, reporting that someone called police to say that they knew of someone else who called Comics World at 5:55 p.m. the day Barbara died to ask about the value of a sports card. A male voice answered, according to the caller. Marlinga said this call was of dire importance whether or not it was Michael answering the phone. If it was, it blew the prosecution's scenario that Michael was lying in wait to kill Barbara at 6 p.m.—after all, she was throwing him a birthday party, and if he was at the store answering the phone in the open, she would have asked him what he was doing there. If it wasn't Michael, it could have been the real killer, Marlinga argued.

"If it's not Michael George, it's somebody who feels in command enough, in control enough, accepted enough in the store, well enough known to Barbara George that he feels free to pick up the phone and answer and say curtly 'no' when they asked him about a hockey card," Marlinga said. "That would have been very important for the jury to know, because as I said, it wrecks the prosecution's theory one way or the other."

Kaplan shook his head. The likelihood that the police report would have been admitted into trial was slim. The caller never identified himself, and because it was hearsay, Sergeant Steckman wouldn't have been able to testify about the report anyway. But Marlinga answered fervently that if the defense had been armed with this police report, Michael's lawyers could have pulled out newspaper advertisements, made public service announcements or held press conferences in hopes of flushing out the mysterious caller. "We would have had a chance to at least find this witness and bring him in," Marlinga said.

Then there was another single-page report, this one dated July 15, which said that a Tina Marie Bochenck called to say she saw two men, ages seventeen to twenty-five, walk into the Comics World store sometime between 6:15 and 6:30 p.m. Marlinga acknowledged that those men likely weren't the killers, but he said the time frame was interesting because the first 911 call came in at 6:22 p.m. The timing of the murder was so compressed, he said, that with more witnesses, it would make it more likely that someone would have recognized Michael had he arrived, killed his wife, then fled the scene.

Additionally, Marlinga said, it would have shown the jury that "the memory of time is a very slippery, subjective thing." If all of the timelines were put together, he said, one conclusion would have to be that Barbara George never died because there wasn't time for anyone to commit the crime.

"Of course, that is an absurdity," Marlinga said. "And so then you have to go to the other side and say quite honestly that, look it, people don't remember times with exactitude."

A third single-page report was generated by Sergeant Donald Lauhoff on July 24. Someone had reported that a kid was selling a variety of vintage 1940s comic books on the cheap—$20 for a whole box when some were worth $385 apiece. Marlinga said the kid likely was fencing them, that they had been stolen, and that if a jury had known someone was selling stolen comics, it would have given more credence to Michael's claim that Barbara died in a robbery.

Marlinga gave some of the documents more weight than others. He mentioned in court almost as an aside a single-page report indicating that Renee Kotula, Michael's lover and future second wife, was married to a man who had developed a mental problem and was sometimes violent. Then Marlinga got to what he called his "smoking gun": the two-page report about Marshall David Prog. In that police report, dated July 20, a man named Patrick Flannery told investigators he was living with a woman whose ex-husband was believed to be involved in the homicide. Prog came into town July 10 or July 11 and was broke, begging his ex-wife, Rita, for money. She refused.

Prog had boasted criminal activities in the past, Marlinga said. When he returned to Florida five days after Barbara's death, he had a lot of money after coming to Michigan empty-handed.

Again, Kaplan shifted. Prog was dead and couldn't defend himself against the accusations. Rita could be allowed to testify, but an ex-wife—especially one who claims her husband had a drug problem—might not be a strong witness. Marlinga acknowledged that this document, like the others, might not be admissible. Still, the defense had the right to know about the reports in hopes of trying to flesh them out, he argued.

Marlinga sat down, and Abbott rose. His job more often than not was to write briefs, not speak before a packed courtroom, and he seemed slightly uncomfortable. He began speaking from the lawyers' table until Biernat asked him to step forward to the podium. He did.

He addressed Marlinga's concerns point-by-point, beginning with Kaplan's summarization of Steckman's testimony. It was a paraphrase, he said, one presented during a part of the trial that jurors are specifically told not to consider as evidence. The law, he said, is clear in situations like that: "If there's no objection and there's instructions given to the jury, that the instructions cure any prejudice whatsoever."

The other reports were unlikely to have been admitted in trial, and likelier less to have affected the outcome of the trial, Abbott said. But Biernat wasn't happy with that argument. Pointing to the two-page report about Marshall Prog, he looked incredulous.

"This is a specific document submitted to the Clinton Township Police Department . . . and it just disappears," he said.

"Okay. Well—" Abbott stuttered.

"Why?" Biernat demanded.

"Even if—I mean, if you put aside the argument that they could have investigated themselves, it's nothing more than this *may* be the person. I mean, there's nothing beyond that at all." His muddled point: The document was speculative hearsay and not likely admissible in trial anyway.

"In a thin case, that might be important," Biernat challenged.

"But how would that come out at trial?" Abbott continued to stumble. He seemed caught off-guard. And spectators in the courtroom began to wonder if this hearing was perfunctory after all.

After forty-five minutes of arguing, Biernat took a break. He instructed everyone to return after lunch, at 1:15 p.m., to hear his ruling. Marlinga shot a hopeful look at Renee, who wasn't sure what to make of the back-and-forth. Biernat had called the case thin and criticized the original investigators' failure to follow up on tips. Twice before, when he turned down the defense's requests for a directed verdict, he'd ultimately sided with the prosecution, saying there was enough evidence for a jury to be able to weigh. Now, he didn't seem so sure.

When court resumed at 1:30 p.m., Biernat issued a familiar-sounding warning: "There's to be no demonstration, no talking in the courtroom, and everyone's expected to conduct themselves in a civil manner."

Brows furrowed. Renee caught her breath. Christina Ball, Barbara's sister, shot a confused look at her brother, Joe. He, too, looked concerned. As Biernat spoke, it was at first legal mumbo-jumbo—People v. Johnson this and People v. Lemmon that. But then he said something everyone understood:

"The Court, in its discretion, is convinced that it would be a miscarriage of justice to allow the verdict to stand," he said.

Renee's eyes squeezed shut. Her husband began to weep.

Biernat began to slam the prosecution: Kaplan had been instructed to limit testimony and talk of Michael's philandering and flirting to show marital discord and motive, but the prosecutor used it in his closing arguments to pass judgment on Michael's character, Biernat said, when he said his behavior at Barbara's funeral was "inconsistent with a grieving husband whose wife had been violently murdered." Also, he said Kaplan tried to shift the burden of proof on the defense by saying if it wasn't Michael, then who was it? The burden of proof always lies with the prosecution.

Biernat agreed with Marlinga about the documents, too—that in a "razor-thin case," those few police reports could have made a difference between a jury finding Michael guilty or innocent. But Biernat's biggest beef was with the photograph Kaplan had used during his closing argument. The photograph, a simple headshot of Michael, was "the most egregious example of prejudicial conduct," Biernat said.

"Because it was the last 'exhibit' the jurors saw, it could be considered the only image of the defendant ingrained in their minds. The damage had been done," Biernat said.

"To summarize," he said, "this is a case where unfortunately the investigation was patently inadequate, witnesses' memories had faded, there was no direct evidence of causation, no other physical evidence linking the defendant to the murder, only inherently conflicting testimony relative to Mr. George's presence between five-fifteen and the time of the murder, several instances of prejudicial prosecutorial misconduct," Biernat said.

"Standing alone, each constitutes grounds for a new trial, but collectively constitute a gross injustice such that the verdict cannot stand."

At 2:22 p.m., he dismissed the court.

Marlinga and his co-counsel, Joe Kosmala, beamed. Renee looked relieved, her smile no longer forced as she walked out of the courtroom.

In the hallway, the sides divided as reporters began asking for their reactions. "Thank you, Jesus," Renee said. "We've been praying for this forever. We all know he's innocent."

Marlinga hailed Biernat's decision as "courageous" and "correct." "It just restores my faith in the judicial system," he said. "This is a model of what a judge should be."

Barbara's family was shocked. They'd come expecting a ho-hum hearing, thinking they would get another glimpse of Michael the Killer in his jail garb before he headed to prison. Now, they faced the real possibility that he could be back on the streets. The judge had set a bond hearing for the next week.

"It's totally ludicrous," said Barbara George's brother, Joe Kowynia. "Marlinga made a mockery of the judicial system."

Prosecutor Eric Smith was too upset to face reporters. He'd been in the job about three years and had learned the hard way that his hot temper could sometimes land him in trouble when he lashed out through the media. Reporters couldn't reach him until late in the day. Even then, he had trouble concealing his ire.

"This judge has hijacked the justice system and made a mockery of this jury's verdict," he seethed. "He's been looking for any excuse to let this convicted killer go free."

He was especially livid at Biernat's charges of misconduct and attack on Kaplan, who he said was among the most respected assistant prosecutors in the state. The photo in the closing statement wasn't "egregious," Smith said; it was simply a visual aid, a piece of drama to help get Kaplan's point across. And the recovered documents were ultimately inconsequential. None, he said, would have been deemed admissible in trial.

Then he noted with irony that the hearing date—September 12, 2008—would have been the Georges' twenty-seventh wedding anniversary. To Smith, it was also the date that Michael George teetered toward getting away with murder—again.

Chapter 37

Relations Deteriorate

Kaplan felt sucker-punched. He'd held his tongue during the hearing and let Smith, who arguably had a hotter head than him, wax indignant to the press about the judge's miscarriage of justice. Kaplan felt he'd done his job, he'd done it well, and all the while, he'd been hamstringed by Biernat's rulings. He'd taken in stride that some of Michael's philandering was sanitized. He'd shrugged it off when Patrice Sartori's tale about the sex tape wasn't allowed or when Biernat said the jury wouldn't hear about the alleged back room blowjob in the Santa suit. Kaplan especially felt the judge had been wrong to rule against admitting allegations of previous insurance frauds—evidence the lawyer felt should have been allowed under Michigan's 404B ruling pertaining to past bad acts. But now the judge had called Kaplan's very credibility into question.

"It stings," Kaplan admitted.

Biernat's use of the term "prosecutorial misconduct" guaranteed that whenever a reporter was forced in short order to sum up why Michael George got a new trial, that would be the reason given, and Kaplan winced at being lumped with low-life attorneys who withheld evidence or bought off witnesses.

In Wayne County, home to ever-turbulent Detroit, an assistant prosecutor had recently been criminally charged with knowingly allowing a witness to perjure himself. Kaplan's big wrongdoing was showing a photograph, yet the same phrase—"prosecutorial misconduct"—was being applied.

"People outside of the Macomb County environment, in reading your article, might think I committed that kind of misconduct," Kaplan told a reporter.

The photograph, he said, was simply a gimmick.

"It's a metaphor," he said. "It means, 'This case is a circumstantial case. It's a puzzle. How do we solve the puzzle? With numerous pieces that all point to the suspect.'"

If it had been so egregious, Kaplan argued, Biernat could have included a caveat in the jury instructions telling jurors to disregard it. Marlinga had even made a motion for a mistrial based on the photograph, which Biernat denied before the verdict. But after the jury made its decision, the judge pounced. Kaplan said he was thunderstruck. He hadn't thought twice about turning over the newly discovered police reports—reports he considered innocuous, though he assumed the defense would use them as the basis of an appeal—and yet he was accused of misconduct for showing a photograph that couldn't even stand upright during his closing arguments.

The irony, he said, was that he'd used the puzzle gimmick before—under Marlinga's leadership.

"He even praised me for it," Kaplan said with a laugh.

In that case, too, the puzzle fell before it was completed.

Smith also continued to steam. Outraged by Biernat's ruling, he took the controversial step of banning all plea deals in the judge's courtroom. Biernat was soft on crime, he argued, and couldn't be trusted to impose harsh enough sentences. The Wednesday after Biernat overturned the verdict, Michael George was due back in court for a bond hearing. A few dozen protesters—upset jurors among them—gathered outside, carrying signs demanding that the verdict be reinstated. Renee, who had packed Michael a bag in case he'd get to come home, quietly walked past the crowd.

Madette Bui, one of the twelve who decided the case, was disgusted with the judge.

"It's insulting," the thirty-nine-year-old registered nurse said while standing near the front steps of the Macomb County Courthouse, which is nestled between the Clinton River and the Mt. Clemens main drag. "Everybody agreed on first-degree murder."

When jurors went back to deliberate, they took a vote to see where they stood. Seven of the twelve were sure George was guilty; the other five were leaning toward not guilty. To reach a consensus, they had gone over the evidence repeatedly. Sure, it was circumstantial, but everything pointed to George, Bui recalled. The sticking points were simple: the timeline, the comment Michael made to police about a box falling on Barb's head and that fated Michael Renaud phone call. Michael's flirtation with other women didn't help his cause, but the jurors knew they had to shake off what they thought of him as a husband and a man and not let that color whether they thought he was a killer.

Outside the courthouse this day, jurors and family members carried homemade signs reading, "Keep Convicted Killers Behind Bars" and "Nothing 'Comical' About Murder."

"Although it was all circumstantial, it was all still evidence, and all of it pointed to him," said Sandra Layne, a fifty-year-old elementary school custodian who sat on the jury. "I was one hundred percent from the day we decided to convict him, and I'll be one hundred percent until the day I die."

As the time neared for Biernat to decide whether George would go free on bond, the protesters packed up their signs and headed to the judge's fourth-floor courtroom, Bui among them. She listened as Kosmala again lambasted the jury's decision, calling it "renegade" and saying he had never in thirty-plus years as a lawyer seen a jury get a decision so outright wrong. Bui's jaw dropped. Her eyes darted around the courtroom, locking with other jurors'. They'd taken their civic duty seriously, and this man was mocking them.

Kosmala accused Eric Smith of staging the protest. (Later, he would note that some of the sign-carriers were county employees who, he said, shouldn't have been protesting on county property during work hours. Smith said the outcry against Biernat's ruling was strong, and he wasn't inclined to tell his staffers, many of them union members, that they couldn't protest the judge's ruling. After all, they get mandated half-hour daily breaks and it was up to them how to use them.)

Biernat, too, slammed Smith's office for what he called "vilifying attacks on the court" since he'd ordered the new trial. He said the prosecutor's ranting could taint a new jury pool and is "contrary to the spirit of the law." Smith scoffed at the allegation; in his mind, overturning a jury's conviction was contrary to the spirit of the law, not protesting a judge who did so.

Some in the community praised Smith's boldness for so publicly denouncing Biernat's ruling. One *Detroit Free Press* reader emailed the reporters on the story praising their "professional demeanor . . . since Kosmala and Marlinga are being world-class jerks by defying the opinion of a jury of twelve citizens in convicting George for killing his wife. What was particularly dumbfounding was Kosmala and Marlinga's motion to muffle Smith since his comments were denying George 'his right to a fair (second) trial.' This would be true if Smith had disparaged the court system before George's first trial, which of course never happened. It appears that Judge Biernat and the defense team succeeded in 'moving the goal posts' after the first jury's conviction, which damn well should bring a protest from Smith."

But Smith took a beating from columnists in the community. A *Macomb Daily* editorial accused Smith of sour grapes, and *Free Press* columnist Brian Dickerson said Smith's outcry was actually a measured move to disguise the case's holes. The award-winning columnist wrote:

> Reversing a unanimous jury verdict is probably the most thankless task a judge can undertake. So we ought to pay attention when any jurist takes that unusual step, especially where the verdict at issue was rendered after a highly publicized trial involving a singularly unsympathetic defendant. It's no surprise that Macomb County Circuit Judge James Biernat is being pilloried for his decision to set aside the conviction of Michael George. . . . No physical evidence or eyewitnesses link George to the killing. But prosecutors argued that his affair with another woman and his status as the beneficiary of a $120,000 [sic] life insurance policy provided the motive for murder. A jury agreed, and some of its members clearly regard Biernat's decision to vacate their unanimous verdict as a personal affront. It is, of course, nothing of the sort—and Macomb County Prosecutor Eric Smith's suggestion that jurors have been dissed seems calculated to distract attention from real shortcomings in his office's case against George.

Dickerson drew parallels to another verdict in metro Detroit that had been overturned the previous year in neighboring Oakland County. James Perry, a kindergarten teacher, was convicted of sexually assaulting two students based on the students' somewhat fluctuating allegations. In the end, charges were dropped. "We're a long way from knowing whether Michael George deserves the same fate," Dickerson concluded. "But Smith's suggestion that Judge Biernat's decision insults the jury's integrity is disingenuous, and his insistence that Macomb County prosecutors henceforth refuse to accept plea deals in cases assigned to Biernat is petty."

In the weeks after the verdict vacation, Smith admitted to the *Free Press* that there was a new rift between his office and the bench. County judges had met twice to vent behind the scenes—once in an emergency meeting soon after Smith said Biernat was looking for an excuse to let a killer walk. He might have been singling out just one judge, but some on the bench took it as an insult to all. Smith acknowledged that it was making life a little unpleasant for him and the assistant prosecutors working daily in the courthouse, but he largely shrugged off the judges' complaints. It's not his job to keep them happy, he said.

"We show up every day, and we prosecute the bad guys," he said. "The only thing that matters to me is whether the victims end up happy with us."

Besides, he said, judges and prosecutors were historically at odds over how harsh a sentence to impose. This was just an extension of a never-ending tug-of-war in the justice system, he reasoned. "In general, prosecutors want judges to be tougher, and judges want prosecutors to be less rigid. When a problem pops up, we deal with it and move on," he said.

Defense lawyers used the tit-for-tat between Biernat and Smith's office as fuel for a motion asking that the entire prosecutor's office be tossed off the Michael George case. They said Smith "has engaged in public comment and demonstrations with the intent and effect of disparaging the court and denying the defendant his right to a fair trial." The lawyers wanted Smith disqualified and replaced by an appointed special prosecutor.

Kosmala told a reporter that Smith was just too personally invested in the case. He was targeting George, he said, to make his dead father happy. He pointed to the comments Smith made in the *Dateline* episode about how his father, who long believed George was the killer, would be proud that he'd nailed the conviction. And he scoffed at the juror-attended demonstration on the courthouse steps, accusing Smith not only of organizing it, but also of instructing that protest signs be assembled using a county conference room.

Biernat denied the defense's motion and kept the prosecutors on board. But he imposed a gag order that forbade either side from talking about the case publicly outside of the courtroom.

Chapter 38

No End in Sight

If parties in the case thought the first stretch progressed impossibly slow, they were in for a shock at the delay they would face post-verdict. Prosecutors thought they had a shot at getting the state appellate court to reverse Biernat's ruling and reinstate the jury's verdict. They filed the paperwork, and then they waited. The state Court of Appeals at first passed on hearing the case, meaning Biernat's ruling would stand, so Smith's office appealed to the state Supreme Court.

The Supreme Court bounced it back to the appellate court and ordered a hearing. In May 2010, that court upheld Biernat's decision to order a new trial. Smith again appealed to the Supreme Court in hopes of getting the jury's guilty verdict reinstated.

Quietly, Smith decided to pull Kaplan off the case and replace him with the office's chief of homicide, Bill Cataldo. Kaplan was tired and his relationship with Biernat had suffered. Cataldo would bring a new energy, Smith thought. Plus, Cataldo was powerful and visceral in the courtroom. He had spent 20 years as a defense lawyer—a do-it-yourselfer, ambulance-chasing past to which his white and wild hair could attest. Defense lawyers were notorious for looking a little looser than their prosecutorial counterparts. When Smith offered him a job as an assistant prosecutor in 2005, he took it on one condition: He refused to cut his hair to fit the staid aesthetic that the job seemed to require.

What Kaplan brought in with intellectualism, Cataldo countered with drama. When the TV cameras were on, he shouted, he whispered, he performed. As a defense lawyer, he had developed a reputation for being over the top, especially in his closing arguments. In one rape case, looking to undermine a victim's claim that she couldn't wash blood out of her panties after the assault, Cataldo nonchalantly took off his sport coat, removed a razor blade from his pocket, sliced his arm, and let the blood drip onto a rag. Then, using some soap and water he had already brought into the courtroom, he washed away the blood. He still lost the case, but it made for an interesting show.

His style was perhaps tempered when he switched from defense to prosecution, but only slightly. One of his first murder cases was a strangulation in which the killer tried to dismiss the death as an accident, a crime of passion. In his closing argument, Cataldo kicked off his shoe, slammed it against a podium, and then pounced on it and throttled it for four agonizingly long minutes—the length of time the medical examiner had estimated it had taken for the victim to die. Cataldo got his conviction. His philosophy was simple: "You have to keep it interesting."

When the George case unfolded in 2007, Cataldo was knee-deep in his own high-profile murder cases. First, there was the gut-wrenching stabbing deaths of two young sisters in Macomb Township. Jennifer Kukla, a thirty-year-old single mother, chased down her doe-eyed daughters, eight-year-old Alexandria and five-year-old Ashley, and viciously slit their throats, nearly decapitating them. She then stacked their bodies in a bedroom of their unkempt trailer, disemboweled the family pets, and sat quietly amongst the carnage for hours. Eventually, a sister came to check on her and discovered the gruesome scene. Kukla had told police she had sat on her porch waiting for a car made of bones to come and take her to hell. The slayings had been in February; by October, when the George case was gaining steam, Cataldo was in trial, dramatically retelling in his opening statement how little Ashley ran from her mother, cowered beneath the kitchen table and yelled, "No, Momma, don't!" (Despite three psychiatrists' testimony that Kukla was legally insane at the time of the slayings, Cataldo persuaded the jury to find her guilty—though mentally ill—of first-degree murder.)

Two months later, Cataldo was on the prosecuting team in the case against a Washington Township father of two, Stephen Grant—arguably the highest-profile case to hit Macomb County in at least a decade. On February 14, 2007, Grant reported that his pretty, curly-haired wife, thirty-four-year-old Tara, had left during an argument never to return. Three weeks later, her torso was discovered in a rubber bin in the couple's garage. The rest of her remains had been scattered in the nearby sprawling park where the Grants regularly took their children for walks and picnics. Grant confessed, but said he had strangled Tara in a fit of rage. He was convicted of second-degree murder.

Thus, when Cataldo stepped into the George case, he knew the basics but had some catching up to do. He told a reporter he would be poring over the trial transcripts and even tracking down the first panel of jurors to learn what worked and what didn't. With the case remaining assigned to the judge who already had ruled against the prosecution, Cataldo said he would have to work even harder than usual.

Meanwhile, George's health was deteriorating in jail, his lawyers told Biernat at every status update. He had lost weight during the trial, but after his conviction, it began peeling off at an alarming rate. Renee quietly told reporters off the record that she was worried he might have the same affliction from which she suffered—multiple sclerosis. It was maddening trying to get information about his welfare, she said, because even as his wife, she had trouble getting past the health-care privacy laws.

On January 27, 2009, a *Free Press* reporter called Marlinga looking for some details on his health. The following story ran on the newspaper's website:

> Michael George, who remains in jail as he awaits a second trial in the 1990 murder of his wife, arrived to court today in a wheelchair, too weak to walk on his own.
>
> George, 48, has lost 50 pounds since his March conviction, said his lawyer, Carl Marlinga.
>
> "His health has been declining over the past couple of months," Marlinga said. "He's having trouble standing. We're hoping it's nothing serious or permanent."
>
> A jury convicted George of first-degree murder in the shooting death of 32-year-old Barbara George. The two owned a comic book store in Clinton Township; Barbara George was found dead in a back room by customers.
>
> Macomb County Circuit Judge James Biernat set aside the conviction, however, saying there hadn't been enough evidence presented to convict George.
>
> A scheduling conference today lasted just minutes, long enough for Biernat to schedule another status hearing for Feb. 11.
>
> The case remains on hold as the state Supreme Court decides whether to get involved. Macomb County Prosecutor Eric Smith, whose cold case unit prosecuted George, has asked the high court to reinstate the conviction.
>
> If the Supreme Court denies prosecutors' request, it will head to a second trial.
>
> Assistant Prosecutor Steve Kaplan, who heads the cold case unit, said there's no way to know how long the court will take to make its decision.

Marlinga said George is undergoing medical tests, including blood work and an MRI, in the Macomb County Jail.

"I know he has once been convicted, but that conviction has been set aside so he's presumed to be innocent, and we believe he actually is innocent," Marlinga said.

"This certainly adds to the tragedy for him to suffer a medical decline for charges that may eventually be shown to not be well founded."

Though the story only ran online and not in the newspaper's print edition, it landed Marlinga in trouble for talking about the case despite Biernat's gag order. Cataldo, in his first official step as new lead prosecutor in the case, filed a motion to find that Marlinga had violated the order. In reality, Marlinga had not said much that could be construed as out of line. He could talk about his client, just not about the case itself. Describing George's medical state was not in violation, but saying that he and Kosmala "believe he actually is innocent" was. In court March 24, Marlinga apologized and said his comment had been off-the-cuff and not meant to stir up trouble.

Just days after that court hearing, prosecutors got their first break in months in the case: The state supreme court had finally made its decision on the office's appeal looking to reinstate the verdict. Even though the appellate court had once passed the George case by, the higher court ruled that it had to look at the case and decide whether it would back the jury's verdict or the judge's move to set it aside. It was both good and bad news for the prosecution. There now was hope that the appellate court would decide to slap George once again with a "guilty" label, but it likely would be six months or more before the decision was made. Any lingering hope that the case might soon wrap up was crushed. The case was officially in limbo.

* * *

Renee kept up her weekly visits, but the situation in Windber was getting unbearable. Now she was paying not just for two lawyers, but for four: Mark Kriger and N. C. Deday LaRene—Marlinga's Detroit-based defense lawyers in his federal indictment—were handling the bulk of her husband's appeal. The Windber comic shop was doing fair enough business to keep afloat, but it just wasn't enough to also foot the lawyer fees, so Renee asked for some help from church friends and had the back of the store slowly converted into living space while she put the couple's home up for sale. She wasn't sure initially whether she would have to follow through, but there were no more collectibles to cash in. She opted not to tell Michael right away what she was up to. His health was too weak, she figured, and she didn't want him to worry about things he couldn't control from his jail cell.

After months of back and forth, Biernat eventually did set bond, but the $2.5 million price tag was beyond Renee's reach. Even if she could find a way to borrow that kind of money, she didn't know if she would someday be able to pay it back. ("What people don't realize is that when you put money up for bond, you never get it back, even if you go to every single court hearing," she fumed.) Marlinga and Kosmala asked Biernat to lower the bond, saying that by setting it so high, he was basically denying bond outright. Cataldo effectively cautioned that George had even more reason now than before to skip town since he already knew it was possible a jury could find him guilty of murder. Biernat handed the prosecution another favorable ruling and agreed with Cataldo. Marlinga and Kosmala appealed to the state supreme court, but in late July 2009, the higher court denied their request. George would have to stay in jail until the court of appeals finally got around to his case.

After a year in stagnation, all sides felt robbed—Smith of a justly earned verdict, Kaplan of a pristine reputation, Barb's family of both her and her daughters from their lives. Michael and Renee, meanwhile, felt robbed of their reputations, of their livelihoods, and of two years and counting. They all said they wanted justice, and they all had different views of what justice entailed.

Just as Renee had helmed the 2008 Pittsburgh Comicon solo eight months after Michael was arrested, she also organized the 2009 event. The three-day convention spanned the September 11 weekend and featured dozens of artists and retailers throughout the Pittsburgh ExpoMart, which technically fell outside of city limits in Monroeville, Pa. On September 12—the anniversary of Biernat's decision to set the guilty verdict aside—the event got a huge boost from legendary comic mastermind Stan Lee, whom Renee had managed to secure as a special guest in a Hail Mary attempt to keep things interesting. Lee, the co-creator of iconic superheroes such as Spider-Man, Iron Man, and the Hulk, arrived, accepted a key to Monroeville from Mayor Greg Erosenko, and signed autographs for a line of fans that snaked outside the VIP entrance and down the parking lot.

Michael was conspicuously absent from the festivities, but his family was well represented: daughters Michelle and Tracie both worked the show, as did four of his stepsons. Renee flitted about, dealing with retailers and artists and helping the Saturday morning rush of fans who arrived to shake Lee's hand. To keep the line moving, she served as go-between, passing along the item Lee was to autograph, then sliding it conveyer-belt style back down to its owner.

"That might go a little easier if you stood closer to me," Lee told Renee, who laughed and said she needed the exercise. Lee mock-scoffed. "I'm always trying to get the girls to get closer to me and they never do," he quipped.

Renee laughed harder. "So that's what you were up to!"

Despite the good humor on the surface, however, it was clear to anyone who knew the Georges that something was missing. Michelle and Tracie looked vacant at their posts, passing out programs and authenticating purchased goods.

When men would stop to ask how Michael was doing, their eyes would well with tears. Renee's smile seemed forced, too. She had told friends that God had a way of pulling off miracles and she was hoping for a Supreme Court ruling just before the convention. It didn't come. Just three days before the convention began, she told a reporter how heartbroken she was that Michael wouldn't be there to see the patriarch of Marvel Comics appear as his special guest. When the verdict was set aside a year earlier, Renee had thanked Jesus and was certain the then-yearlong ordeal was drawing to a close. A full year later, nothing had progressed. The limbo was driving her crazy, she said. The morning after the convention, she had the meltdown she'd been holding back all weekend.

"I really thought I would have Michael home by now," she said.

Then she prayed her husband would soon be back in court.